Mometrix
TEST PREPARATION

MTTC
Language Arts (Elementary) (90) Test Secrets Study Guide

Dear Future Exam Success Story

First of all, **THANK YOU** for purchasing Mometrix study materials!

Second, congratulations! You are one of the few determined test-takers who are committed to doing whatever it takes to excel on your exam. **You have come to the right place.** We developed these study materials with one goal in mind: to deliver you the information you need in a format that's concise and easy to use.

In addition to optimizing your guide for the content of the test, we've outlined our recommended steps for breaking down the preparation process into small, attainable goals so you can make sure you stay on track.

We've also analyzed the entire test-taking process, identifying the most common pitfalls and showing how you can overcome them and be ready for any curveball the test throws you.

Standardized testing is one of the biggest obstacles on your road to success, which only increases the importance of doing well in the high-pressure, high-stakes environment of test day. Your results on this test could have a significant impact on your future, and this guide provides the information and practical advice to help you achieve your full potential on test day.

Your success is our success

We would love to hear from you! If you would like to share the story of your exam success or if you have any questions or comments in regard to our products, please contact us at **800-673-8175** or **support@mometrix.com**.

Thanks again for your business and we wish you continued success!

Sincerely,
The Mometrix Test Preparation Team

Need more help? Check out our flashcards at:
http://MometrixFlashcards.com/MTTC

TABLE OF CONTENTS

Introduction

Thank you for purchasing this resource! You have made the choice to prepare yourself for a test that could have a huge impact on your future, and this guide is designed to help you be fully ready for test day. Obviously, it's important to have a solid understanding of the test material, but you also need to be prepared for the unique environment and stressors of the test, so that you can perform to the best of your abilities.

For this purpose, the first section that appears in this guide is the **Secret Keys**. We've devoted countless hours to meticulously researching what works and what doesn't, and we've boiled down our findings to the five most impactful steps you can take to improve your performance on the test. We start at the beginning with study planning and move through the preparation process, all the way to the testing strategies that will help you get the most out of what you know when you're finally sitting in front of the test.

We recommend that you start preparing for your test as far in advance as possible. However, if you've bought this guide as a last-minute study resource and only have a few days before your test, we recommend that you skip over the first two Secret Keys since they address a long-term study plan.

If you struggle with **test anxiety**, we strongly encourage you to check out our recommendations for how you can overcome it. Test anxiety is a formidable foe, but it can be beaten, and we want to make sure you have the tools you need to defeat it.

1

Secret Key #1 – Plan Big, Study Small

There's a lot riding on your performance. If you want to ace this test, you're going to need to keep your skills sharp and the material fresh in your mind. You need a plan that lets you review everything you need to know while still fitting in your schedule. We'll break this strategy down into three categories.

Information Organization

Start with the information you already have: the official test outline. From this, you can make a complete list of all the concepts you need to cover before the test. Organize these concepts into groups that can be studied together, and create a list of any related vocabulary you need to learn so you can brush up on any difficult terms. You'll want to keep this vocabulary list handy once you actually start studying since you may need to add to it along the way.

Time Management

Once you have your set of study concepts, decide how to spread them out over the time you have left before the test. Break your study plan into small, clear goals so you have a manageable task for each day and know exactly what you're doing. Then just focus on one small step at a time. When you manage your time this way, you don't need to spend hours at a time studying. Studying a small block of content for a short period each day helps you retain information better and avoid stressing over how much you have left to do. You can relax knowing that you have a plan to cover everything in time. In order for this strategy to be effective though, you have to start studying early and stick to your schedule. Avoid the exhaustion and futility that comes from last-minute cramming!

Study Environment

The environment you study in has a big impact on your learning. Studying in a coffee shop, while probably more enjoyable, is not likely to be as fruitful as studying in a quiet room. It's important to keep distractions to a minimum. You're only planning to study for a short block of time, so make the most of it. Don't pause to check your phone or get up to find a snack. It's also important to **avoid multitasking**. Research has consistently shown that multitasking will make your studying dramatically less effective. Your study area should also be comfortable and well-lit so you don't have the distraction of straining your eyes or sitting on an uncomfortable chair.

The time of day you study is also important. You want to be rested and alert. Don't wait until just before bedtime. Study when you'll be most likely to comprehend and remember. Even better, if you know what time of day your test will be, set that time aside for study. That way your brain will be used to working on that subject at that specific time and you'll have a better chance of recalling information.

Finally, it can be helpful to team up with others who are studying for the same test. Your actual studying should be done in as isolated an environment as possible, but the work of organizing the information and setting up the study plan can be divided up. In between study sessions, you can discuss with your teammates the concepts that you're all studying and quiz each other on the details. Just be sure that your teammates are as serious about the test as you are. If you find that your study time is being replaced with social time, you might need to find a new team.

Secret Key #2 – Make Your Studying Count

You're devoting a lot of time and effort to preparing for this test, so you want to be absolutely certain it will pay off. This means doing more than just reading the content and hoping you can remember it on test day. It's important to make every minute of study count. There are two main areas you can focus on to make your studying count.

Retention

It doesn't matter how much time you study if you can't remember the material. You need to make sure you are retaining the concepts. To check your retention of the information you're learning, try recalling it at later times with minimal prompting. Try carrying around flashcards and glance at one or two from time to time or ask a friend who's also studying for the test to quiz you.

To enhance your retention, look for ways to put the information into practice so that you can apply it rather than simply recalling it. If you're using the information in practical ways, it will be much easier to remember. Similarly, it helps to solidify a concept in your mind if you're not only reading it to yourself but also explaining it to someone else. Ask a friend to let you teach them about a concept you're a little shaky on (or speak aloud to an imaginary audience if necessary). As you try to summarize, define, give examples, and answer your friend's questions, you'll understand the concepts better and they will stay with you longer. Finally, step back for a big picture view and ask yourself how each piece of information fits with the whole subject. When you link the different concepts together and see them working together as a whole, it's easier to remember the individual components.

Finally, practice showing your work on any multi-step problems, even if you're just studying. Writing out each step you take to solve a problem will help solidify the process in your mind, and you'll be more likely to remember it during the test.

Modality

Modality simply refers to the means or method by which you study. Choosing a study modality that fits your own individual learning style is crucial. No two people learn best in exactly the same way, so it's important to know your strengths and use them to your advantage.

For example, if you learn best by visualization, focus on visualizing a concept in your mind and draw an image or a diagram. Try color-coding your notes, illustrating them, or creating symbols that will trigger your mind to recall a learned concept. If you learn best by hearing or discussing information, find a study partner who learns the same way or read aloud to yourself. Think about how to put the information in your own words. Imagine that you are giving a lecture on the topic and record yourself so you can listen to it later.

For any learning style, flashcards can be helpful. Organize the information so you can take advantage of spare moments to review. Underline key words or phrases. Use different colors for different categories. Mnemonic devices (such as creating a short list in which every item starts with the same letter) can also help with retention. Find what works best for you and use it to store the information in your mind most effectively and easily.

3

Secret Key #3 – Practice the Right Way

Your success on test day depends not only on how many hours you put into preparing, but also on whether you prepared the right way. It's good to check along the way to see if your studying is paying off. One of the most effective ways to do this is by taking practice tests to evaluate your progress. Practice tests are useful because they show exactly where you need to improve. Every time you take a practice test, pay special attention to these three groups of questions:

- The questions you got wrong
- The questions you had to guess on, even if you guessed right
- The questions you found difficult or slow to work through

This will show you exactly what your weak areas are, and where you need to devote more study time. Ask yourself why each of these questions gave you trouble. Was it because you didn't understand the material? Was it because you didn't remember the vocabulary? Do you need more repetitions on this type of question to build speed and confidence? Dig into those questions and figure out how you can strengthen your weak areas as you go back to review the material.

 Additionally, many practice tests have a section explaining the answer choices. It can be tempting to read the explanation and think that you now have a good understanding of the concept. However, an explanation likely only covers part of the question's broader context. Even if the explanation makes perfect sense, **go back and investigate** every concept related to the question until you're positive you have a thorough understanding.

As you go along, keep in mind that the practice test is just that: practice. Memorizing these questions and answers will not be very helpful on the actual test because it is unlikely to have any of the same exact questions. If you only know the right answers to the sample questions, you won't be prepared for the real thing. **Study the concepts** until you understand them fully, and then you'll be able to answer any question that shows up on the test.

It's important to wait on the practice tests until you're ready. If you take a test on your first day of study, you may be overwhelmed by the amount of material covered and how much you need to learn. Work up to it gradually.

On test day, you'll need to be prepared for answering questions, managing your time, and using the test-taking strategies you've learned. It's a lot to balance, like a mental marathon that will have a big impact on your future. Like training for a marathon, you'll need to start slowly and work your way up. When test day arrives, you'll be ready.

Start with the strategies you've read in the first two Secret Keys—plan your course and study in the way that works best for you. If you have time, consider using multiple study resources to get different approaches to the same concepts. It can be helpful to see difficult concepts from more than one angle. Then find a good source for practice tests. Many times, the test website will suggest potential study resources or provide sample tests.

Practice Test Strategy

If you're able to find at least three practice tests, we recommend this strategy:

UNTIMED AND OPEN-BOOK PRACTICE

Take the first test with no time constraints and with your notes and study guide handy. Take your time and focus on applying the strategies you've learned.

TIMED AND OPEN-BOOK PRACTICE

Take the second practice test open-book as well, but set a timer and practice pacing yourself to finish in time.

TIMED AND CLOSED-BOOK PRACTICE

Take any other practice tests as if it were test day. Set a timer and put away your study materials. Sit at a table or desk in a quiet room, imagine yourself at the testing center, and answer questions as quickly and accurately as possible.

Keep repeating timed and closed-book tests on a regular basis until you run out of practice tests or it's time for the actual test. Your mind will be ready for the schedule and stress of test day, and you'll be able to focus on recalling the material you've learned.

5

Secret Key #4 – Pace Yourself

Once you're fully prepared for the material on the test, your biggest challenge on test day will be managing your time. Just knowing that the clock is ticking can make you panic even if you have plenty of time left. Work on pacing yourself so you can build confidence against the time constraints of the exam. Pacing is a difficult skill to master, especially in a high-pressure environment, so **practice is vital**.

Set time expectations for your pace based on how much time is available. For example, if a section has 60 questions and the time limit is 30 minutes, you know you have to average 30 seconds or less per question in order to answer them all. Although 30 seconds is the hard limit, set 25 seconds per question as your goal, so you reserve extra time to spend on harder questions. When you budget extra time for the harder questions, you no longer have any reason to stress when those questions take longer to answer.

Don't let this time expectation distract you from working through the test at a calm, steady pace, but keep it in mind so you don't spend too much time on any one question. Recognize that taking extra time on one question you don't understand may keep you from answering two that you do understand later in the test. If your time limit for a question is up and you're still not sure of the answer, mark it and move on, and come back to it later if the time and the test format allow. If the testing format doesn't allow you to return to earlier questions, just make an educated guess; then put it out of your mind and move on.

On the easier questions, be careful not to rush. It may seem wise to hurry through them so you have more time for the challenging ones, but it's not worth missing one if you know the concept and just didn't take the time to read the question fully. Work efficiently but make sure you understand the question and have looked at all of the answer choices, since more than one may seem right at first.

Even if you're paying attention to the time, you may find yourself a little behind at some point. You should speed up to get back on track, but do so wisely. Don't panic; just take a few seconds less on each question until you're caught up. Don't guess without thinking, but do look through the answer choices and eliminate any you know are wrong. If you can get down to two choices, it is often worthwhile to guess from those. Once you've chosen an answer, move on and don't dwell on any that you skipped or had to hurry through. If a question was taking too long, chances are it was one of the harder ones, so you weren't as likely to get it right anyway.

On the other hand, if you find yourself getting ahead of schedule, it may be beneficial to slow down a little. The more quickly you work, the more likely you are to make a careless mistake that will affect your score. You've budgeted time for each question, so don't be afraid to spend that time. Practice an efficient but careful pace to get the most out of the time you have.

Secret Key #5 – Have a Plan for Guessing

When you're taking the test, you may find yourself stuck on a question. Some of the answer choices seem better than others, but you don't see the one answer choice that is obviously correct. What do you do?

The scenario described above is very common, yet most test takers have not effectively prepared for it. Developing and practicing a plan for guessing may be one of the single most effective uses of your time as you get ready for the exam.

In developing your plan for guessing, there are three questions to address:

- When should you start the guessing process?
- How should you narrow down the choices?
- Which answer should you choose?

When to Start the Guessing Process

Unless your plan for guessing is to select C every time (which, despite its merits, is not what we recommend), you need to leave yourself enough time to apply your answer elimination strategies. Since you have a limited amount of time for each question, that means that if you're going to give yourself the best shot at guessing correctly, you have to decide quickly whether or not you will guess.

Of course, the best-case scenario is that you don't have to guess at all, so first, see if you can answer the question based on your knowledge of the subject and basic reasoning skills. Focus on the key words in the question and try to jog your memory of related topics. Give yourself a chance to bring the knowledge to mind, but once you realize that you don't have (or you can't access) the knowledge you need to answer the question, it's time to start the guessing process.

It's almost always better to start the guessing process too early than too late. It only takes a few seconds to remember something and answer the question from knowledge. Carefully eliminating wrong answer choices takes longer. Plus, going through the process of eliminating answer choices can actually help jog your memory.

Summary: Start the guessing process as soon as you decide that you can't answer the question based on your knowledge.

7

How to Narrow Down the Choices

The next chapter in this book (**Test-Taking Strategies**) includes a wide range of strategies for how to approach questions and how to look for answer choices to eliminate. You will definitely want to read those carefully, practice them, and figure out which ones work best for you. Here though, we're going to address a mindset rather than a particular strategy.

Your odds of guessing an answer correctly depend on how many options you are choosing from.

Number of options left	5	4	3	2	1
Odds of guessing correctly	20%	25%	33%	50%	100%

You can see from this chart just how valuable it is to be able to eliminate incorrect answers and make an educated guess, but there are two things that many test takers do that cause them to miss out on the benefits of guessing:

- Accidentally eliminating the correct answer
- Selecting an answer based on an impression

We'll look at the first one here, and the second one in the next section.

To avoid accidentally eliminating the correct answer, we recommend a thought exercise called **the $5 challenge**. In this challenge, you only eliminate an answer choice from contention if you are willing to bet $5 on it being wrong. Why $5? Five dollars is a small but not insignificant amount of money. It's an amount you could afford to lose but wouldn't want to throw away. And while losing

$5 once might not hurt too much, doing it twenty times will set you back $100. In the same way, each small decision you make—eliminating a choice here, guessing on a question there—won't by itself impact your score very much, but when you put them all together, they can make a big difference. By holding each answer choice elimination decision to a higher standard, you can reduce the risk of accidentally eliminating the correct answer.

The $5 challenge can also be applied in a positive sense: If you are willing to bet $5 that an answer choice *is* correct, go ahead and mark it as correct.

Summary: Only eliminate an answer choice if you are willing to bet $5 that it is wrong.

8

Which Answer to Choose

You're taking the test. You've run into a hard question and decided you'll have to guess. You've eliminated all the answer choices you're willing to bet $5 on. Now you have to pick an answer. Why do we even need to talk about this? Why can't you just pick whichever one you feel like when the time comes?

The answer to these questions is that if you don't come into the test with a plan, you'll rely on your impression to select an answer choice, and if you do that, you risk falling into a trap. The test writers know that everyone who takes their test will be guessing on some of the questions, so they intentionally write wrong answer choices to seem plausible. You still have to pick an answer though, and if the wrong answer choices are designed to look right, how can you ever be sure that you're not falling for their trap? The best solution we've found to this dilemma is to take the decision out of your hands entirely. Here is the process we recommend:

Once you've eliminated any choices that you are confident (willing to bet $5) are wrong, select the first remaining choice as your answer.

Whether you choose to select the first remaining choice, the second, or the last, the important thing is that you use some preselected standard. Using this approach guarantees that you will not be enticed into selecting an answer choice that looks right, because you are not basing your decision on how the answer choices look.

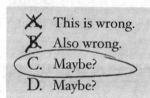

This is not meant to make you question your knowledge. Instead, it is to help you recognize the difference between your knowledge and your impressions. There's a huge difference between thinking an answer is right because of what you know, and thinking an answer is right because it looks or sounds like it should be right.

Summary: To ensure that your selection is appropriately random, make a predetermined selection from among all answer choices you have not eliminated.

Test-Taking Strategies

This section contains a list of test-taking strategies that you may find helpful as you work through the test. By taking what you know and applying logical thought, you can maximize your chances of answering any question correctly!

It is very important to realize that every question is different and every person is different: no single strategy will work on every question, and no single strategy will work for every person. That's why we've included all of them here, so you can try them out and determine which ones work best for different types of questions and which ones work best for you.

Question Strategies

⊘ READ CAREFULLY

Read the question and the answer choices carefully. Don't miss the question because you misread the terms. You have plenty of time to read each question thoroughly and make sure you understand what is being asked. Yet a happy medium must be attained, so don't waste too much time. You must read carefully and efficiently.

⊘ CONTEXTUAL CLUES

Look for contextual clues. If the question includes a word you are not familiar with, look at the immediate context for some indication of what the word might mean. Contextual clues can often give you all the information you need to decipher the meaning of an unfamiliar word. Even if you can't determine the meaning, you may be able to narrow down the possibilities enough to make a solid guess at the answer to the question.

⊘ PREFIXES

If you're having trouble with a word in the question or answer choices, try dissecting it. Take advantage of every clue that the word might include. Prefixes can be a huge help. Usually, they allow you to determine a basic meaning. *Pre-* means before, *post-* means after, *pro-* is positive, *de-* is negative. From prefixes, you can get an idea of the general meaning of the word and try to put it into context.

⊘ HEDGE WORDS

Watch out for critical hedge words, such as *likely, may, can, sometimes, often, almost, mostly, usually, generally, rarely,* and *sometimes.* Question writers insert these hedge phrases to cover every possibility. Often an answer choice will be wrong simply because it leaves no room for exception. Be on guard for answer choices that have definitive words such as *exactly* and *always.*

⊘ SWITCHBACK WORDS

Stay alert for *switchbacks.* These are the words and phrases frequently used to alert you to shifts in thought. The most common switchback words are *but, although,* and *however.* Others include *nevertheless, on the other hand, even though, while, in spite of, despite,* and *regardless of.* Switchback words are important to catch because they can change the direction of the question or an answer choice.

⊘ FACE VALUE

When in doubt, use common sense. Accept the situation in the problem at face value. Don't read too much into it. These problems will not require you to make wild assumptions. If you have to go beyond creativity and warp time or space in order to have an answer choice fit the question, then you should move on and consider the other answer choices. These are normal problems rooted in reality. The applicable relationship or explanation may not be readily apparent, but it is there for you to figure out. Use your common sense to interpret anything that isn't clear.

Answer Choice Strategies

⊘ ANSWER SELECTION

The most thorough way to pick an answer choice is to identify and eliminate wrong answers until only one is left, then confirm it is the correct answer. Sometimes an answer choice may immediately seem right, but be careful. The test writers will usually put more than one reasonable answer choice on each question, so take a second to read all of them and make sure that the other choices are not equally obvious. As long as you have time left, it is better to read every answer choice than to pick the first one that looks right without checking the others.

⊘ ANSWER CHOICE FAMILIES

An answer choice family consists of two (in rare cases, three) answer choices that are very similar in construction and cannot all be true at the same time. If you see two answer choices that are direct opposites or parallels, one of them is usually the correct answer. For instance, if one answer choice says that quantity x increases and another either says that quantity x decreases (opposite) or says that quantity y increases (parallel), then those answer choices would fall into the same family. An answer choice that doesn't match the construction of the answer choice family is more likely to be incorrect. Most questions will not have answer choice families, but when they do appear, you should be prepared to recognize them.

⊘ ELIMINATE ANSWERS

Eliminate answer choices as soon as you realize they are wrong, but make sure you consider all possibilities. If you are eliminating answer choices and realize that the last one you are left with is also wrong, don't panic. Start over and consider each choice again. There may be something you missed the first time that you will realize on the second pass.

⊘ AVOID FACT TRAPS

Don't be distracted by an answer choice that is factually true but doesn't answer the question. You are looking for the choice that answers the question. Stay focused on what the question is asking for so you don't accidentally pick an answer that is true but incorrect. Always go back to the question and make sure the answer choice you've selected actually answers the question and is not merely a true statement.

⊘ EXTREME STATEMENTS

In general, you should avoid answers that put forth extreme actions as standard practice or proclaim controversial ideas as established fact. An answer choice that states the "process should be used in certain situations, if…" is much more likely to be correct than one that states the "process should be discontinued completely." The first is a calm rational statement and doesn't even make a definitive, uncompromising stance, using a hedge word *if* to provide wiggle room, whereas the second choice is far more extreme.

11

⊘ BENCHMARK

As you read through the answer choices and you come across one that seems to answer the question well, mentally select that answer choice. This is not your final answer, but it's the one that will help you evaluate the other answer choices. The one that you selected is your benchmark or standard for judging each of the other answer choices. Every other answer choice must be compared to your benchmark. That choice is correct until proven otherwise by another answer choice beating it. If you find a better answer, then that one becomes your new benchmark. Once you've decided that no other choice answers the question as well as your benchmark, you have your final answer.

⊘ PREDICT THE ANSWER

Before you even start looking at the answer choices, it is often best to try to predict the answer. When you come up with the answer on your own, it is easier to avoid distractions and traps because you will know exactly what to look for. The right answer choice is unlikely to be word-for-word what you came up with, but it should be a close match. Even if you are confident that you have the right answer, you should still take the time to read each option before moving on.

General Strategies

⊘ TOUGH QUESTIONS

If you are stumped on a problem or it appears too hard or too difficult, don't waste time. Move on! Remember though, if you can quickly check for obviously incorrect answer choices, your chances of guessing correctly are greatly improved. Before you completely give up, at least try to knock out a couple of possible answers. Eliminate what you can and then guess at the remaining answer choices before moving on.

⊘ CHECK YOUR WORK

Since you will probably not know every term listed and the answer to every question, it is important that you get credit for the ones that you do know. Don't miss any questions through careless mistakes. If at all possible, try to take a second to look back over your answer selection and make sure you've selected the correct answer choice and haven't made a costly careless mistake (such as marking an answer choice that you didn't mean to mark). This quick double check should more than pay for itself in caught mistakes for the time it costs.

⊘ PACE YOURSELF

It's easy to be overwhelmed when you're looking at a page full of questions; your mind is confused and full of random thoughts, and the clock is ticking down faster than you would like. Calm down and maintain the pace that you have set for yourself. Especially as you get down to the last few minutes of the test, don't let the small numbers on the clock make you panic. As long as you are on track by monitoring your pace, you are guaranteed to have time for each question.

⊘ DON'T RUSH

It is very easy to make errors when you are in a hurry. Maintaining a fast pace in answering questions is pointless if it makes you miss questions that you would have gotten right otherwise. Test writers like to include distracting information and wrong answers that seem right. Taking a little extra time to avoid careless mistakes can make all the difference in your test score. Find a pace that allows you to be confident in the answers that you select.

⊘ Keep Moving

Panicking will not help you pass the test, so do your best to stay calm and keep moving. Taking deep breaths and going through the answer elimination steps you practiced can help to break through a stress barrier and keep your pace.

Final Notes

The combination of a solid foundation of content knowledge and the confidence that comes from practicing your plan for applying that knowledge is the key to maximizing your performance on test day. As your foundation of content knowledge is built up and strengthened, you'll find that the strategies included in this chapter become more and more effective in helping you quickly sift through the distractions and traps of the test to isolate the correct answer.

Now that you're preparing to move forward into the test content chapters of this book, be sure to keep your goal in mind. As you read, think about how you will be able to apply this information on the test. If you've already seen sample questions for the test and you have an idea of the question format and style, try to come up with questions of your own that you can answer based on what you're reading. This will give you valuable practice applying your knowledge in the same ways you can expect to on test day.

Good luck and good studying!

Meaning and Communication

Reading Comprehension

UNDERSTANDING A PASSAGE

One of the most important skills in reading comprehension is the identification of **topics** and **main ideas**. There is a subtle difference between these two features. The topic is the subject of a text (i.e., what the text is all about). The main idea, on the other hand, is the most important point being made by the author. The topic is usually expressed in a few words at the most while the main idea often needs a full sentence to be completely defined. As an example, a short passage might be written on the topic of penguins, and the main idea could be written as *Penguins are different from other birds in many ways*. In most nonfiction writing, the topic and the main idea will be **stated directly** and often appear in a sentence at the very beginning or end of the text. When being tested on an understanding of the author's topic, you may be able to skim the passage for the general idea by reading only the first sentence of each paragraph. A body paragraph's first sentence is often—but not always—the main **topic sentence** which gives you a summary of the content in the paragraph.

However, there are cases in which the reader must figure out an **unstated** topic or main idea. In these instances, you must read every sentence of the text and try to come up with an overarching idea that is supported by each of those sentences.

Note: The main idea should not be confused with the thesis statement. While the main idea gives a brief, general summary of a text, the thesis statement provides a **specific perspective** on an issue that the author supports with evidence.

> **Review Video: Topics and Main Ideas**
> Visit mometrix.com/academy and enter code: 407801

Supporting details are smaller pieces of evidence that provide backing for the main point. In order to show that a main idea is correct or valid, an author must add details that prove their point. All texts contain details, but they are only classified as supporting details when they serve to reinforce some larger point. Supporting details are most commonly found in informative and persuasive texts. In some cases, they will be clearly indicated with terms like *for example* or *for instance*, or they will be enumerated with terms like *first*, *second*, and *last*. However, you need to be prepared for texts that do not contain those indicators. As a reader, you should consider whether the author's supporting details really back up his or her main point. Details can be factual and correct, yet they may not be **relevant** to the author's point. Conversely, details can be relevant, but be ineffective because they are based on opinion or assertions that cannot be proven.

> **Review Video: Supporting Details**
> Visit mometrix.com/academy and enter code: 396297

An example of a main idea is: *Giraffes live in the Serengeti of Africa*. A supporting detail about giraffes could be: *A giraffe in this region benefits from a long neck by reaching twigs and leaves on tall trees*. The main idea gives the general idea that the text is about giraffes. The supporting detail gives a specific fact about how the giraffes eat.

15

ORGANIZATION OF THE TEXT

The way a text is organized can help readers understand the author's intent and his or her conclusions. There are various ways to organize a text, and each one has a purpose and use. Usually, authors will organize information logically in a passage so the reader can follow and locate the information within the text. However, since not all passages are written with the same logical structure, you need to be familiar with several different types of passage structure.

> **Review Video: Organizational Methods to Structure Text**
> Visit mometrix.com/academy and enter code: 606263
>
> **Review Video: Sequence of Events in a Story**
> Visit mometrix.com/academy and enter code: 807512

CHRONOLOGICAL

When using **chronological** order, the author presents information in the order that it happened. For example, biographies are typically written in chronological order. The subject's birth and childhood are presented first, followed by their adult life, and lastly the events leading up to the person's death.

CAUSE AND EFFECT

One of the most common text structures is **cause and effect**. A **cause** is an act or event that makes something happen, and an **effect** is the thing that happens as a result of the cause. A cause-and-effect relationship is not always explicit, but there are some terms in English that signal causes, such as *since*, *because*, and *due to*. Furthermore, terms that signal effects include *consequently, therefore, this leads to*. As an example, consider the sentence *Because the sky was clear, Ron did not bring an umbrella*. The cause is the clear sky, and the effect is that Ron did not bring an umbrella. However, readers may find that sometimes the cause-and-effect relationship will not be clearly noted. For instance, the sentence *He was late and missed the meeting* does not contain any signaling words, but the sentence still contains a cause (he was late) and an effect (he missed the meeting).

> **Review Video: Cause and Effect**
> Visit mometrix.com/academy and enter code: 868099

MULTIPLE EFFECTS

Be aware of the possibility for a single cause to have **multiple effects.** (e.g., *Single cause*: Because you left your homework on the table, your dog engulfed the assignment. *Multiple effects*: As a result, you receive a failing grade, your parents do not allow you to go out with your friends, you miss out on the new movie, and one of your classmates spoils it for you before you have another chance to watch it).

MULTIPLE CAUSES

Also, there is the possibility for a single effect to have **multiple causes.** (e.g., *Single effect*: Alan has a fever. *Multiple causes*: An unexpected cold front came through the area, and Alan forgot to take his multi-vitamin to avoid getting sick.) Additionally, an effect can in turn be the cause of another effect, in what is known as a cause-and-effect chain. (e.g., As a result of her disdain for procrastination, Lynn prepared for her exam. This led to her passing her test with high marks. Hence, her resume was accepted and her application was approved.)

CAUSE AND EFFECT IN PERSUASIVE ESSAYS

Persuasive essays, in which an author tries to make a convincing argument and change the minds of readers, usually include cause-and-effect relationships. However, these relationships should not always be taken at face value. Frequently, an author will assume a cause or take an effect for granted. To read a persuasive essay effectively, readers need to judge the cause-and-effect relationships that the author is presenting. For instance, imagine an author wrote the following: *The parking deck has been unprofitable because people would prefer to ride their bikes.* The relationship is clear: the cause is that people prefer to ride their bikes, and the effect is that the parking deck has been unprofitable. However, readers should consider whether this argument is conclusive. Perhaps there are other reasons for the failure of the parking deck: a down economy, excessive fees, etc. Too often, authors present causal relationships as if they are fact rather than opinion. Readers should be on the alert for these dubious claims.

PROBLEM-SOLUTION

Some nonfiction texts are organized to **present a problem** followed by a solution. For this type of text, the problem is often explained before the solution is offered. In some cases, as when the problem is well known, the solution may be introduced briefly at the beginning. Other passages may focus on the solution, and the problem will be referenced only occasionally. Some texts will outline multiple solutions to a problem, leaving readers to choose among them. If the author has an interest or an allegiance to one solution, he or she may fail to mention or describe accurately some of the other solutions. Readers should be careful of the author's agenda when reading a problem-solution text. Only by understanding the author's perspective and interests can one develop a proper judgment of the proposed solution.

COMPARE AND CONTRAST

Many texts follow the **compare-and-contrast** model in which the similarities and differences between two ideas or things are explored. Analysis of the similarities between ideas is called **comparison**. In an ideal comparison, the author places ideas or things in an equivalent structure, i.e., the author presents the ideas in the same way. If an author wants to show the similarities between cricket and baseball, then he or she may do so by summarizing the equipment and rules for each game. Be mindful of the similarities as they appear in the passage and take note of any differences that are mentioned. Often, these small differences will only reinforce the more general similarity.

> **Review Video: Compare and Contrast**
> Visit mometrix.com/academy and enter code: 798319

Thinking critically about ideas and conclusions can seem like a daunting task. One way to ease this task is to understand the basic elements of ideas and writing techniques. Looking at the ways different ideas relate to each other can be a good way for readers to begin their analysis. For instance, sometimes authors will write about two ideas that are in opposition to each other. Or, one author will provide his or her ideas on a topic, and another author may respond in opposition. The analysis of these opposing ideas is known as **contrast**. Contrast is often marred by the author's obvious partiality to one of the ideas. A discerning reader will be put off by an author who does not engage in a fair fight. In an analysis of opposing ideas, both ideas should be presented in clear and reasonable terms. If the author does prefer a side, you need to read carefully to determine the areas where the author shows or avoids this preference. In an analysis of opposing ideas, you should proceed through the passage by marking the major differences point by point with an eye that is looking for an explanation of each side's view. For instance, in an analysis of capitalism and communism, there is an importance in outlining each side's view on labor, markets, prices, personal

17

responsibility, etc. Additionally, as you read through the passages, you should note whether the opposing views present each side in a similar manner.

SEQUENCE

Readers must be able to identify a text's **sequence**, or the order in which things happen. Often, when the sequence is very important to the author, the text is indicated with signal words like *first*, *then*, *next*, and *last*. However, a sequence can be merely implied and must be noted by the reader. Consider the sentence *He walked through the garden and gave water and fertilizer to the plants*. Clearly, the man did not walk through the garden before he collected water and fertilizer for the plants. So, the implied sequence is that he first collected water, then he collected fertilizer, next he walked through the garden, and last he gave water or fertilizer as necessary to the plants. Texts do not always proceed in an orderly sequence from first to last. Sometimes they begin at the end and start over at the beginning. As a reader, you can enhance your understanding of the passage by taking brief notes to clarify the sequence.

MAKING CONNECTIONS TO ENHANCE COMPREHENSION

Reading involves thinking. For good comprehension, readers make **text-to-self**, **text-to-text**, and **text-to-world connections**. Making connections helps readers understand text better and predict what might occur next based on what they already know, such as how characters in the story feel or what happened in another text. Text-to-self connections with the reader's life and experiences make literature more personally relevant and meaningful to readers. Readers can make connections before, during, and after reading—including whenever the text reminds them of something similar they have encountered in life or other texts. The genre, setting, characters, plot elements, literary structure and devices, and themes an author uses allow a reader to make connections to other works of literature or to people and events in their own lives. Venn diagrams and other graphic organizers help visualize connections. Readers can also make double-entry notes: key content, ideas, events, words, and quotations on one side, and the connections with these on the other.

SUMMARIZING LITERATURE TO SUPPORT COMPREHENSION

When reading literature, especially demanding works, **summarizing** helps readers identify important information and organize it in their minds. They can also identify themes, problems, and solutions, and can sequence the story. Readers can summarize before, during, and after they read. They should use their own words, as they do when describing a personal event or giving directions. Previewing a text's organization before reading by examining the book cover, table of contents, and illustrations also aids summarizing. Making notes of key words and ideas in a graphic organizer while reading can benefit readers in the same way. Graphic organizers are another useful method; readers skim the text to determine main ideas and then narrow the list with the aid of the organizer. Unimportant details should be omitted in summaries. Summaries can be organized using description, problem-solution, comparison-contrast, sequence, main ideas, or cause-and-effect.

> **Review Video: Summarizing Text**
> Visit mometrix.com/academy and enter code: 172903

PARAPHRASING

Paraphrasing is another method that the reader can use to aid in comprehension. When paraphrasing, one puts what they have read into their own words by rephrasing what the author has written, or one "translates" all of what the author shared into their own words by including as many details as they can.

18

Making Predictions and Inferences

MAKING PREDICTIONS

When we read literature, **making predictions** about what will happen in the writing reinforces our purpose for reading and prepares us mentally. A **prediction** is a guess about what will happen next. Readers constantly make predictions based on what they have read and what they already know. We can make predictions before we begin reading and during our reading. Consider the following sentence: *Staring at the computer screen in shock, Kim blindly reached over for the brimming glass of water on the shelf to her side.* The sentence suggests that Kim is distracted, and that she is not looking at the glass that she is going to pick up. So, a reader might predict that Kim is going to knock over the glass. Of course, not every prediction will be accurate: perhaps Kim will pick the glass up cleanly. Nevertheless, the author has certainly created the expectation that the water might be spilled.

As we read on, we can test the accuracy of our predictions, revise them in light of additional reading, and confirm or refute our predictions. Predictions are always subject to revision as the reader acquires more information. A reader can make predictions by observing the title and illustrations; noting the structure, characters, and subject; drawing on existing knowledge relative to the subject; and asking "why" and "who" questions. Connecting reading to what we already know enables us to learn new information and construct meaning. For example, before third-graders read a book about Johnny Appleseed, they may start a KWL chart—a list of what they *Know*, what they *Want* to know or learn, and what they have *Learned* after reading. Activating existing background knowledge and thinking about the text before reading improves comprehension.

> **Review Video: Predictive Reading**
> Visit mometrix.com/academy and enter code: 437248

Test-taking tip: To respond to questions requiring future predictions, your answers should be based on evidence of past or present behavior and events.

EVALUATING PREDICTIONS

When making predictions, readers should be able to explain how they developed their prediction. One way readers can defend their thought process is by citing textual evidence. Textual evidence to evaluate reader predictions about literature includes specific synopses of the work, paraphrases of the work or parts of it, and direct quotations from the work. These references to the text must support the prediction by indicating, clearly or unclearly, what will happen later in the story. A text may provide these indications through literary devices such as foreshadowing. Foreshadowing is anything in a text that gives the reader a hint about what is to come by emphasizing the likelihood of an event or development. Foreshadowing can occur through descriptions, exposition, and dialogue. Foreshadowing in dialogue usually occurs when a character gives a warning or expresses a strong feeling that a certain event will occur. Foreshadowing can also occur through irony. However, unlike other forms of foreshadowing, the events that seem the most likely are the opposite of what actually happens. Instances of foreshadowing and irony can be summarized, paraphrased, or quoted to defend a reader's prediction.

> **Review Video: Textual Evidence for Predictions**
> Visit mometrix.com/academy and enter code: 261070

DRAWING CONCLUSIONS FROM INFERENCES

Inferences about literary text are logical conclusions that readers make based on their observations and previous knowledge. An inference is based on both what is found in a passage or a story and what is known from personal experience. For instance, a story may say that a character is frightened and can hear howling in the distance. Based on both what is in the text and personal knowledge, it is a logical conclusion that the character is frightened because he hears the sound of wolves. A good inference is supported by the information in a passage.

IMPLICIT AND EXPLICIT INFORMATION

By inferring, readers construct meanings from text that are personally relevant. By combining their own schemas or concepts and their background information pertinent to the text with what they read, readers interpret it according to both what the author has conveyed and their own unique perspectives. Inferences are different from **explicit information**, which is clearly stated in a passage. Authors do not always explicitly spell out every meaning in what they write; many meanings are implicit. Through inference, readers can comprehend implied meanings in the text, and also derive personal significance from it, making the text meaningful and memorable to them. Inference is a natural process in everyday life. When readers infer, they can draw conclusions about what the author is saying, predict what may reasonably follow, amend these predictions as they continue to read, interpret the import of themes, and analyze the characters' feelings and motivations through their actions.

EXAMPLE OF DRAWING CONCLUSIONS FROM INFERENCES

Read the excerpt and decide why Jana finally relaxed.

> Jana loved her job, but the work was very demanding. She had trouble relaxing. She called a friend, but she still thought about work. She ordered a pizza, but eating it did not help. Then, her kitten jumped on her lap and began to purr. Jana leaned back and began to hum a little tune. She felt better.

You can draw the conclusion that Jana relaxed because her kitten jumped on her lap. The kitten purred, and Jana leaned back and hummed a tune. Then she felt better. The excerpt does not explicitly say that this is the reason why she was able to relax. The text leaves the matter unclear, but the reader can infer or make a "best guess" that this is the reason she is relaxing. This is a logical conclusion based on the information in the passage. It is the best conclusion a reader can make based on the information he or she has read. Inferences are based on the information in a passage, but they are not directly stated in the passage.

Test-taking tip: While being tested on your ability to make correct inferences, you must look for **contextual clues**. An answer can be true, but not the best or most correct answer. The contextual clues will help you find the answer that is the **best answer** out of the given choices. Be careful in your reading to understand the context in which a phrase is stated. When asked for the implied meaning of a statement made in the passage, you should immediately locate the statement and read the **context** in which the statement was made. Also, look for an answer choice that has a similar phrase to the statement in question.

> **Review Video: Inference**
> Visit mometrix.com/academy and enter code: 379203
>
> **Review Video: How to Support a Conclusion**
> Visit mometrix.com/academy and enter code: 281653

Interactions with Texts

PURPOSES FOR WRITING

In order to be an effective reader, one must pay attention to the author's **position** and **purpose**. Even those texts that seem objective and impartial, like textbooks, have a position and bias. Readers need to take these positions into account when considering the author's message. When an author uses emotional language or clearly favors one side of an argument, his or her position is clear. However, the author's position may be evident not only in what he or she writes, but also in what he or she doesn't write. In a normal setting, a reader would want to review some other texts on the same topic in order to develop a view of the author's position. If this was not possible, then you would want to at least acquire some background about the author. However, since you are in the middle of an exam and the only source of information is the text, you should look for language and argumentation that seems to indicate a particular stance on the subject.

> **Review Video: Author's Position**
> Visit mometrix.com/academy and enter code: 827954

Usually, identifying the author's **purpose** is easier than identifying his or her position. In most cases, the author has no interest in hiding his or her purpose. A text that is meant to entertain, for instance, should be written to please the reader. Most narratives, or stories, are written to entertain, though they may also inform or persuade. Informative texts are easy to identify, while the most difficult purpose of a text to identify is persuasion because the author has an interest in making this purpose hard to detect. When a reader discovers that the author is trying to persuade, he or she should be skeptical of the argument. For this reason, persuasive texts often try to establish an entertaining tone and hope to amuse the reader into agreement. On the other hand, an informative tone may be implemented to create an appearance of authority and objectivity.

An author's purpose is evident often in the organization of the text (e.g., section headings in bold font points to an informative text). However, you may not have such organization available to you in your exam. Instead, if the author makes his or her main idea clear from the beginning, then the likely purpose of the text is to inform. If the author begins by making a claim and provides various arguments to support that claim, then the purpose is probably to persuade. If the author tells a story or wants to gain the reader's attention more than to push a particular point or deliver information, then his or her purpose is most likely to entertain. As a reader, you must judge authors on how well they accomplish their purpose. In other words, you need to consider the type of passage (e.g., technical, persuasive, etc.) that the author has written and if the author has followed the requirements of the passage type.

MAKING LOGICAL CONCLUSIONS ABOUT A PASSAGE

A reader should always be drawing conclusions from the text. Sometimes conclusions are **implied** from written information, and other times the information is **stated directly** within the passage. One should always aim to draw conclusions from information stated within a passage, rather than to draw them from mere implications. At times an author may provide some information and then describe a counterargument. Readers should be alert for direct statements that are subsequently rejected or weakened by the author. Furthermore, you should always read through the entire passage before drawing conclusions. Many readers are trained to expect the author's conclusions at either the beginning or the end of the passage, but many texts do not adhere to this format.

Drawing conclusions from information implied within a passage requires confidence on the part of the reader. **Implications** are things that the author does not state directly, but readers can assume based on what the author does say. Consider the following passage: *I stepped outside and opened my umbrella. By the time I got to work, the cuffs of my pants were soaked*. The author never states that it is raining, but this fact is clearly implied. Conclusions based on implication must be well supported by the text. In order to draw a solid conclusion, readers should have **multiple pieces of evidence**. If readers have only one piece, they must be assured that there is no other possible explanation than their conclusion. A good reader will be able to draw many conclusions from information implied by the text, which will be a great help on the exam.

DRAWING CONCLUSIONS

A common type of inference that a reader has to make is **drawing a conclusion**. The reader makes this conclusion based on the information provided within a text. Certain facts are included to help a reader come to a specific conclusion. For example, a story may open with a man trudging through the snow on a cold winter day, dragging a sled behind him. The reader can logically **infer** from the setting of the story that the man is wearing heavy winter clothes in order to stay warm. Information is implied based on the setting of a story, which is why **setting** is an important element of the text. If the same man in the example was trudging down a beach on a hot summer day, dragging a surf board behind him, the reader would assume that the man is not wearing heavy clothes. The reader makes inferences based on their own experiences and the information presented to them in the story.

Test-taking tip: When asked to identify a conclusion that may be drawn, look for critical "hedge" phrases, such as *likely*, *may*, *can*, and *will often*, among many others. When you are being tested on this knowledge, remember the question that writers insert into these hedge phrases to cover every possibility. Often an answer will be wrong simply because there is no room for exception. Extreme positive or negative answers (such as always or never) are usually not correct. When answering these questions, the reader **should not** use any outside knowledge that is not gathered directly or reasonably inferred from the passage. Correct answers can be derived straight from the passage.

EXAMPLE

Read the following sentence from *Little Women* by Louisa May Alcott and draw a conclusion based upon the information presented:

> *You know the reason Mother proposed not having any presents this Christmas was because it is going to be a hard winter for everyone; and she thinks we ought not to spend money for pleasure, when our men are suffering so in the army.*

Based on the information in the sentence, the reader can conclude, or **infer**, that the men are away at war while the women are still at home. The pronoun *our* gives a clue to the reader that the character is speaking about men she knows. In addition, the reader can assume that the character is speaking to a brother or sister, since the term "Mother" is used by the character while speaking to another person. The reader can also come to the conclusion that the characters celebrate Christmas, since it is mentioned in the **context** of the sentence. In the sentence, the mother is presented as an unselfish character who is opinionated and thinks about the wellbeing of other people.

COMPARING TWO STORIES

When presented with two different stories, there will be **similarities** and **differences** between the two. A reader needs to make a list, or other graphic organizer, of the points presented in each story. Once the reader has written down the main point and supporting points for each story, the two sets of ideas can be compared. The reader can then present each idea and show how it is the same or different in the other story. This is called **comparing and contrasting ideas**.

The reader can compare ideas by stating, for example: "In Story 1, the author believes that humankind will one day land on Mars, whereas in Story 2, the author believes that Mars is too far away for humans to ever step foot on." Note that the two viewpoints are different in each story that the reader is comparing. A reader may state that: "Both stories discussed the likelihood of humankind landing on Mars." This statement shows how the viewpoint presented in both stories is based on the same topic, rather than how each viewpoint is different. The reader will complete a comparison of two stories with a conclusion.

> **Review Video: Comparing Two Stories**
> Visit mometrix.com/academy and enter code: 833765

OUTLINING A PASSAGE

As an aid to drawing conclusions, **outlining** the information contained in the passage should be a familiar skill to readers. An effective outline will reveal the structure of the passage and will lead to solid conclusions. An effective outline will have a title that refers to the basic subject of the text, though the title does not need to restate the main idea. In most outlines, the main idea will be the first major section. Each major idea in the passage will be established as the head of a category. For instance, the most common outline format calls for the main ideas of the passage to be indicated with Roman numerals. In an effective outline of this kind, each of the main ideas will be represented by a Roman numeral and none of the Roman numerals will designate minor details or secondary ideas. Moreover, all supporting ideas and details should be placed in the appropriate place on the outline. An outline does not need to include every detail listed in the text, but it should feature all of those that are central to the argument or message. Each of these details should be listed under the corresponding main idea.

> **Review Video: Outlining**
> Visit mometrix.com/academy and enter code: 584445

USING GRAPHIC ORGANIZERS

Ideas from a text can also be organized using **graphic organizers**. A graphic organizer is a way to simplify information and take key points from the text. A graphic organizer such as a timeline may have an event listed for a corresponding date on the timeline, while an outline may have an event listed under a key point that occurs in the text. Each reader needs to create the type of graphic organizer that works the best for him or her in terms of being able to recall information from a story. Examples include a spider-map, which takes a main idea from the story and places it in a bubble with supporting points branching off the main idea. An outline is useful for diagramming the main and supporting points of the entire story, and a Venn diagram compares and contrasts characteristics of two or more ideas.

> **Review Video: Graphic Organizers**
> Visit mometrix.com/academy and enter code: 665513

SUMMARIZING

A helpful tool is the ability to **summarize** the information that you have read in a paragraph or passage format. This process is similar to creating an effective outline. First, a summary should accurately define the main idea of the passage, though the summary does not need to explain this main idea in exhaustive detail. The summary should continue by laying out the most important supporting details or arguments from the passage. All of the significant supporting details should be included, and none of the details included should be irrelevant or insignificant. Also, the summary should accurately report all of these details. Too often, the desire for brevity in a summary leads to the sacrifice of clarity or accuracy. Summaries are often difficult to read because they omit all of the graceful language, digressions, and asides that distinguish great writing. However, an effective summary should communicate the same overall message as the original text.

EVALUATING A PASSAGE

It is important to understand the logical conclusion of the ideas presented in an informational text. **Identifying a logical conclusion** can help you determine whether you agree with the writer or not. Coming to this conclusion is much like making an inference: the approach requires you to combine the information given by the text with what you already know and make a logical conclusion. If the author intended for the reader to draw a certain conclusion, then you can expect the author's argumentation and detail to be leading in that direction.

One way to approach the task of drawing conclusions is to make brief **notes** of all the points made by the author. When the notes are arranged on paper, they may clarify the logical conclusion. Another way to approach conclusions is to consider whether the reasoning of the author raises any pertinent questions. Sometimes you will be able to draw several conclusions from a passage. On occasion these will be conclusions that were never imagined by the author. Therefore, be aware that these conclusions must be **supported directly by the text**.

EVALUATION OF SUMMARIES

A summary of a literary passage is a condensation in the reader's own words of the passage's main points. Several guidelines can be used in evaluating a summary. The summary should be complete yet concise. It should be accurate, balanced, fair, neutral, and objective, excluding the reader's own opinions or reactions. It should reflect in similar proportion how much each point summarized was covered in the original passage. Summary writers should include tags of attribution, like "Macaulay argues that" to reference the original author whose ideas are represented in the summary. Summary writers should not overuse quotations; they should only quote central concepts or phrases they cannot precisely convey in words other than those of the original author. Another aspect of evaluating a summary is considering whether it can stand alone as a coherent, unified composition. In addition, evaluation of a summary should include whether its writer has cited the original source of the passage they have summarized so that readers can find it.

Developmental Literacy

LITERACY

Literacy is commonly understood as the **ability to read and write**. UNESCO, the United Nations Educational, Scientific, and Cultural Organization, has further defined literacy as the "ability to identify, understand, interpret, create, communicate, compute, and use printed and written materials associated with varying contexts." Under the UNESCO definition, understanding cultural, political, and historical contexts of communities falls under the definition of literacy. While **reading literacy** may be gauged simply by the ability to read a newspaper, **writing literacy** includes spelling, grammar, and sentence structure. To be literate in a foreign language, one would also need to be able to understand a language by listening and be able to speak the language. Some argue that visual representation and numeracy should be included in the requirements one must meet to be considered literate. **Computer literacy** refers to one's ability to utilize the basic functions of computers and other technologies. Subsets of reading literacy include phonological awareness, decoding, comprehension, and vocabulary.

PHONOLOGICAL AWARENESS

A subskill of literacy, phonological awareness is the ability to perceive sound structures in a spoken word, such as syllables and the individual phonemes within syllables. **Phonemes** are the sounds represented by the letters in the alphabet. The ability to separate, blend, and manipulate sounds is critical to developing reading and spelling skills. Phonological awareness is concerned with not only syllables, but also **onset sounds** (the initial sound in a word, such as /k/ in 'cat') and **rime** (the sounds that follow the onset in a word, such as /at/ in 'cat'). Phonological awareness is an auditory skill that does not necessarily involve print. It should be developed before the student has learned letter to sound correspondences. A student's phonological awareness is an indicator of future reading success.

> **Review Video: <u>Phonological and Phonemic Awareness, and Phonics</u>**
> Visit mometrix.com/academy and enter code: 197017
>
> **Review Video: <u>Components of Oral Language Development</u>**
> Visit mometrix.com/academy and enter code: 480589

COMMUNICATION DEVELOPMENT NORMALLY OCCURRING WITHIN A CHILD'S FIRST FIVE YEARS OF LIFE

Language and communication development depend strongly on the language a child develops within the first five years of life. During this time, three developmental periods are observed. At birth, the first period begins. This period is characterized by infant crying and gazing. Babies communicate their sensations and emotions through these behaviors, so they are expressive; however, they are not yet intentional. They indirectly indicate their needs through expressing how they feel, and when these needs are met, these communicative behaviors are reinforced. These expressions and reinforcement are the foundations for the later development of intentional communication. This becomes possible in the second developmental period, between 6 and 18 months. At this time, infants become able to coordinate their attention visually with other people relative to things and events, enabling purposeful communication with adults. During the third developmental period, from 18 months on, children come to use language as their main way of communicating and learning. Preschoolers can carry on conversations, exercise self-control through language use, and conduct verbal negotiations.

MILESTONES OF NORMAL LANGUAGE DEVELOPMENT BY THE 2 YEARS OLD

By the time most children reach the age of 2 years, they have acquired a vocabulary of about 150 to 300 words. They can name various familiar objects found in their environments. They are able to use at least two prepositions in their speech (e.g., *in*, *on*, and/or *under*). Two-year-olds typically combine the words they know into short sentences. These sentences tend to be mostly noun-verb or verb-noun combinations (e.g., "Daddy work," "Watch this"). They may also include verb-preposition combinations (e.g., "Go out," "Come in"). By the age of 2 years, children use pronouns, such as *I*, *me*, and *you*. They typically can use at least two such pronouns correctly. A normally developing 2-year-old will respond to some commands, directions, or questions, such as "Show me your eyes" or "Where are your ears?"

SALIENT GENERAL ASPECTS OF HUMAN LANGUAGE ABILITIES FROM BEFORE BIRTH TO 5 YEARS OF AGE

Language and communication abilities are integral parts of human life that are central to learning, successful school performance, successful social interactions, and successful living. Human language ability begins before birth: the developing fetus can hear not only internal maternal sounds, but also the mother's voice, others' voices, and other sounds outside the womb. Humans have a natural sensitivity to human sounds and languages from before they are born until they are about 4½ years old. These years are critical for developing language and communication. Babies and young children are predisposed to greater sensitivity to human sounds than other sounds, orienting them toward the language spoken around them. Children absorb their environmental language completely, including vocal tones, syntax, usage, and emphasis. This linguistic absorption occurs very rapidly. Children's first 2½ years particularly involve amazing abilities to learn language, including grammatical expression.

6 MONTHS, 12 MONTHS, AND 18 MONTHS

Individual differences dictate a broad range of language development that is still normal. However, parents observing noticeably delayed language development in their children should consult professionals. Typically, babies respond to hearing their names by 6 months of age, turn their heads and eyes toward the sources of human voices they hear, and respond accordingly to friendly and angry tones of voice. By the age of 12 months, toddlers can usually understand and follow simple directions, especially when these are accompanied by physical and/or vocal cues. They can intentionally use one or more words with the correct meaning. By the age of 18 months, a normally developing child usually has acquired a vocabulary of roughly 5 to 20 words. Eighteen-month-old children use nouns in their speech most of the time. They are very likely to repeat certain words and/or phrases over and over. At this age, children typically are able to follow simple verbal commands without needing as many visual or auditory cues as at 12 months.

THREE YEARS

By the time they are 3 years old, most normally developing children have acquired vocabularies of between 900 and 1,000 words. Typically, they correctly use the pronouns *I*, *me*, and *you*. They use more verbs more frequently. They apply past tenses to some verbs and plurals to some nouns. 3-year-olds usually can use at least three prepositions; the most common are *in*, *on*, and *under*. The normally developing 3-year-old knows the major body parts and can name them. 3-year-olds typically use 3-word sentences with ease. Normally, parents should find approximately 75 to 100 percent of what a 3-year-old says to be intelligible, while strangers should find between 50 and 75 percent of a 3-year-old's speech intelligible. Children this age comprehend most simple questions about their activities and environments and can answer questions about what they should do when they are thirsty, hungry, sleepy, hot, or cold. They can tell about their experiences in ways that

26

adults can generally follow. By the age of 3 years, children should also be able to tell others their name, age, and sex.

FOUR YEARS

When normally developing children are 4 years old, most know the names of animals familiar to them. They can use at least four prepositions in their speech (e.g., *in, on, under, to, from,* etc.). They can name familiar objects in pictures, and they know and can identify one color or more. Usually, they are able to repeat four-syllable words they hear. They verbalize as they engage in their activities, which Vygotsky dubbed "private speech." Private speech helps young children think through what they are doing, solve problems, make decisions, and reinforce the correct sequences in multistep activities. When presented with contrasting items, 4-year-olds can understand comparative concepts like bigger and smaller. At this age, they are able to comply with simple commands without the target stimuli being in their sight (e.g., "Put those clothes in the hamper" [upstairs]). Four-year-old children will also frequently repeat speech sounds, syllables, words, and phrases, similar to 18-month-olds' repetitions but at higher linguistic and developmental levels.

FIVE YEARS

Once most children have reached the age of 5 years, their speech has expanded from the emphasis of younger children on nouns, verbs, and a few prepositions, and is now characterized by many more descriptive words, including adjectives and adverbs. Five-year-olds understand common antonyms, such as big/little, heavy/light, long/short, and hot/cold. They can now repeat longer sentences they hear, up to about 9 words. When given three consecutive, uninterrupted commands, the typical 5-year-old can follow these without forgetting one or two. At age 5, most children have learned simple concepts of time like today, yesterday, and tomorrow; day, morning, afternoon, and night; and before, after, and later. Five-year-olds typically speak in relatively long sentences and normally should be incorporating some compound sentences (with more than one independent clause) and complex sentences (with one or more independent and dependent clauses). Five-year-old children's speech is also grammatically correct most of the time.

ACTIVITIES THAT TEACH PHONOLOGICAL AWARENESS

Classroom activities that teach phonological awareness include language play and exposure to a variety of sounds and the contexts of sounds. Activities that teach phonological awareness include:

- Clapping to the sounds of individual words, names, or all words in a sentence
- Practicing saying blended phonemes
- Singing songs that involve phoneme replacement (e.g., The Name Game)
- Reading poems, songs, and nursery rhymes out loud
- Reading patterned and predictable texts out loud
- Listening to environmental sounds or following verbal directions
- Playing games with rhyming chants or fingerplays
- Reading alliterative texts out loud
- Grouping objects by beginning sounds
- Reordering words in a well-known sentence or making silly phrases by deleting words from a well-known sentence (perhaps from a favorite storybook)

TEACHING OF READING THROUGH PHONICS

Phonics is the process of learning to read by learning how spoken language is represented by letters. Students learn to read phonetically by sounding out the **phonemes** in words and then blending them together to produce the correct sounds in words. In other words, the student connects speech sounds with letters or groups of letters and blends the sounds together to determine the pronunciation of an unknown word. Phonics is a method commonly used to teach **decoding and reading**, but it has been challenged by other methods, such as the whole language approach. Despite the complexity of pronunciation and combined sounds in the English language, phonics is a highly effective way to teach reading. Being able to read or pronounce a word does not mean the student comprehends the meaning of the word, but context aids comprehension. When phonics is used as a foundation for decoding, children eventually learn to recognize words automatically and advance to decoding multisyllable words with practice.

ALPHABETIC PRINCIPLE AND ALPHABET WRITING SYSTEMS

The **alphabetic principle** refers to the use of letters and combinations of letters to represent speech sounds. The way letters are combined and pronounced is guided by a system of rules that establishes relationships between written and spoken words and their letter symbols. Alphabet writing systems are common around the world. Some are **phonological** in that each letter stands for an individual sound and words are spelled just as they sound. However, keep in mind that there are other writing systems as well, such as the Chinese **logographic** system and the Japanese **syllabic** system.

> **Review Video: Print Awareness and Alphabet Knowledge**
> Visit mometrix.com/academy and enter code: 541069

FACTS CHILDREN SHOULD KNOW ABOUT LETTERS

To be appropriately prepared to learn to read and write, a child should learn:

- That each letter is **distinct** in appearance
- What **direction and shape** must be used to write each letter
- That each letter has a **name**, which can be associated with the shape of a letter
- That there are **26** letters in the English alphabet, and letters are grouped in a certain order
- That letters represent **sounds of speech**
- That **words** are composed of letters and have meaning
- That one must be able to **correspond** letters and sounds to read

DEVELOPMENT OF LANGUAGE SKILLS

Children learn language through interacting with others, by experiencing language in daily and relevant context, and through understanding that speaking and listening are necessary for effective communication. Teachers can promote **language development** by intensifying the opportunities a child has to experience and understand language.

Teachers can assist language development by:

- Modeling enriched vocabulary and teaching new words
- Using questions and examples to extend a child's descriptive language skills
- Providing ample response time to encourage children to practice speech
- Asking for clarification to provide students with the opportunity to develop communication skills
- Promoting conversations among children
- Providing feedback to let children know they have been heard and understood, and providing further explanation when needed

RELATIONSHIP BETWEEN ORAL AND WRITTEN LANGUAGE DEVELOPMENT

Oral and written language development occur simultaneously. The acquisition of skills in one area supports the acquisition of skills in the other. However, oral language is not a prerequisite to written language. An immature form of oral language development is babbling, and an immature form of written language development is scribbling. **Oral language development** does not occur naturally, but does occur in a social context. This means it is best to include children in conversations rather than simply talk at them. **Written language development** can occur without direct instruction. In fact, reading and writing do not necessarily need to be taught through formal lessons if the child is exposed to a print-rich environment. A teacher can assist a child's language development by building on what the child already knows, discussing relevant and meaningful events and experiences, teaching vocabulary and literacy skills, and providing opportunities to acquire more complex language.

PRINT-RICH ENVIRONMENT

A teacher can provide a **print-rich environment** in the classroom in a number of ways. These include:

- **Displaying** the following in the classroom:
  - Children's names in print or cursive
  - Children's written work
  - Newspapers and magazines
  - Instructional charts
  - Written schedules
  - Signs and labels
  - Printed songs, poems, and rhymes
- Using **graphic organizers** such as KWL charts or story road maps to:
  - Remind students about what was read and discussed
  - Expand on the lesson topic or theme
  - Show the relationships among books, ideas, and words
- Using **big books** to:
  - Point out features of print, such as specific letters and punctuation
  - Track print from right to left
  - Emphasize the concept of words and the fact that they are used to communicate

BENEFITS OF PRINT AND BOOK AWARENESS

Print and book awareness helps a child understand:

- That there is a **connection** between print and messages contained on signs, labels, and other print forms in the child's environment
- That reading and writing are ways to obtain information and communicate ideas
- That **print** written in English runs from left to right and from top to bottom
- That a book has **parts**, such as a title, a cover, a title page, and a table of contents
- That a book has an **author** and contains a **story**
- That **illustrations** can carry meaning
- That **letters and words** are different
- That **words and sentences** are separated by spaces and punctuation
- That different **text forms** are used for different functions

- That print represents **spoken language**
- How to **hold** a book

DECODING

Decoding is the method or strategy used to make sense of printed words and figure out how to correctly pronounce them. In order to **decode**, a student needs to know the relationships between letters and sounds, including letter patterns; that words are constructed from phonemes and phoneme blends; and that a printed word represents a word that can be spoken. This knowledge will help the student recognize familiar words and make informed guesses about the pronunciation of unfamiliar words. Decoding is not the same as comprehension. It does not require an understanding of the meaning of a word, only a knowledge of how to recognize and pronounce it. Decoding can also refer to the skills a student uses to determine the meaning of a **sentence**. These skills include applying knowledge of vocabulary, sentence structure, and context.

ROLE OF FLUENCY IN LITERACY DEVELOPMENT

Fluency is the goal of literacy development. It is the ability to read accurately and quickly. Evidence of fluency includes the ability to recognize words automatically and group words for comprehension. At this point, the student no longer needs to decode words except for complex, unfamiliar ones. He or she is able to move to the next level and understand the **meaning** of a text. The student should be able to self-check for comprehension and should feel comfortable expressing ideas in writing. Teachers can help students build fluency by continuing to provide:

- Reading experiences and discussions about text that gradually increase in level of difficulty
- Reading practice, both silently and out loud
- Word analysis practice
- Instruction on reading comprehension strategies
- Opportunities to express responses to readings through writing

> **Review Video: Fluency**
> Visit mometrix.com/academy and enter code: 531179

ROLE OF VOCABULARY IN LITERACY DEVELOPMENT

When students do not know the meaning of words in a text, their comprehension is limited. As a result, the text becomes boring or confusing. The larger a student's **vocabulary** is, the better their reading comprehension will be. A larger vocabulary is also associated with an enhanced ability to **communicate** in speech and writing. It is the teacher's role to help students develop a good working vocabulary. Students learn most of the words they use and understand by listening to the world around them (adults, other students, media, etc.) They also learn from their reading experiences, which include being read to and reading independently. Carefully designed activities can also stimulate vocabulary growth, and should emphasize useful words that students see frequently, important words necessary for understanding text, and difficult words and phrases, such as idioms or words with more than one meaning.

TEACHING TECHNIQUES PROMOTING VOCABULARY DEVELOPMENT

A student's **vocabulary** can be developed by:

- Calling upon a student's **prior knowledge** and making comparisons to that knowledge
- **Defining** a word and providing multiple examples of the use of the word in context
- Showing a student how to use **context clues** to discover the meaning of a word

- Providing instruction on **prefixes**, **roots**, and **suffixes** to help students break a word into its parts and decipher its meaning
- Showing students how to use a **dictionary and a thesaurus**
- Asking students to **practice** new vocabulary by using the words in their own writing
- Providing a **print-rich environment** with a word wall
- Studying a group of words related to a **single subject**, such as farm words, transportation words, etc. so that concept development is enhanced

AFFIXES, PREFIXES, AND ROOT WORDS

Affixes are syllables attached to the beginning or end of a word to make a derivative or inflectional form of a word. Both prefixes and suffixes are affixes. A **prefix** is a syllable that appears at the beginning of a word that creates a specific meaning in combination with the root or base word. For example, the prefix *mis* means wrong. When combined with the root word *spelling*, the word *misspelling* is created, which means wrong spelling. A **root word** is the base of a word to which affixes can be added. For example, the prefix *in-* or *pre-* can be added to the latin root word *vent* to create *invent* or *prevent*, respectively. The suffix *-er* can be added to the root word *manage* to create *manager*, which means one who manages. The suffix *-able*, meaning capable of, can be added to *manage* to create *managable*, which means capable of being managed.

SUFFIXES

A **suffix** is a syllable that appears at the end of a word that creates a specific meaning in combination with the root or base word. There are three types of suffixes:

- **Noun suffixes**—Noun suffixes can change a verb or adjective to a noun. They can denote the act of, state of, quality of, or result of something. For example, *-ment* added to *argue* becomes *argument*, which can be understood as the act the act of resulting state from arguing or the reasons given to prove an idea. Noun suffixes can also denote the doer, or one who acts. For example, *-eer* added to *auction* becomes *auctioneer*, meaning one who auctions. Other examples include *-hood*, *-ness*, *-tion*, *-ship*, and *-ism*.
- **Verb suffixes**—These change other words to verbs and denote to make or to perform the act of. For example, *-en* added to *soft* makes *soften*, which means to make soft. Other verb suffixes are *-ate* (perpetuate), *-fy* (dignify), and *-ize* (sterilize).
- **Adjectival suffixes**—These suffixes change other words to adjectives and include suffixes such as *-ful*, which means full of. When added to *care*, the word *careful* is formed, which means full of care. Other examples are *-ish* and *-less*.

STRATEGIES TO IMPROVE READING COMPREHENSION

Teachers can model the strategies students can use on their own to better comprehend a text through a read-aloud. First, the teacher should do a walk-through of the story **illustrations** and ask, "What's happening here?" The teacher should then ask students to **predict** what the story will be about based on what they have seen. As the book is read, the teacher should ask open-ended questions such as, "Why do you think the character did this?" and "How do you think the character feels?" The teacher should also ask students if they can **relate** to the story or have background knowledge of something similar. After the reading, the teacher should ask the students to **retell** the story in their own words to check for comprehension. Possible methods of retelling include performing a puppet show or summarizing the story to a partner.

Review Video: The Link Between Grammar Skills and Reading Comprehension
Visit mometrix.com/academy and enter code: 411287

ROLE OF PRIOR KNOWLEDGE IN DETERMINING APPROPRIATE LITERACY EDUCATION

Even preschool children have some literacy skills, and the extent and type of these skills have implications for instructional approaches. **Comprehension** results from relating two or more pieces of information. One piece comes from the text, and another piece might come from **prior knowledge** (something from a student's long-term memory). For a child, that prior knowledge comes from being read to at home; taking part in other literacy experiences, such as playing computer or word games; being exposed to a print-rich environment at home; and observing parents' reading habits. Children who have had **extensive literacy experience** are better prepared to further develop their literacy skills in school than children who have not been read to, have few books or magazines in their homes, are seldom exposed to high-level oral or written language activities, and seldom witness adults engaged in reading and writing. Children with a scant literacy background are at a disadvantage. The teacher must not make any assumptions about their prior knowledge, and should use intense, targeted instruction. Otherwise, the student may have trouble improving their reading comprehension.

English Language Learning

THEORIES OF LANGUAGE DEVELOPMENT

Four theories of language development are:

- **Learning approach**—This theory assumes that language is first learned by imitating the speech of adults. It is then solidified in school through drills about the rules of language structures.
- **Linguistic approach**—Championed by Noam Chomsky in the 1950s, this theory proposes that the ability to use a language is innate. This is a biological approach rather than one based on cognition or social patterning.
- **Cognitive approach**—Developed in the 1970s and based on the work of Piaget, this theory states that children must develop appropriate cognitive skills before they can acquire language.
- **Sociocognitive approach**—In the 1970s, some researchers proposed that language development is a complex interaction of linguistic, social, and cognitive influences. This theory best explains the lack of language skills among children who are neglected, have uneducated parents, or live in poverty.

CLASSROOM PRACTICES BENEFITING SECOND LANGUAGE ACQUISITION

Since some students may have a limited understanding of English, a teacher should employ the following practices to promote second language acquisition:

- Make all instruction as **understandable** as possible and use simple and repeated terms.
- Relate instruction to the **cultures** of ESL children.
- Increase **interactive activities** and use gestures or nonverbal actions when modeling.
- Provide language and literacy development instruction in **all curriculum areas**.
- Establish **consistent routines** that help children connect words and events.
- Use a **schedule** so children know what will happen next and will not feel lost.
- Integrate ESL children into **group activities** with non-ESL children.
- Appoint bilingual students to act as **student translators**.
- Explain actions as activities happen so that a **word to action relationship** is established.
- Initiate opportunities for ESL children to **experiment** with and practice new language.
- Employ multisensory learning.

TEACHING STRATEGIES TO PROMOTE LISTENING SKILLS OF ESL STUDENTS

Listening is a critical skill when learning a new language. Students spend a great deal more time listening than they do speaking, and far less time reading and writing than speaking. One way to encourage ESL students to listen is to talk about topics that are of **interest** to the ESL learner. Otherwise, students may tune out the speaker because they don't want to put in that much effort to learn about a topic they find boring. Another way to encourage ESL students to listen is to talk about content or give examples that are **easy** to understand or are **related** to a topic that is familiar to ESL students. Culturally relevant materials will be more interesting to ESL students, will make them feel more comfortable, and will contain vocabulary that they may already be familiar with.

Considerations Relevant to ESL Students Related to Learning by Listening

Listening is not a passive skill, but an **active** one. Therefore, a teacher needs to make the listening experience as rewarding as possible and provide as many auditory and visual clues as possible. Three ways that the teacher can make the listening experience rewarding for ESL students are:

- Avoid **colloquialisms** and **abbreviated or slang terms** that may be confusing to the ESL listener, unless there is enough time to define them and explain their use.
- Make the spoken English understandable by stopping to **clarify** points, **repeating** new or difficult words, and **defining** words that may not be known.
- Support the spoken word with as many **visuals** as possible. Pictures, diagrams, gestures, facial expressions, and body language can help the ESL learner correctly interpret the spoken language more easily and also leaves an image impression that helps them remember the words.

Top-Down and Bottom-Up Processing

ESL students need to be given opportunities to practice both top-down and bottom-up processing. If they are old enough to understand these concepts, they should be made aware that these are two processes that affect their listening comprehension. In **top-down processing**, the listener refers to **background and global knowledge** to figure out the meaning of a message. For example, when asking an ESL student to perform a task, the steps of the task should be explained and accompanied by a review of the vocabulary terms the student already understands so that the student feels comfortable tackling new steps and new words. The teacher should also allow students to ask questions to verify comprehension. In **bottom-up processing**, the listener figures out the meaning of a message by using "**data**" obtained from what is said. This data includes sounds (stress, rhythm, and intonation), words, and grammatical relationships. All data can be used to make conclusions or interpretations. For example, the listener can develop bottom-up skills by learning how to detect differences in intonation between statements and questions.

Listening Lessons

All students, but especially ESL students, can be taught **listening** through specific training. During listening lessons, the teacher should guide students through three steps:

- **Pre-listening activity**—This establishes the purpose of the lesson and engages students' background knowledge. This activity should ask students to think about and discuss something they already know about the topic. Alternatively, the teacher can provide background information.
- **The listening activity**—This requires the listener to obtain information and then immediately do something with that information. For example, the teacher can review the schedule for the day or the week. In this example, students are being given information about a routine they already know, and need to be able to identify names, tasks, and times.
- **Post-listening activity**—This is an evaluation process that allows students to judge how well they did with the listening task. Other language skills can be included in the activity. For example, this activity could involve asking questions about who will do what according to the classroom schedule (Who is the lunch monitor today?) and could also involve asking students to produce whole sentence replies.

HELPING ESL STUDENTS UNDERSTAND SUBJECT MATTER

SPEAKING

To help ESL students better understand subject matter, the following teaching strategies using spoken English can be used:

- **Read aloud** from a textbook, and then ask ESL students to **verbally summarize** what was read. The teacher should assist by providing new words as needed to give students the opportunity to practice vocabulary and speaking skills. The teacher should then read the passage again to students to verify accuracy and details.
- The teacher could ask ESL students to explain why the subject matter is important to them and where they see it fitting into their lives. This verbalization gives them speaking practice and helps them relate to the subject.
- Whenever small group activities are being conducted, ESL students can be placed with **English-speaking students**. It is best to keep the groups to two or three students so that the ESL student will be motivated by the need to be involved. English-speaking students should be encouraged to include ESL students in the group work.

READING

There are supplemental printed materials that can be used to help ESL students understand subject matter. The following strategies can be used to help ESL students develop English reading skills.

- Make sure all ESL students have a **bilingual dictionary** to use. A thesaurus would also be helpful.
- Try to keep **content area books** written in the ESL students' native languages in the classroom. Students can use them side-by-side with English texts. Textbooks in other languages can be ordered from the school library or obtained from the classroom textbook publisher.
- If a student lacks confidence in his or her ability to read the textbook, the teacher can read a passage to the student and have him or her **verbally summarize** the passage. The teacher should take notes on what the student says and then read them back. These notes can be a substitute, short-form, in-their-own-words textbook that the student can understand.

GENERAL TEACHING STRATEGIES TO HELP ESL STUDENTS

Some strategies can help students develop more than one important skill. They may involve a combination of speaking, listening, and viewing. Others are mainly classroom management aids. General teaching strategies for ESL students include:

- **Partner** English-speaking students with ESL students as study buddies and ask the English-speaking students to share notes.
- Encourage ESL students to ask **questions** whenever they don't understand something. They should be aware that they don't have to be able to interpret every word of text to understand the concept.
- Dictate **key sentences** related to the content area being taught and ask ESL students to write them down. This gives them practice in listening and writing, and also helps them identify what is important.
- **Alternate** difficult and easy tasks so that ESL students can experience academic success.
- Ask ESL students to **label** objects associated with content areas, such as maps, diagrams, parts of a leaf, or parts of a sentence. This gives students writing and reading experience and helps them remember key vocabulary.

Literature, Genre, and Craft

Parts of Speech

THE EIGHT PARTS OF SPEECH

NOUNS

When you talk about a person, place, thing, or idea, you are talking about a **noun**. The two main types of nouns are **common** and **proper** nouns. Also, nouns can be abstract (i.e., general) or concrete (i.e., specific).

COMMON NOUNS

Common nouns are generic names for people, places, and things. Common nouns are not usually capitalized.

Examples of common nouns:

> *People*: boy, girl, worker, manager

> *Places*: school, bank, library, home

> *Things*: dog, cat, truck, car

> **Review Video: What is a Noun?**
> Visit mometrix.com/academy and enter code: 344028

PROPER NOUNS

Proper nouns name specific people, places, or things. All proper nouns are capitalized.

Examples of proper nouns:

> *People*: Abraham Lincoln, George Washington, Martin Luther King, Jr.

> *Places*: Los Angeles, California; New York; Asia

> *Things*: Statue of Liberty, Earth, Lincoln Memorial

Note: When referring to the planet that we live on, capitalize *Earth*. When referring to the dirt, rocks, or land, lowercase *earth*.

GENERAL AND SPECIFIC NOUNS

General nouns are the names of conditions or ideas. **Specific nouns** name people, places, and things that are understood by using your senses.

General nouns:

> *Condition*: beauty, strength

> *Idea*: truth, peace

Specific nouns:

People: baby, friend, father

Places: town, park, city hall

Things: rainbow, cough, apple, silk, gasoline

COLLECTIVE NOUNS

Collective nouns are the names for a group of people, places, or things that may act as a whole. The following are examples of collective nouns: *class, company, dozen, group, herd, team,* and *public.* Collective nouns usually require an article, which denotes the noun as being a single unit. For instance, a choir is a group of singers. Even though there are many singers in a choir, the word choir is grammatically treated as a single unit. If we refer to the members of the group, and not the group itself, it is no longer a collective noun.

Incorrect: The *choir are* going to compete nationally this year.

Correct: The *choir is* going to compete nationally this year.

Incorrect: The *members* of the choir *is* competing nationally this year.

Correct: The *members* of the choir *are* competing nationally this year.

PRONOUNS

Pronouns are words that are used to stand in for nouns. A pronoun may be classified as personal, intensive, relative, interrogative, demonstrative, indefinite, and reciprocal.

Personal: *Nominative* is the case for nouns and pronouns that are the subject of a sentence. *Objective* is the case for nouns and pronouns that are an object in a sentence. *Possessive* is the case for nouns and pronouns that show possession or ownership.

Singular

	Nominative	Objective	Possessive
First Person	I	me	my, mine
Second Person	you	you	your, yours
Third Person	he, she, it	him, her, it	his, her, hers, its

Plural

	Nominative	Objective	Possessive
First Person	we	us	our, ours
Second Person	you	you	your, yours
Third Person	they	them	their, theirs

Intensive: I myself, you yourself, he himself, she herself, the (thing) itself, we ourselves, you yourselves, they themselves

Relative: which, who, whom, whose

Interrogative: what, which, who, whom, whose

Demonstrative: this, that, these, those

Indefinite: all, any, each, everyone, either/neither, one, some, several

Reciprocal: each other, one another

VERBS

If you want to write a sentence, then you need a verb. Without a verb, you have no sentence. The verb of a sentence indicates action or being. In other words, the verb shows something's action or state of being or the action that has been done to something.

TRANSITIVE AND INTRANSITIVE VERBS

A **transitive verb** is a verb whose action (e.g., drive, run, jump) indicates a receiver (e.g., car, dog, kangaroo). **Intransitive verbs** do not indicate a receiver of an action. In other words, the action of the verb does not point to a subject or object.

Transitive: He plays the piano. | The piano was played by him.

Intransitive: He plays. | John plays well.

A dictionary will tell you whether a verb is transitive or intransitive. Some verbs can be transitive and intransitive.

ACTION VERBS AND LINKING VERBS

Action verbs show what the subject is doing. In other words, an action verb shows action. Unlike most types of words, a single action verb, in the right context, can be an entire sentence. **Linking verbs** link the subject of a sentence to a noun or pronoun, or they link a subject with an adjective. You always need a verb if you want a complete sentence. However, linking verbs on their own cannot be a complete sentence.

Common linking verbs include *appear, be, become, feel, grow, look, seem, smell, sound,* and *taste*. However, any verb that shows a condition and connects to a noun, pronoun, or adjective that describes the subject of a sentence is a linking verb.

Action: He sings. | Run! | Go! | I talk with him every day. | She reads.

Linking:

Incorrect: I am.

Correct: I am John. | The roses smell lovely. | I feel tired.

Note: Some verbs are followed by words that look like prepositions, but they are a part of the verb and a part of the verb's meaning. These are known as phrasal verbs, and examples include *call off, look up,* and *drop off*.

VOICE

Transitive verbs come in active or passive **voice**. If something does an action or is acted upon, then you will know whether a verb is active or passive. When the subject of the sentence is doing the action, the verb is in **active voice**. When the subject is acted upon, the verb is in **passive voice**.

Active: Jon drew the picture. (The subject *Jon* is doing the action of *drawing a picture*.)

Passive: The picture is drawn by Jon. (The subject *picture* is receiving the action from Jon.)

VERB TENSES

A verb **tense** shows the different form of a verb to point to the time of an action. The present and past tense are indicated by the verb's form. An action in the present, *I talk*, can change form for the past: *I talked*. However, for the other tenses, an auxiliary (i.e., helping) verb is needed to show the change in form. These helping verbs include *am, are, is | have, has, had | was, were, will* (or *shall*).

Present: I talk	Present perfect: I have talked
Past: I talked	Past perfect: I had talked
Future: I will talk	Future perfect: I will have talked

Present: The action happens at the current time.

Example: He *walks* to the store every morning.

To show that something is happening right now, use the progressive present tense: I *am walking*.

Past: The action happened in the past.

Example: He *walked* to the store an hour ago.

Future: The action is going to happen later.

Example: I *will walk* to the store tomorrow.

Present perfect: The action started in the past and continues into the present or took place previously at an unspecified time.

Example: I *have walked* to the store three times today.

Past perfect: The second action happened in the past. The first action came before the second.

Example: Before I walked to the store (Action 2), I *had walked* to the library (Action 1).

Future perfect: An action that uses the past and the future. In other words, the action is complete before a future moment.

Example: When she comes for the supplies (future moment), I *will have walked* to the store (action completed before the future moment).

> **Review Video: <u>Present Perfect, Past Perfect, and Future Perfect Verb Tenses</u>**
> Visit mometrix.com/academy and enter code: 269472

CONJUGATING VERBS

When you need to change the form of a verb, you are **conjugating** a verb. The key forms of a verb are singular, present tense (dream); singular, past tense (dreamed); and the past participle (have dreamed). Note: the past participle needs a helping verb to make a verb tense. For example, I *have dreamed* of this day. The following tables demonstrate some of the different ways to conjugate a verb:

Singular

Tense	First Person	Second Person	Third Person
Present	I dream	You dream	He, she, it dreams
Past	I dreamed	You dreamed	He, she, it dreamed
Past Participle	I have dreamed	You have dreamed	He, she, it has dreamed

Plural

Tense	First Person	Second Person	Third Person
Present	We dream	You dream	They dream
Past	We dreamed	You dreamed	They dreamed
Past Participle	We have dreamed	You have dreamed	They have dreamed

MOOD

There are three **moods** in English: the indicative, the imperative, and the subjunctive.

The **indicative mood** is used for facts, opinions, and questions.

Fact: You can do this.

Opinion: I think that you can do this.

Question: Do you know that you can do this?

The **imperative** is used for orders or requests.

Order: You are going to do this!

Request: Will you do this for me?

The **subjunctive mood** is for wishes and statements that go against fact.

Wish: I wish that I were famous.

Statement against fact: If I were you, I would do this. (This goes against fact because I am not you. You have the chance to do this, and I do not have the chance.)

ADJECTIVES

An **adjective** is a word that is used to modify a noun or pronoun. An adjective answers a question: *Which one? What kind?* or *How many?* Usually, adjectives come before the words that they modify, but they may also come after a linking verb.

Which one? The *third* suit is my favorite.

What kind? This suit is *navy blue*.

How many? I am going to buy *four* pairs of socks to match the suit.

> **Review Video: Descriptive Text**
> Visit mometrix.com/academy and enter code: 174903

ARTICLES

Articles are adjectives that are used to distinguish nouns as definite or indefinite. **Definite** nouns are preceded by the article *the* and indicate a specific person, place, thing, or idea. **Indefinite** nouns are preceded by *a* or *an* and do not indicate a specific person, place, thing, or idea. *A*, *an*, and *the* are the only articles. Note: *An* comes before words that start with a vowel sound. For example, "Are you going to get an **u**mbrella?"

Definite: I lost *the* bottle that belongs to me.

Indefinite: Does anyone have *a* bottle to share?

> **Review Video: Function of Articles**
> Visit mometrix.com/academy and enter code: 449383

COMPARISON WITH ADJECTIVES

Some adjectives are relative and other adjectives are absolute. Adjectives that are **relative** can show the comparison between things. **Absolute** adjectives can also show comparison, but they do so in a different way. Let's say that you are reading two books. You think that one book is perfect, and the other book is not exactly perfect. It is not possible for one book to be more perfect than the other. Either you think that the book is perfect, or you think that the book is imperfect. In this case, perfect and imperfect are absolute adjectives.

Relative adjectives will show the different **degrees** of something or someone to something else or someone else. The three degrees of adjectives include positive, comparative, and superlative.

The **positive** degree is the normal form of an adjective.

Example: This work is *difficult*. | She is *smart*.

The **comparative** degree compares one person or thing to another person or thing.

Example: This work is *more difficult* than your work. | She is *smarter* than me.

41

The **superlative** degree compares more than two people or things.

Example: This is the *most difficult* work of my life. | She is the *smartest* lady in school.

> **Review Video: What is an Adjective?**
> Visit mometrix.com/academy and enter code: 470154

ADVERBS

An **adverb** is a word that is used to **modify** a verb, adjective, or another adverb. Usually, adverbs answer one of these questions: *When? Where? How?* and *Why?* The negatives *not* and *never* are considered adverbs. Adverbs that modify adjectives or other adverbs **strengthen** or **weaken** the words that they modify.

Examples:

He walks *quickly* through the crowd.

The water flows *smoothly* on the rocks.

Note: Adverbs are usually indicated by the morpheme *-ly*, which has been added to the root word. For instance, *quick* can be made into an adverb by adding *-ly* to construct *quickly*. Some words that end in *-ly* do not follow this rule and can behave as other parts of speech. Examples of adjectives ending in *-ly* include: *early, friendly, holy, lonely, silly*, and *ugly*. To know if a word that ends in *-ly* is an adjective or adverb, check your dictionary. Also, while many adverbs end in *-ly*, you need to remember that not all adverbs end in *-ly*.

Examples:

He is *never* angry.

You walked *across* the bridge.

> **Review Video: What is an Adverb?**
> Visit mometrix.com/academy and enter code: 713951
>
> **Review Video: Adverbs that Modify Adjectives**
> Visit mometrix.com/academy and enter code: 122570

COMPARISON WITH ADVERBS

The rules for comparing adverbs are the same as the rules for adjectives.

The **positive** degree is the standard form of an adverb.

Example: He arrives *soon*. | She speaks *softly* to her friends.

The **comparative** degree compares one person or thing to another person or thing.

Example: He arrives *sooner* than Sarah. | She speaks *more softly* than him.

The **superlative** degree compares more than two people or things.

Example: He arrives *soonest* of the group. | She speaks the *most softly* of any of her friends.

PREPOSITIONS

A **preposition** is a word placed before a noun or pronoun that shows the relationship between an object and another word in the sentence.

Common prepositions:

about	before	during	on	under
after	beneath	for	over	until
against	between	from	past	up
among	beyond	in	through	with
around	by	of	to	within
at	down	off	toward	without

Examples:

The napkin is *in* the drawer.

The Earth rotates *around* the Sun.

The needle is *beneath* the haystack.

Can you find "me" *among* the words?

> **Review Video: Prepositions**
> Visit mometrix.com/academy and enter code: 946763

CONJUNCTIONS

Conjunctions join words, phrases, or clauses and they show the connection between the joined pieces. **Coordinating conjunctions** connect equal parts of sentences. **Correlative conjunctions** show the connection between pairs. **Subordinating conjunctions** join subordinate (i.e., dependent) clauses with independent clauses.

COORDINATING CONJUNCTIONS

The **coordinating conjunctions** include: *and, but, yet, or, nor, for,* and *so*

Examples:

The rock was small, *but* it was heavy.

She drove in the night, *and* he drove in the day.

CORRELATIVE CONJUNCTIONS

The **correlative conjunctions** are: *either...or* | *neither...nor* | *not only...but also*

Examples:

Either you are coming *or* you are staying.

He *not only* ran three miles *but also* swam 200 yards.

> **Review Video: Coordinating and Correlative Conjunctions**
> Visit mometrix.com/academy and enter code: 390329
>
> **Review Video: Adverb Equal Comparisons**
> Visit mometrix.com/academy and enter code: 231291

SUBORDINATING CONJUNCTIONS

Common **subordinating conjunctions** include:

after	since	whenever
although	so that	where
because	unless	wherever
before	until	whether
in order that	when	while

Examples:

I am hungry *because* I did not eat breakfast.

He went home *when* everyone left.

> **Review Video: Subordinating Conjunctions**
> Visit mometrix.com/academy and enter code: 958913

INTERJECTIONS

Interjections are words of exclamation (i.e., audible expression of great feeling) that are used alone or as a part of a sentence. Often, they are used at the beginning of a sentence for an introduction. Sometimes, they can be used in the middle of a sentence to show a change in thought or attitude.

Common Interjections: Hey! | Oh, | Ouch! | Please! | Wow!

Agreement and Sentence Structure

SUBJECTS AND PREDICATES
SUBJECTS

The **subject** of a sentence names who or what the sentence is about. The subject may be directly stated in a sentence, or the subject may be the implied *you*. The **complete subject** includes the simple subject and all of its modifiers. To find the complete subject, ask *Who* or *What* and insert the verb to complete the question. The answer, including any modifiers (adjectives, prepositional phrases, etc.), is the complete subject. To find the **simple subject**, remove all of the modifiers in the complete subject. Being able to locate the subject of a sentence helps with many problems, such as those involving sentence fragments and subject-verb agreement.

Examples:

simple
subject

The small, red car is the one that he wants for Christmas.
complete
subject

simple
subject

The young artist is coming over for dinner.
complete
subject

> **Review Video: Subjects in English**
> Visit mometrix.com/academy and enter code: 444771

In **imperative** sentences, the verb's subject is understood (e.g., [You] Run to the store), but is not actually present in the sentence. Normally, the subject comes before the verb. However, the subject comes after the verb in sentences that begin with *There are* or *There was*.

Direct:

John knows the way to the park.	Who knows the way to the park?	John
The cookies need ten more minutes.	What needs ten minutes?	The cookies
By five o'clock, Bill will need to leave.	Who needs to leave?	Bill
There are five letters on the table for him.	What is on the table?	Five letters
There were coffee and doughnuts in the house.	What was in the house?	Coffee and doughnuts

Implied:

Go to the post office for me.	Who is going to the post office?	You
Come and sit with me, please?	Who needs to come and sit?	You

PREDICATES

In a sentence, you always have a predicate and a subject. The subject tells what the sentence is about, and the **predicate** explains or describes the subject.

45

Think about the sentence *He sings.* In this sentence, we have a subject (He) and a predicate (sings). This is all that is needed for a sentence to be complete. Most sentences contain more information, but if this is all the information that you are given, then you have a complete sentence.

Now, let's look at another sentence: *John and Jane sing on Tuesday nights at the dance hall.*

       subject   predicate

John and Jane sing on Tuesday nights at the dance hall.

SUBJECT-VERB AGREEMENT

Verbs **agree** with their subjects in number. In other words, singular subjects need singular verbs. Plural subjects need plural verbs. **Singular** is for **one** person, place, or thing. **Plural** is for **more than one** person, place, or thing. Subjects and verbs must also share the same point of view, as in first, second, or third person. The present tense ending *-s* is used on a verb if its subject is third person singular; otherwise, the verb's ending is not modified.

Review Video: **Subject-Verb Agreement**
Visit mometrix.com/academy and enter code: 479190

NUMBER AGREEMENT EXAMPLES:

                           singular singular
                            subject   verb

Single Subject and Verb: Dan   calls home.

Dan is one person. So, the singular verb *calls* is needed.

                        plural   plural
                        subject   verb

Plural Subject and Verb: Dan and Bob call home.

More than one person needs the plural verb *call*.

PERSON AGREEMENT EXAMPLES:

First Person: I *am* walking.

Second Person: You *are* walking.

Third Person: He *is* walking.

COMPLICATIONS WITH SUBJECT-VERB AGREEMENT
WORDS BETWEEN SUBJECT AND VERB

Words that come between the simple subject and the verb have no bearing on subject-verb agreement.

Examples:

     singular   singular
     subject   verb

The joy of my life returns home tonight.

The phrase *of my life* does not influence the verb *returns*.

singular subject   singular verb

The question that still remains unanswered is "Who are you?"

Don't let the phrase "*that still remains*..." trouble you. The subject *question* goes with *is*.

COMPOUND SUBJECTS

A compound subject is formed when two or more nouns joined by *and*, *or*, or *nor* jointly act as the subject of the sentence.

JOINED BY AND

When a compound subject is joined by *and*, it is treated as a plural subject and requires a plural verb.

Examples:

plural subject   plural verb

You and Jon are invited to come to my house.

plural subject   plural verb

The pencil and paper belong to me.

JOINED BY OR/NOR

For a compound subject joined by *or* or *nor*, the verb must agree in number with the part of the subject that is closest to the verb (italicized in the examples below).

Examples:

subject   verb

Today or tomorrow is the day.

subject   verb

Stan or Phil wants to read the book.

subject   verb

Neither the pen nor the book is on the desk.

subject   verb

Either the blanket or pillows arrive this afternoon.

INDEFINITE PRONOUNS AS SUBJECT

An indefinite pronoun is a pronoun that does not refer to a specific noun. Different indefinite pronouns may only function as a singular noun, only function as a plural noun, or change depending on how they are used.

ALWAYS SINGULAR

Pronouns such as *each*, *either*, *everybody*, *anybody*, *somebody*, and *nobody* are always singular.

Examples:

singular subject · singular verb

Each of the runners has a different bib number.

singular verb · singular subject

Is either of you ready for the game?

Note: The words *each* and *either* can also be used as adjectives (e.g., *each* person is unique). When one of these adjectives modifies the subject of a sentence, it is always a singular subject.

singular subject · singular verb

Everybody grows a day older every day.

singular subject · singular verb

Anybody is welcome to bring a tent.

ALWAYS PLURAL

Pronouns such as *both*, *several*, and *many* are always plural.

Examples:

plural subject · plural verb

Both of the siblings were too tired to argue.

plural subject · plural verb

Many have tried, but none have succeeded.

DEPEND ON CONTEXT

Pronouns such as *some*, *any*, *all*, *none*, *more*, and *most* can be either singular or plural depending on what they are representing in the context of the sentence.

Examples:

singular subject · singular verb

All of my dog's food was still there in his bowl.

plural subject · plural verb

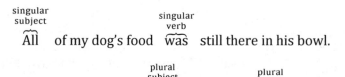

By the end of the night, all of my guests were already excited about coming to my next party.

OTHER CASES INVOLVING PLURAL OR IRREGULAR FORM

Some nouns are **singular in meaning but plural in form**: news, mathematics, physics, and economics.

> The *news is* coming on now.

> *Mathematics is* my favorite class.

Some nouns are plural in form and meaning, and have **no singular equivalent**: scissors and pants.

> Do these *pants come* with a shirt?

> The *scissors are* for my project.

Mathematical operations are **irregular** in their construction, but are normally considered to be **singular in meaning**.

> *One plus one is* two.

> *Three times three is* nine.

Note: Look to your **dictionary** for help when you aren't sure whether a noun with a plural form has a singular or plural meaning.

COMPLEMENTS

A complement is a noun, pronoun, or adjective that is used to give more information about the subject or verb in the sentence.

DIRECT OBJECTS

A direct object is a noun or pronoun that takes or receives the **action** of a verb. (Remember: a complete sentence does not need a direct object, so not all sentences will have them. A sentence needs only a subject and a verb.) When you are looking for a direct object, find the verb and ask *who* or *what*.

Examples:

> I took *the blanket*.

> Jane read *books*.

INDIRECT OBJECTS

An indirect object is a word or group of words that show how an action had an **influence** on someone or something. If there is an indirect object in a sentence, then you always have a direct object in the sentence. When you are looking for the indirect object, find the verb and ask *to/for whom or what*.

Examples:

indirect   direct
object   object
We taught the old dog a new trick.

indirect   direct
object   object
I gave them a math lesson.

PREDICATE NOMINATIVES AND PREDICATE ADJECTIVES

As we looked at previously, verbs may be classified as either action verbs or linking verbs. A linking verb is so named because it links the subject to words in the predicate that describe or define the subject. These words are called predicate nominatives (if nouns or pronouns) or predicate adjectives (if adjectives).

Examples:

subject   predicate nominative
My father is a lawyer.

subject   predicate adjective
Your mother is patient.

PRONOUN USAGE

The **antecedent** is the noun that has been replaced by a pronoun. A pronoun and its antecedent **agree** when they have the same number (singular or plural) and gender (male, female, or neutral).

Examples:

antecedent   pronoun
Singular agreement: John came into town, and he played for us.

antecedent   pronoun
Plural agreement: John and Rick came into town, and they played for us.

To determine which is the correct pronoun to use in a compound subject or object, try each pronoun **alone** in place of the compound in the sentence. Your knowledge of pronouns will tell you which one is correct.

Example:

Bob and (I, me) will be going.

Test: (1) *I will be going* or (2) *Me will be going*. The second choice cannot be correct because *me* cannot be used as the subject of a sentence. Instead, *me* is used as an object.

Answer: Bob and I will be going.

When a pronoun is used with a noun immediately following (as in "we boys"), try the sentence **without the added noun**.

Example:

(We/Us) boys played football last year.

Test: (1) *We played football last year* or (2) *Us played football last year*. Again, the second choice cannot be correct because *us* cannot be used as a subject of a sentence. Instead, *us* is used as an object.

Answer: We boys played football last year.

> **Review Video: <u>Pronoun Usage</u>**
> Visit mometrix.com/academy and enter code: 666500
>
> **Review Video: <u>What is Pronoun-Antecedent Agreement?</u>**
> Visit mometrix.com/academy and enter code: 919704

A pronoun should point clearly to the **antecedent**. Here is how a pronoun reference can be unhelpful if it is puzzling or not directly stated.

                    antecedent   pronoun
Unhelpful: Ron and Jim went to the store, and he bought soda.

Who bought soda? Ron or Jim?

              antecedent   pronoun
Helpful: Jim went to the store, and he bought soda.

The sentence is clear. Jim bought the soda.

Some pronouns change their form by their placement in a sentence. A pronoun that is a **subject** in a sentence comes in the **subjective case**. Pronouns that serve as **objects** appear in the **objective case**. Finally, the pronouns that are used as **possessives** appear in the **possessive case**.

Examples:

Subjective case: *He* is coming to the show.

The pronoun *He* is the subject of the sentence.

Objective case: Josh drove *him* to the airport.

The pronoun *him* is the object of the sentence.

Possessive case: The flowers are *mine*.

The pronoun *mine* shows ownership of the flowers.

The word *who* is a subjective-case pronoun that can be used as a **subject**. The word *whom* is an objective-case pronoun that can be used as an **object**. The words *who* and *whom* are common in subordinate clauses or in questions.

Examples:

$$\text{He knows } \underset{\text{subject}}{\underbrace{\text{who}}} \; \underset{\text{verb}}{\underbrace{\text{wants}}} \text{ to come.}$$

$$\text{He knows the man } \underset{\text{object}}{\underbrace{\text{whom}}} \text{ we } \underset{\text{verb}}{\underbrace{\text{want}}} \text{ at the party.}$$

CLAUSES

A clause is a group of words that contains both a subject and a predicate (verb). There are two types of clauses: independent and dependent. An **independent clause** contains a complete thought, while a **dependent (or subordinate) clause** does not. A dependent clause includes a subject and a verb, and may also contain objects or complements, but it cannot stand as a complete thought without being joined to an independent clause. Dependent clauses function within sentences as adjectives, adverbs, or nouns.

Example:

$$\underset{\substack{\text{independent} \\ \text{clause}}}{\underbrace{\text{I am running}}} \; \underset{\substack{\text{dependent} \\ \text{clause}}}{\underbrace{\text{because I want to stay in shape.}}}$$

The clause *I am running* is an independent clause: it has a subject and a verb, and it gives a complete thought. The clause *because I want to stay in shape* is a dependent clause: it has a subject and a verb, but it does not express a complete thought. It adds detail to the independent clause to which it is attached.

> **Review Video: What is a Clause?**
> Visit mometrix.com/academy and enter code: 940170
>
> **Review Video: Independent and Dependent Clauses**
> Visit mometrix.com/academy and enter code: 556903

TYPES OF DEPENDENT CLAUSES

ADJECTIVE CLAUSES

An **adjective clause** is a dependent clause that modifies a noun or a pronoun. Adjective clauses begin with a relative pronoun (*who, whose, whom, which,* and *that*) or a relative adverb (*where, when,* and *why*).

Also, adjective clauses come after the noun that the clause needs to explain or rename. This is done to have a clear connection to the independent clause.

Examples:

$$\underset{\substack{\text{independent} \\ \text{clause}}}{\underbrace{\text{I learned the reason}}} \; \underset{\substack{\text{adjective} \\ \text{clause}}}{\underbrace{\text{why I won the award.}}}$$

$$\underset{\substack{\text{independent} \\ \text{clause}}}{\underbrace{\text{This is the place}}} \; \underset{\substack{\text{adjective} \\ \text{clause}}}{\underbrace{\text{where I started my first job.}}}$$

An adjective clause can be an essential or nonessential clause. An essential clause is very important to the sentence. **Essential clauses** explain or define a person or thing. **Nonessential clauses** give more information about a person or thing but are not necessary to define them. Nonessential clauses are set off with commas while essential clauses are not.

Examples:

essential
clause

A person who works hard at first can often rest later in life.

nonessential
clause

Neil Armstrong, who walked on the moon, is my hero.

> **Review Video: Adjective Clauses and Phrases**
> Visit mometrix.com/academy and enter code: 520888

ADVERB CLAUSES

An **adverb clause** is a dependent clause that modifies a verb, adjective, or adverb. In sentences with multiple dependent clauses, adverb clauses are usually placed immediately before or after the independent clause. An adverb clause is introduced with words such as *after, although, as, before, because, if, since, so, unless, when, where,* and *while.*

Examples:

adverb
clause

When you walked outside, I called the manager.

adverb
clause

I will go with you unless you want to stay.

NOUN CLAUSES

A **noun clause** is a dependent clause that can be used as a subject, object, or complement. Noun clauses begin with words such as *how, that, what, whether, which, who,* and *why.* These words can also come with an adjective clause. Unless the noun clause is being used as the subject of the sentence, it should come after the verb of the independent clause.

Examples:

noun
clause

The real mystery is how you avoided serious injury.

noun
clause

What you learn from each other depends on your honesty with others.

SUBORDINATION

When two related ideas are not of equal importance, the ideal way to combine them is to make the more important idea an independent clause and the less important idea a dependent or subordinate clause. This is called **subordination**.

Example:

> **Separate ideas**: The team had a perfect regular season. The team lost the championship.

> **Subordinated**: Despite having a perfect regular season, *the team lost the championship.*

PHRASES

A phrase is a group of words that functions as a single part of speech, usually a noun, adjective, or adverb. A **phrase** is not a complete thought, but it adds detail or explanation to a sentence, or renames something within the sentence.

PREPOSITIONAL PHRASES

One of the most common types of phrases is the prepositional phrase. A **prepositional phrase** begins with a preposition and ends with a noun or pronoun that is the object of the preposition. Normally, the prepositional phrase functions as an **adjective** or an **adverb** within the sentence.

Examples:

prepositional
phrase
The picnic is on the blanket.

prepositional
phrase
I am sick with a fever today.

prepositional
phrase
Among the many flowers, John found a four-leaf clover.

VERBAL PHRASES

A **verbal** is a word or phrase that is formed from a verb but does not function as a verb. Depending on its particular form, it may be used as a noun, adjective, or adverb. A verbal does **not** replace a verb in a sentence.

Examples:

verb
Correct: Walk a mile daily.

This is a complete sentence with the implied subject *you*.

verbal
Incorrect: To walk a mile.

This is not a sentence since there is no functional verb.

There are three types of verbal: **participles**, **gerunds**, and **infinitives**. Each type of verbal has a corresponding **phrase** that consists of the verbal itself along with any complements or modifiers.

PARTICIPLES

A **participle** is a type of verbal that always functions as an adjective. The present participle always ends with *-ing*. Past participles end with *-d, -ed, -n,* or *-t*.

Examples: dance | dancing | danced
(verb | present participle | past participle)

Participial phrases most often come right before or right after the noun or pronoun that they modify.

Examples:

Shipwrecked on an island, (participial phrase) the boys started to fish for food.

Having been seated for five hours, (participial phrase) we got out of the car to stretch our legs.

Praised for their work, (participial phrase) the group accepted the first-place trophy.

GERUNDS

A **gerund** is a type of verbal that always functions as a **noun**. Like present participles, gerunds always end with *-ing*, but they can be easily distinguished from one another by the part of speech they represent (participles always function as adjectives). Since a gerund or gerund phrase always functions as a noun, it can be used as the subject of a sentence, the predicate nominative, or the object of a verb or preposition.

Examples:

We want to be known for teaching the poor. (gerund / object of preposition)

Coaching this team is the best job of my life. (gerund / subject)

We like practicing our songs in the basement. (gerund / object of verb)

INFINITIVES

An **infinitive** is a type of verbal that can function as a noun, an adjective, or an adverb. An infinitive is made of the word *to* and the basic form of the verb. As with all other types of verbal phrases, an infinitive phrase includes the verbal itself and all of its complements or modifiers.

Examples:

infinitive
To join the team is my goal in life.
noun

infinitive
The animals have enough food to eat for the night.
adjective

infinitive
People lift weights to exercise their muscles.
adverb

Review Video: Gerunds, Infinitives, and Participles
Visit mometrix.com/academy and enter code: 634263

APPOSITIVE PHRASES

An **appositive** is a word or phrase that is used to explain or rename nouns or pronouns. Noun phrases, gerund phrases, and infinitive phrases can all be used as appositives.

Examples:

appositive
Terriers, hunters at heart, have been dressed up to look like lap dogs.

The noun phrase *hunters at heart* renames the noun *terriers*.

appositive
His plan, to save and invest his money, was proven as a safe approach.

The infinitive phrase explains what the plan is.

Appositive phrases can be **essential** or **nonessential**. An appositive phrase is essential if the person, place, or thing being described or renamed is too general for its meaning to be understood without the appositive.

Examples:

essential
Two of America's Founding Fathers, George Washington and Thomas Jefferson, served as presidents.

nonessential
George Washington and Thomas Jefferson, two Founding Fathers, served as presidents.

ABSOLUTE PHRASES

An absolute phrase is a phrase that consists of **a noun followed by a participle**. An absolute phrase provides **context** to what is being described in the sentence, but it does not modify or explain any particular word; it is essentially independent.

Examples:

noun   participle
The alarm ringing, he pushed the snooze button.
absolute
phrase

noun   participle
The music paused, she continued to dance through the crowd.
absolute
phrase

PARALLELISM

When multiple items or ideas are presented in a sentence in series, such as in a list, the items or ideas must be stated in grammatically equivalent ways. In other words, if one idea is stated in gerund form, the second cannot be stated in infinitive form. For example, to write, *I enjoy reading and to study* would be incorrect. An infinitive and a gerund are not equivalent. Instead, you should write *I enjoy reading and studying*. In lists of more than two, all items must be parallel.

Example:

Incorrect: He stopped at the office, grocery store, and the pharmacy before heading home.

The first and third items in the list of places include the article *the*, so the second item needs it as well.

Correct: He stopped at the office, *the* grocery store, and the pharmacy before heading home.

Example:

Incorrect: While vacationing in Europe, she went biking, skiing, and climbed mountains.

The first and second items in the list are gerunds, so the third item must be as well.

Correct: While vacationing in Europe, she went biking, skiing, and *mountain climbing*.

> **Review Video: Parallel Sentence Construction**
> Visit mometrix.com/academy and enter code: 831988

SENTENCE PURPOSE

There are four types of sentences: declarative, imperative, interrogative, and exclamatory.

A **declarative** sentence states a fact and ends with a period.

The football game starts at seven o'clock.

An **imperative** sentence tells someone to do something and generally ends with a period. An urgent command might end with an exclamation point instead.

Don't forget to buy your ticket.

An **interrogative** sentence asks a question and ends with a question mark.

Are you going to the game on Friday?

An **exclamatory** sentence shows strong emotion and ends with an exclamation point.

I can't believe we won the game!

> **Review Video: Functions of a Sentence**
> Visit mometrix.com/academy and enter code: 475974

SENTENCE STRUCTURE

Sentences are classified by structure based on the type and number of clauses present. The four classifications of sentence structure are the following:

Simple: A simple sentence has one independent clause with no dependent clauses. A simple sentence may have **compound elements** (i.e., compound subject or verb).

Examples:

single   single
subject   verb
Judy watered the lawn.

compound   single
subject   verb
Judy and Alan watered the lawn.

single   compound   compound
subject   verb   verb
Judy watered the lawn and pulled weeds.

compound   compound   compound
subject   verb   verb
Judy and Alan watered the lawn and pulled weeds.

Compound: A compound sentence has two or more independent clauses with no dependent clauses. Usually, the independent clauses are joined with a comma and a coordinating conjunction or with a semicolon.

Examples:

independent   independent
clause   clause
The time has come, and we are ready.

independent   independent
clause   clause
I woke up at dawn; the sun was just coming up.

Complex: A complex sentence has one independent clause and at least one dependent clause.

Examples:

dependent   independent
clause   clause
Although he had the flu, Harry went to work.

independent   dependent
clause   clause
Marcia got married, after she finished college.

58

Compound-Complex: A compound-complex sentence has at least two independent clauses and at least one dependent clause.

Examples:

independent   dependent   independent
clause   clause   clause

John is my friend who went to India, and he brought back souvenirs.

independent   independent   dependent
clause   clause   clause

You may not realize this, but we heard the music that you played last night.

> **Review Video: Sentence Structure**
> Visit mometrix.com/academy and enter code: 700478

Sentence variety is important to consider when writing an essay or speech. A variety of sentence lengths and types creates rhythm, makes a passage more engaging, and gives writers an opportunity to demonstrate their writing style. Writing that uses the same length or type of sentence without variation can be boring or difficult to read. To evaluate a passage for effective sentence variety, it is helpful to note whether the passage contains diverse sentence structures and lengths. It is also important to pay attention to the way each sentence starts and avoid beginning with the same words or phrases.

SENTENCE FRAGMENTS

Recall that a group of words must contain at least one **independent clause** in order to be considered a sentence. If it doesn't contain even one independent clause, it is called a **sentence fragment**.

The appropriate process for **repairing** a sentence fragment depends on what type of fragment it is. If the fragment is a dependent clause, it can sometimes be as simple as removing a subordinating word (e.g., when, because, if) from the beginning of the fragment. Alternatively, a dependent clause can be incorporated into a closely related neighboring sentence. If the fragment is missing some required part, like a subject or a verb, the fix might be as simple as adding the missing part.

Examples:

Fragment: Because he wanted to sail the Mediterranean.

Removed subordinating word: He wanted to sail the Mediterranean.

Combined with another sentence: Because he wanted to sail the Mediterranean, he booked a Greek island cruise.

RUN-ON SENTENCES

Run-on sentences consist of multiple independent clauses that have not been joined together properly. Run-on sentences can be corrected in several different ways:

Join clauses properly: This can be done with a comma and coordinating conjunction, with a semicolon, or with a colon or dash if the second clause is explaining something in the first.

59

Example:

> **Incorrect**: I went on the trip, we visited lots of castles.

> **Corrected**: I went on the trip, and we visited lots of castles.

Split into separate sentences: This correction is most effective when the independent clauses are very long or when they are not closely related.

Example:

> **Incorrect**: The drive to New York takes ten hours, my uncle lives in Boston.

> **Corrected**: The drive to New York takes ten hours. My uncle lives in Boston.

Make one clause dependent: This is the easiest way to make the sentence correct and more interesting at the same time. It's often as simple as adding a subordinating word between the two clauses or before the first clause.

Example:

> **Incorrect**: I finally made it to the store and I bought some eggs.

> **Corrected**: When I finally made it to the store, I bought some eggs.

Reduce to one clause with a compound verb: If both clauses have the same subject, remove the subject from the second clause, and you now have just one clause with a compound verb.

Example:

> **Incorrect**: The drive to New York takes ten hours, it makes me very tired.

> **Corrected**: The drive to New York takes ten hours and makes me very tired.

Note: While these are the simplest ways to correct a run-on sentence, often the best way is to completely reorganize the thoughts in the sentence and rewrite it.

> **Review Video: Fragments and Run-on Sentences**
> Visit mometrix.com/academy and enter code: 541989

DANGLING AND MISPLACED MODIFIERS

DANGLING MODIFIERS

A dangling modifier is a dependent clause or verbal phrase that does not have a clear logical connection to a word in the sentence.

Example:

Incorrect: Reading each magazine article, the stories caught my attention.

(dangling modifier: Reading each magazine article)

The word *stories* cannot be modified by *Reading each magazine article*. People can read, but stories cannot read. Therefore, the subject of the sentence must be a person.

Corrected: Reading each magazine article, I was entertained by the stories.

(dependent clause: Reading each magazine article)

Example:

Incorrect: Ever since childhood, my grandparents have visited me for Christmas.

(dangling modifier: Ever since childhood)

The speaker in this sentence can't have been visited by her grandparents when *they* were children, since she wouldn't have been born yet. Either the modifier should be clarified or the sentence should be rearranged to specify whose childhood is being referenced.

Clarified: Ever since I was a child, my grandparents have visited for Christmas.

(dependent clause: Ever since I was a child)

Rearranged: I have enjoyed my grandparents visiting for Christmas, ever since childhood.

(dependent clause: ever since childhood)

MISPLACED MODIFIERS

Because modifiers are grammatically versatile, they can be put in many different places within the structure of a sentence. The danger of this versatility is that a modifier can accidentally be placed where it is modifying the wrong word or where it is not clear which word it is modifying.

Example:

Incorrect: She read the book to a crowd that was filled with beautiful pictures.

(modifier: that was filled with beautiful pictures)

The book was filled with beautiful pictures, not the crowd.

Corrected: She read the book that was filled with beautiful pictures to a crowd.

(modifier: that was filled with beautiful pictures)

61

Example:

Ambiguous: Derek saw a bus nearly hit a man $\overbrace{\text{on his way to work.}}^{\text{modifier}}$

Was Derek on his way to work or was the other man?

Derek: $\overbrace{\text{On his way to work,}}^{\text{modifier}}$ Derek saw a bus nearly hit a man.

The other man: Derek saw a bus nearly hit a man $\overbrace{\text{who was on his way to work.}}^{\text{modifier}}$

SPLIT INFINITIVES

A split infinitive occurs when a modifying word comes between the word *to* and the verb that pairs with *to*.

Example: To *clearly* explain vs. *To explain* clearly | To *softly* sing vs. *To sing* softly

Though considered improper by some, split infinitives may provide better clarity and simplicity in some cases than the alternatives. As such, avoiding them should not be considered a universal rule.

DOUBLE NEGATIVES

Standard English allows **two negatives** only when a **positive** meaning is intended. For example, *The team was not displeased with their performance*. Double negatives to emphasize negation are not used in standard English.

Negative modifiers (e.g., never, no, and not) should not be paired with other negative modifiers or negative words (e.g., none, nobody, nothing, or neither). The modifiers *hardly, barely*, and *scarcely* are also considered negatives in standard English, so they should not be used with other negatives.

Punctuation

END PUNCTUATION

PERIODS

Use a period to end all sentences except direct questions and exclamations. Periods are also used for abbreviations.

Examples: 3 p.m. | 2 a.m. | Mr. Jones | Mrs. Stevens | Dr. Smith | Bill, Jr. | Pennsylvania Ave.

Note: An abbreviation is a shortened form of a word or phrase.

QUESTION MARKS

Question marks should be used following a **direct question**. A polite request can be followed by a period instead of a question mark.

Direct Question: What is for lunch today? | How are you? | Why is that the answer?

Polite Requests: Can you please send me the item tomorrow. | Will you please walk with me on the track.

Review Video: **Question Marks**
Visit mometrix.com/academy and enter code: 118471

EXCLAMATION MARKS

Exclamation marks are used after a word group or sentence that shows much feeling or has special importance. Exclamation marks should not be overused. They are saved for proper **exclamatory interjections**.

Example: We're going to the finals! | You have a beautiful car! | "That's crazy!" she yelled.

Review Video: **Exclamation Points**
Visit mometrix.com/academy and enter code: 199367

COMMAS

The comma is a punctuation mark that can help you understand connections in a sentence. Not every sentence needs a comma. However, if a sentence needs a comma, you need to put it in the right place. A comma in the wrong place (or an absent comma) will make a sentence's meaning unclear. These are some of the rules for commas:

Use Case	Example
Before a **coordinating conjunction** joining independent clauses	Bob caught three fish, and I caught two fish.
After an **introductory phrase**	After the final out, we went to a restaurant to celebrate.
After an **adverbial clause**	Studying the stars, I was awed by the beauty of the sky.
Between **items in a series**	I will bring the turkey, the pie, and the coffee.
For **interjections**	Wow, you know how to play this game.
After *yes* and *no* responses	No, I cannot come tomorrow.
Separate **nonessential modifiers**	John Frank, who coaches the team, was promoted today.
Separate **nonessential appositives**	Thomas Edison, an American inventor, was born in Ohio.
Separate **nouns of direct address**	You, John, are my only hope in this moment.
Separate **interrogative tags**	This is the last time, correct?
Separate **contrasts**	You are my friend, not my enemy.
Writing **dates**	July 4, 1776, is an important date to remember.
Writing **addresses**	He is meeting me at 456 Delaware Avenue, Washington, D.C., tomorrow morning.
Writing **geographical names**	Paris, France, is my favorite city.
Writing **titles**	John Smith, PhD, will be visiting your class today.
Separate **expressions like *he said***	"You can start," she said, "with an apology."

Also, you can use a comma **between coordinate adjectives** not joined with *and*. However, not all adjectives are coordinate (i.e., equal or parallel).

Incorrect: The kind, brown dog followed me home.

Correct: The kind, loyal dog followed me home.

There are two simple ways to know if your adjectives are coordinate. One, you can join the adjectives with *and*: *The kind and loyal dog*. Two, you can change the order of the adjectives: *The loyal, kind dog*.

> **Review Video: When to Use a Comma**
> Visit mometrix.com/academy and enter code: 786797

SEMICOLONS

The semicolon is used to connect major sentence pieces of equal value. Some rules for semicolons include:

Use Case	Example
Between closely connected independent clauses **not connected with a coordinating conjunction**	You are right; we should go with your plan.
Between independent clauses **linked with a transitional word**	I think that we can agree on this; however, I am not sure about my friends.
Between items in a **series that has internal punctuation**	I have visited New York, New York; Augusta, Maine; and Baltimore, Maryland.

> **Review Video: How to Use Semicolons**
> Visit mometrix.com/academy and enter code: 370605

COLONS

The colon is used to call attention to the words that follow it. A colon must come after a **complete independent clause**. The rules for colons are as follows:

Use Case	Example
After an independent clause to **make a list**	I want to learn many languages: Spanish, German, and Italian.
For **explanations**	There is one thing that stands out on your resume: responsibility.
To give a **quote**	He started with an idea: "We are able to do more than we imagine."
After the **greeting in a formal letter**	To Whom It May Concern:
Show **hours and minutes**	It is 3:14 p.m.
Separate a **title and subtitle**	The essay is titled "America: A Short Introduction to a Modern Country."

> **Review Video: Colons**
> Visit mometrix.com/academy and enter code: 868673

PARENTHESES

Parentheses are used for additional information. Also, they can be used to put labels for letters or numbers in a series. Parentheses should be not be used very often. If they are overused, parentheses can be a distraction instead of a help.

Examples:

> **Extra Information**: The rattlesnake (see Image 2) is a dangerous snake of North and South America.

> **Series**: Include in the email (1) your name, (2) your address, and (3) your question for the author.

> **Review Video: Parentheses**
> Visit mometrix.com/academy and enter code: 947743

QUOTATION MARKS

Use quotation marks to close off **direct quotations** of a person's spoken or written words. Do not use quotation marks around indirect quotations. An indirect quotation gives someone's message without using the person's exact words. Use **single quotation marks** to close off a quotation inside a quotation.

> **Direct Quote**: Nancy said, "I am waiting for Henry to arrive."

> **Indirect Quote**: Henry said that he is going to be late to the meeting.

> **Quote inside a Quote**: The teacher asked, "Has everyone read 'The Gift of the Magi'?"

Quotation marks should be used around the titles of **short works**: newspaper and magazine articles, poems, short stories, songs, television episodes, radio programs, and subdivisions of books or websites.

Examples:

"Rip Van Winkle" (short story by Washington Irving)

"O Captain! My Captain!" (poem by Walt Whitman)

Although it is not standard usage, quotation marks are sometimes used to highlight **irony** or the use of words to mean something other than their dictionary definition. This type of usage should be employed sparingly, if at all.

Examples:

The boss warned Frank that he was walking on "thin ice."	Frank is not walking on real ice. Instead, he is being warned to avoid mistakes.
The teacher thanked the young man for his "honesty."	The quotation marks around *honesty* show that the teacher does not believe the young man's explanation.

> **Review Video: Quotation Marks**
> Visit mometrix.com/academy and enter code: 884918

Periods and commas are put **inside** quotation marks. Colons and semicolons are put **outside** the quotation marks. Question marks and exclamation points are placed inside quotation marks when they are part of a quote. When the question or exclamation mark goes with the whole sentence, the mark is left outside of the quotation marks.

Examples:

Period and comma	We read "The Gift of the Magi," "The Skylight Room," and "The Cactus."
Semicolon	They watched "The Nutcracker"; then, they went home.
Exclamation mark that is a part of a quote	The crowd cheered, "Victory!"
Question mark that goes with the whole sentence	Is your favorite short story "The Tell-Tale Heart"?

APOSTROPHES

An apostrophe is used to show **possession** or the **deletion of letters in contractions**. An apostrophe is not needed with the possessive pronouns *his, hers, its, ours, theirs, whose*, and *yours*.

Singular Nouns: David's car | a book's theme | my brother's board game

Plural Nouns that end with *-s*: the scissors' handle | boys' basketball

Plural Nouns that end without *-s*: Men's department | the people's adventure

> **Review Video: When to Use an Apostrophe**
> Visit mometrix.com/academy and enter code: 213068
>
> **Review Video: Punctuation Errors in Possessive Pronouns**
> Visit mometrix.com/academy and enter code: 221438

HYPHENS

Hyphens are used to **separate compound words**. Use hyphens in the following cases:

Use Case	Example
Compound numbers from 21 to 99 when written out in words	This team needs twenty-five points to win the game.
Written-out fractions that are used as adjectives	The recipe says that we need a three-fourths cup of butter.
Compound adjectives that come before a noun	The well-fed dog took a nap.
Unusual compound words that would be hard to read or easily confused with other words	This is the best anti-itch cream on the market.

Note: This is not a complete set of the rules for hyphens. A dictionary is the best tool for knowing if a compound word needs a hyphen.

> **Review Video: Hyphens**
> Visit mometrix.com/academy and enter code: 981632

DASHES

Dashes are used to show a **break** or a **change in thought** in a sentence or to act as parentheses in a sentence. When typing, use two hyphens to make a dash. Do not put a space before or after the dash. The following are the functions of dashes:

Use Case	Example
Set off parenthetical statements or an **appositive with internal punctuation**	The three trees—oak, pine, and magnolia—are coming on a truck tomorrow.
Show a **break or change in tone or thought**	The first question—how silly of me—does not have a correct answer.

ELLIPSIS MARKS

The ellipsis mark has **three** periods (...) to show when **words have been removed** from a quotation. If a **full sentence or more** is removed from a quoted passage, you need to use **four** periods to show the removed text and the end punctuation mark. The ellipsis mark should not be used at the beginning of a quotation. The ellipsis mark should also not be used at the end of a quotation unless some words have been deleted from the end of the final sentence.

Example:

"Then he picked up the groceries...paid for them...later he went home."

BRACKETS

There are two main reasons to use brackets:

Use Case	Example
Placing **parentheses inside of parentheses**	The hero of this story, Paul Revere (a silversmith and industrialist [see Ch. 4]), rode through towns of Massachusetts to warn of advancing British troops.
Adding **clarification or detail to a quotation** that is not part of the quotation	The father explained, "My children are planning to attend my alma mater [State University]."

Review Video: Brackets
Visit mometrix.com/academy and enter code: 727546

Common Usage Mistakes

WORD CONFUSION

WHICH, THAT, AND WHO

The words *which*, *that*, and *who* can act as **relative pronouns** to help clarify or describe a noun.

Which is used for things only.

> Example: Andrew's car, *which is old and rusty*, broke down last week.

That is used for people or things. *That* is usually informal when used to describe people.

> Example: Is this the only book *that Louis L'Amour wrote?*

> Example: Is Louis L'Amour the author *that wrote Western novels?*

Who is used for people or for animals that have an identity or personality.

> Example: Mozart was the composer *who wrote those operas.*

> Example: John's dog, *who is called Max,* is large and fierce.

HOMOPHONES

Homophones are words that sound alike (or similar) but have different **spellings** and **definitions**. A homophone is a type of **homonym**, which is a pair or group of words that are pronounced or spelled the same, but do not mean the same thing.

TO, TOO, AND TWO

To can be an adverb or a preposition for showing direction, purpose, and relationship. See your dictionary for the many other ways to use *to* in a sentence.

> Examples: I went to the store. | I want to go with you.

Too is an adverb that means *also, as well, very,* or *in excess.*

> Examples: I can walk a mile too. | You have eaten too much.

Two is a number.

> Example: You have two minutes left.

THERE, THEIR, AND THEY'RE

There can be an adjective, adverb, or pronoun. Often, *there* is used to show a place or to start a sentence.

> Examples: I went there yesterday. | There is something in his pocket.

Their is a pronoun that is used to show ownership.

> Examples: He is their father. | This is their fourth apology this week.

They're is a contraction of *they are.*

> Example: Did you know that they're in town?

KNEW AND NEW

Knew is the past tense of *know*.

> Example: I knew the answer.

New is an adjective that means something is current, has not been used, or is modern.

> Example: This is my new phone.

THEN AND THAN

Then is an adverb that indicates sequence or order:

> Example: I'm going to run to the library and then come home.

Than is special-purpose word used only for comparisons:

> Example: Susie likes chips more than candy.

ITS AND IT'S

Its is a pronoun that shows ownership.

> Example: The guitar is in its case.

It's is a contraction of *it is*.

> Example: It's an honor and a privilege to meet you.

Note: The *h* in honor is silent, so *honor* starts with the vowel sound *o*, which must have the article *an*.

YOUR AND YOU'RE

Your is a pronoun that shows ownership.

> Example: This is your moment to shine.

You're is a contraction of *you are*.

> Example: Yes, you're correct.

SAW AND SEEN

Saw is the past-tense form of *see*.

> Example: I saw a turtle on my walk this morning.

Seen is the past participle of *see*.

> Example: I have seen this movie before.

AFFECT AND EFFECT

There are two main reasons that *affect* and *effect* are so often confused: 1) both words can be used as either a noun or a verb, and 2) unlike most homophones, their usage and meanings are closely related to each other. Here is a quick rundown of the four usage options:

Affect (n): feeling, emotion, or mood that is displayed

Example: The patient had a flat *affect*. (i.e., his face showed little or no emotion)

Affect (v): to alter, to change, to influence

Example: The sunshine *affects* the plant's growth.

Effect (n): a result, a consequence

Example: What *effect* will this weather have on our schedule?

Effect (v): to bring about, to cause to be

Example: These new rules will *effect* order in the office.

The noun form of *affect* is rarely used outside of technical medical descriptions, so if a noun form is needed on the test, you can safely select *effect*. The verb form of *effect* is not as rare as the noun form of *affect*, but it's still not all that likely to show up on your test. If you need a verb and you can't decide which to use based on the definitions, choosing *affect* is your best bet.

HOMOGRAPHS

Homographs are words that share the same spelling, but have different meanings and sometimes different pronunciations. To figure out which meaning is being used, you should be looking for context clues. The context clues give hints to the meaning of the word. For example, the word *spot* has many meanings. It can mean "a place" or "a stain or blot." In the sentence "After my lunch, I saw a spot on my shirt," the word *spot* means "a stain or blot." The context clues of "After my lunch" and "on my shirt" guide you to this decision. A homograph is another type of homonym.

BANK

(noun): an establishment where money is held for savings or lending

(verb): to collect or pile up

CONTENT

(noun): the topics that will be addressed within a book

(adjective): pleased or satisfied

(verb): to make someone pleased or satisfied

FINE

(noun): an amount of money that acts a penalty for an offense

(adjective): very small or thin

(adverb): in an acceptable way

(verb): to make someone pay money as a punishment

INCENSE

(noun): a material that is burned in religious settings and makes a pleasant aroma

(verb): to frustrate or anger

LEAD

(noun): the first or highest position

(noun): a heavy metallic element

(verb): to direct a person or group of followers

(adjective): containing lead

OBJECT

(noun): a lifeless item that can be held and observed

(verb): to disagree

PRODUCE

(noun): fruits and vegetables

(verb): to make or create something

REFUSE

(noun): garbage or debris that has been thrown away

(verb): to not allow

SUBJECT

(noun): an area of study

(verb): to force or subdue

TEAR

(noun): a fluid secreted by the eyes

(verb): to separate or pull apart

Prose

COMMON FORMS OF PROSE FICTION

HISTORICAL, PICARESQUE, GOTHIC, AND PSYCHOLOGICAL FICTION

Historical fiction is set in particular historical periods, including prehistoric and mythological. Examples include Walter Scott's *Rob Roy* and *Ivanhoe*; Leo Tolstoy's *War and Peace*; Robert Graves' *I, Claudius;* Mary Renault's *The King Must Die* and *The Bull from the Sea* (an historical novel using Greek mythology); Virginia Woolf's *Orlando* and *Between the Acts*; and John Dos Passos's *U.S.A* trilogy. **Picaresque** novels recount episodic adventures of a rogue protagonist or *pícaro,* like Miguel de Cervantes' *Don Quixote* or Henry Fielding's *Tom Jones.* **Gothic** novels originated as a reaction against 18th-century Enlightenment rationalism, featuring horror, mystery, superstition, madness, supernatural elements, and revenge. Early examples include Horace Walpole's *Castle of Otranto,* Matthew Gregory Lewis' *Monk*, Mary Shelley's *Frankenstein*, and Bram Stoker's *Dracula.* In America, Edgar Allan Poe wrote many Gothic works. Contemporary novelist Anne Rice has penned many Gothic novels under the pseudonym A. N. Roquelaure. **Psychological** novels, originating in 17th-century France, explore characters' motivations. Examples include Abbé Prévost's *Manon Lescaut;* George Eliot's novels; Fyodor Dostoyevsky's *Crime and Punishment;* Tolstoy's *Anna Karenina;* Gustave Flaubert's *Madame Bovary;* and the novels of Henry James, James Joyce, and Vladimir Nabokov.

NOVELS OF MANNERS

Novels of manners are fictional stories that observe, explore, and analyze the social behaviors of a specific time and place. While deep psychological themes are more universal across different historical periods and countries, the manners of a particular society are shorter-lived and more varied; the **novel of manners** captures these societal details. Novels of manners can also be regarded as symbolically representing, in artistic form, certain established and secure social orders. Characteristics of novels of manners include descriptions of a society with defined behavioral codes; language that uses standardized, impersonal formulas; and inhibition of emotional expression, as contrasted with the strong emotions expressed in romantic or sentimental novels. Jane Austen's detailed descriptions of English society and characters struggling with the definitions and restrictions placed on them by society are excellent models of the novel of manners. In the 20th century, Evelyn Waugh's *Handful of Dust* is a novel of social manners, and his *Sword of Honour* trilogy contains novels of military manners. Another 20th-century example is *The Unbearable Bassington* by Saki (the pen name of writer H. H. Munro), focusing on Edwardian society.

WESTERN-WORLD SENTIMENTAL NOVELS

Sentimental love novels originated in the movement of Romanticism. Eighteenth-century examples of novels that emphasize the emotional aspect of love include Samuel Richardson's *Pamela* (1740) and Jean-Jacques Rousseau's *Nouvelle Héloïse* (1761). Also in the 18th century, Laurence Sterne's novel *Tristram Shandy* (1760-1767) is an example of a novel with elements of sentimentality. The Victorian era's rejection of emotionalism caused the term "sentimental" to have undesirable connotations. However, even non-sentimental novelists such as William Makepeace Thackeray and Charles Dickens incorporated sentimental elements in their writing. A 19th-century author of genuinely sentimental novels was Mrs. Henry Wood (e.g., *East Lynne,* 1861). In the 20th century, Erich Segal's sentimental novel *Love Story* (1970) was a popular bestseller.

EPISTOLARY NOVELS

Epistolary novels are told in the form of letters written by their characters rather than in typical narrative form. Samuel Richardson, the best-known author of epistolary novels like *Pamela* (1740)

73

and *Clarissa* (1748), widely influenced early Romantic epistolary novels throughout Europe that freely expressed emotions. Richardson, a printer, published technical manuals on letter-writing for young gentlewomen; his epistolary novels were fictional extensions of those nonfictional instructional books. Nineteenth-century English author Wilkie Collins' *The Moonstone* (1868) was a mystery written in epistolary form. By the 20th century, the format of well-composed written letters came to be regarded as artificial and outmoded. A 20th-century evolution of letters was tape-recording transcripts, such as in French playwright Samuel Beckett's drama *Krapp's Last Tape*. Though evoking modern alienation, Beckett still created a sense of fictional characters' direct communication without author intervention as Richardson had.

PASTORAL NOVELS

Pastoral novels lyrically idealize country life as idyllic and utopian, akin to the Garden of Eden. *Daphnis and Chloe*, written by Greek novelist Longus around the second or third century, influenced Elizabethan pastoral romances like Thomas Lodge's *Rosalynde* (1590), which inspired Shakespeare's *As You Like It*, and Philip Sidney's *Arcadia* (1590). Jacques-Henri Bernardin de St. Pierre's French work *Paul et Virginie* (1787) demonstrated the early Romantic view of the innocence and goodness of nature. Though the style lost popularity by the 20th century, pastoral elements can still be seen in novels like *The Rainbow* (1915) and *Lady Chatterley's Lover* (1928), both by D. H. Lawrence. Growing realism transformed pastoral writing into less ideal and more dystopian, distasteful and ironic depictions of country life in George Eliot's and Thomas Hardy's novels. Saul Bellow's novel *Herzog* (1964) may demonstrate how urban ills highlight an alternative pastoral ideal. The pastoral style is commonly thought to be overly idealized and outdated today, as seen in Stella Gibbons' pastoral satire, Cold Comfort Farm (1932).

BILDUNGSROMAN

Bildungsroman is German for "education novel." This term is also used in English to describe "apprenticeship" novels focusing on coming-of-age stories, including youth's struggles and searches for things such as identity, spiritual understanding, or the meaning in life. Johann Wolfgang von Goethe's *Wilhelm Meisters Lehrjahre* (1796) is credited as the origin of this genre. Two of Charles Dickens' novels, *David Copperfield* (1850) and *Great Expectations* (1861), also fit this form. H. G. Wells wrote *bildungsromans* about questing for apprenticeships to address the complications of modern life in *Joan and Peter* (1918) and from a Utopian perspective in *The Dream* (1924). School *bildungsromans* include Thomas Hughes' *Tom Brown's School Days* (1857) and Alain-Fournier's *Le Grand Meaulnes* (1913). Many Hermann Hesse novels, including *Demian, Steppenwolf, Siddhartha, Magister Ludi,* and *Beneath the Wheel* are *bildungsromans* about a struggling, searching youth. Samuel Butler's *The Way of All Flesh* (1903) and James Joyce's *A Portrait of the Artist as a Young Man* (1916) are two modern examples. Variations include J. D. Salinger's *The Catcher in the Rye* (1951), set both within and beyond school, and William Golding's *Lord of the Flies* (1955), a novel not set in a school but one that is a coming-of-age story nonetheless.

ROMAN À CLEF

Roman à clef, French for "novel with a key," refers to books that require a real-life frame of reference, or key, for full comprehension. In Geoffrey Chaucer's *Canterbury Tales,* the Nun's Priest's Tale contains details that confuse readers unaware of history about the Earl of Bolingbroke's involvement in an assassination plot. Other literary works fitting this form include John Dryden's political satirical poem "Absalom and Achitophel" (1681), Jonathan Swift's satire "A Tale of a Tub" (1704), and George Orwell's political allegory *Animal Farm* (1945), all of which cannot be understood completely without knowing their camouflaged historical contents. *Roman à clefs* disguise truths too dangerous for authors to state directly. Readers must know about the enemies of D. H. Lawrence and Aldous Huxley to appreciate their respective novels: *Aaron's Rod* (1922) and

Point Counter Point (1928). Marcel Proust's *Remembrance of Things Past (À la recherché du temps perdu,* 1871-1922) is informed by his social context. James Joyce's *Finnegans Wake* is an enormous *roman à clef* containing multitudinous personal references.

> **Review Video: Major Forms of Prose**
> Visit mometrix.com/academy and enter code: 565543

OTHER COMMON TYPES OF PROSE

- A **narrative** is any composition that tells a story. Narratives have characters, settings, and a structure. Narratives may be fiction or nonfiction stories and may follow a linear or nonlinear structure. The purpose of a narrative is generally to entertain, but nonfiction narratives can be informative, as well. Narratives also appear in a variety of structures and formats.

- **Biographies** are books written about another person's life. Biographies can be valuable historical resources. Though they provide a narrow view of the relevant time period and culture, their specificity can also provide a unique context for that period or culture. Biographies, especially those whose subject was a well-known and influential figure, can provide a more complete picture of the figure's life or contributions. Biographies can also serve as a source of inspiration or communicate a moral because of their focus on one person over an extended period of time.

- **Myths**, or stories from mythology, exist in most ancient cultures and continue to influence modern cultures. Mythology is so influential that it has even inspired numerous pieces of modern literature and media in popular culture. While popular culture most clearly references mythology from the Ancient Greek and Roman cultures, literature has been influenced by mythologies from around the entire world. Since mythology is so prevalent in ancient literature, it makes sense that universal themes and morals often appear in mythology and even drive some myths. This suggests connections between cultures through the stories they pass down.

- **Fables** are short, didactic stories that typically feature imaginary creatures or talking animals. The famous story "The Tortoise and the Hare" is a fable. Fables are still told and used today because of their universally understandable morals and characters, making them suitable for children's literature and media.

- **Fairy tales** are stories that involve fictional creatures or realistic characters with fantastical traits and abilities. Fairy tales often end happily and depict the victory of good over evil. The plots and characters in fairy tales are often far-fetched and whimsical.

- **Folk Tales** are stories that have withstood time and are usually popular in a particular region or culture. Folk tales often depict the clever success of a common person, though the story may, alternatively, end poorly for the protagonist. Folk tales are easily confused with fairytales because fairytales can be a type of folk tale.

- **Legends** are stories that typically focus on one character and highlight their victory over a particular enemy or obstacle. Legends often feature some facts or are inspired by true events, but are still understood to be either exaggerated or partially fictional. Heroes are often the protagonists of legends as they often save or protect others as they conquer enemies and obstacles.

- A **short story** is a fictional narrative that is shorter than a novel. However, there is not a definite page or word count that defines the short story category. Short stories tend to focus on one or few elements of a story in order to efficiently tell the story. Though they are often brief, short stories may still contain a moral or impact their readers.

> **Review Video: Myths, Fables, Legends, and Fairy Tales**
> Visit mometrix.com/academy and enter code: 347199

COMMON GENRES IN PROSE

- The **mystery** genre includes stories with plots that follow a protagonist as they work to solve an unexplained situation, such as a murder, disappearance, or robbery. Protagonists of mysteries may be hired professionals or amateurs who solve the mystery despite their lack of experience and resources. Mysteries allow the reader to solve the case along with the protagonist, and often grant the reader an advantageous perspective, creating dramatic irony. The *Sherlock Holmes* novels by Sir Arthur Conan Doyle are examples of mystery novels.
- **Science fiction** is a genre that is based on the manipulation and exaggeration of real scientific discoveries and processes. These works are speculative and frequently depict a world where scientific discoveries and society have progressed beyond the point reached at the time of the work's creation. Works of science fiction often take place in a distant location or time, allowing for the dramatic advancements and conveniences they often depict. *Dune*, written by Frank Herbert, is an example of a science-fiction novel.
- The **fantasy** genre includes stories that feature imaginary creatures and supernatural abilities, but often take place in settings that resemble real places and cultures in history. Fantasy novels usually follow a gifted protagonist from humble beginnings as they embark on a quest, journey, or adventure and encounter mystical beings and personally challenging obstacles. Common themes in the fantasy genre include personal growth, good versus evil, and the value of the journey. J.R.R. Tolkien's *The Lord of the Rings* trilogy belongs to the fantasy genre.
- **Realistic fiction** describes fictional narratives that include events and characters that do not exist, but could appear in reality. Within the narrative, these characters and events may be depicted in real places. For example, Pip, the protagonist of Charles Dickens's *Great Expectations*, was not a real person, but the novel shows him living in London, England for much of his young adulthood. Realistic fiction contains no far-fetched or impossible elements and presents situations that can or do occur in real life. A contemporary example of realistic fiction is *Wonder* by R.J. Palacio.
- **Historical fiction** includes works that take place in the past and model their setting after real historical cultures, societies, and time periods. These works may include real historical figures and events, but they also may not. Works of historical fiction must be fully informed by the period and location they are set in, meaning both the major and minor details of the work must be historically compatible with the work's setting. Examples of historical fiction include Kathryn Stockett's *The Help* and Markus Zusak's *The Book Thief*.
- The phrase **literary nonfiction** describes nonfiction narratives that present true facts and events in a way that entertains readers and displays creativity. Literary nonfiction, also called creative nonfiction, may resemble fiction in its style and flow, but the truth of the events it describes sets it apart from fictional literature. Different types of books may be considered literary nonfiction, such as biographies, if they appear to employ creativity in their writing. An example of literary nonfiction is *The Immortal Life of Henrietta Lacks* by Rebecca Skloot.

REALISM AND SATIRE

REALISM

Realism is a literary form with the goal of representing reality as faithfully as possible. Its genesis in Western literature was a reaction against the sentimentality and extreme emotionalism of the works written during the Romantic literary movement, which championed feelings and emotional expression. Realists focused in great detail on immediacy of time and place, on specific actions of their characters, and the justifiable consequences of those actions. Some techniques of **realism** include writing in vernacular (conversational language), using specific dialects, and placing an emphasis on character rather than plot. Realistic literature also often addresses ethical issues. Historically, realistic works have often concentrated on the middle classes of the authors' societies. Realists eschew treatments that are too dramatic or sensationalistic as exaggerations of the reality that they strive to portray as closely as they are able. Influenced by his own bleak past, Fyodor Dostoevsky wrote several novels, such as *Crime and Punishment* (1866) that shunned romantic ideals and sought to portray a stark reality. Henry James was a prominent writer of realism in novels such as *Daisy Miller* (1879). Samuel Clemens (Mark Twain) skillfully represented the language and culture of lower-class Mississippi in his novel *The Adventures of Huckleberry Finn* (1885).

SATIRE

Satire uses sarcasm, irony, and humor as social criticism to lampoon human folly. Unlike realism, which intends to depict reality as it exists without exaggeration, **satire** often involves creating situations or ideas that deliberately exaggerate reality to appear ridiculous to illuminate flawed behaviors. Ancient Roman satirists included Horace and Juvenal. Alexander Pope's poem "The Rape of the Lock" satirized the values of fashionable members of the 18th-century upper-middle class, which Pope found shallow and trivial. The theft of a lock of hair from a young woman is blown out of proportion: the poem's characters regard it as seriously as they would a rape. Irishman Jonathan Swift satirized British society, politics, and religion in works like "A Modest Proposal" and *Gulliver's Travels*. In "A Modest Proposal," Swift used essay form and mock-serious tone, satirically "proposing" cannibalism of babies and children as a solution to poverty and overpopulation. He satirized petty political disputes in *Gulliver's Travels*.

77

Poetry

POETRY TERMINOLOGY

Unlike prose, which traditionally (except in forms like stream of consciousness) consists of complete sentences connected into paragraphs, poetry is written in **verses**. These may form complete sentences, clauses, or phrases. Poetry may be written with or without rhyme. It can be metered, following a particular rhythmic pattern such as iambic, dactylic, spondaic, trochaic, or **anapestic**, or may be without regular meter. The terms **iamb** and **trochee**, among others, identify stressed and unstressed syllables in each verse. Meter is also described by the number of beats or stressed syllables per verse: **dimeter** (2), **trimeter** (3), **tetrameter** (4), **pentameter** (5), and so forth. Using the symbol ◡ to denote unstressed and / to denote stressed syllables, **iambic** = ◡/; **trochaic** = /◡; **spondaic** = //; **dactylic** = /◡◡; **anapestic** = ◡◡/. **Rhyme schemes** identify which lines rhyme, such as ABAB, ABCA, AABA, and so on. Poetry with neither rhyme nor meter is called **free verse**. Poems may be in free verse, metered but unrhymed, rhymed but without meter, or using both rhyme and meter. In English, the most common meter is iambic pentameter. Unrhymed iambic pentameter is called **blank verse**.

> **Review Video: Different Types of Rhyme**
> Visit mometrix.com/academy and enter code: 999342
>
> **Review Video: Evocative Words and Rhythm**
> Visit mometrix.com/academy and enter code: 894610

MAJOR FORMS OF POETRY

From man's earliest days, he expressed himself with poetry. A large percentage of the surviving literature from ancient times is in **epic poetry**, utilized by Homer and other Greco-Roman poets. Epic poems typically recount heroic deeds and adventures, using stylized language and combining dramatic and lyrical conventions. **Epistolary poems**, poems that are written and read as letters, also developed in ancient times. In the fourteenth and fifteenth centuries, the **ballad** became a popular convention. Ballads often follow a rhyme scheme and meter and focus on subjects such as love, death, and religion. Many ballads tell stories, and several modern ballads are put to music. From these early conventions, numerous other poetic forms developed, such as **elegies**, **odes**, and **pastoral poems**. Elegies are mourning poems written in three parts: lament, praise of the deceased, and solace for loss. Odes evolved from songs to the typical poem of the Romantic time period, expressing strong feelings and contemplative thoughts. Pastoral poems idealize nature and country living. Poetry can also be used to make short, pithy statements. **Epigrams** (memorable rhymes with one or two lines) and **limericks** (two lines of iambic dimeter followed by two lines of iambic dimeter and another of iambic trimeter) are known for humor and wit.

HAIKU

Haiku was originally a Japanese poetry form. In the 13th century, haiku was the opening phrase of renga, a 100-stanza oral poem. By the 16th century, haiku diverged into a separate short poem. When Western writers discovered haiku, the form became popular in English, as well as other languages. A haiku has 17 syllables, traditionally distributed across three lines as 5/7/5, with a pause after the first or second line. Haiku are syllabic and unrhymed. Haiku philosophy and technique are that brevity's compression forces writers to express images concisely, depict a moment in time, and evoke illumination and enlightenment. An example is 17th-century haiku master Matsuo Basho's classic: "An old silent pond… / A frog jumps into the pond, / splash! Silence again." Modern American poet Ezra Pound revealed the influence of haiku in his two-line poem "In a Station of the Metro." In this poem, line 1 has 12 syllables (combining the syllable count of the first two lines of a haiku) and line 2 has 7, but it still preserves haiku's philosophy and imagistic technique: "The apparition of these faces in the crowd; / Petals on a wet, black bough."

SONNETS

The sonnet traditionally has 14 lines of iambic pentameter, tightly organized around a theme. The Petrarchan sonnet, named for 14th-century Italian poet Petrarch, has an eight-line stanza, the octave, and a six-line stanza, the sestet. There is a change or turn, known as the volta, between the eighth and ninth verses, setting up the sestet's answer or summary. The rhyme scheme is ABBA/ABBA/CDECDE or CDCDCD. The English or Shakespearean sonnet has three quatrains and one couplet, with the rhyme scheme ABAB/CDCD/EFEF/GG. This format better suits English, which has fewer rhymes than Italian. The final couplet often contrasts sharply with the preceding quatrains, as in Shakespeare's sonnets—for example, Sonnet 130, "My mistress' eyes are nothing like the sun...And yet, by heaven, I think my love as rare / As any she belied with false compare." Variations on the sonnet form include Edmund Spenser's Spenserian sonnet in the 16th century, John Milton's Miltonic sonnet in the 17th century, and sonnet sequences. Sonnet sequences are seen in works such as John Donne's *La Corona* and Elizabeth Barrett Browning's *Sonnets from the Portuguese*.

> **Review Video: Structural Elements of Poetry**
> Visit mometrix.com/academy and enter code: 265216

Poetic Themes and Devices

CARPE DIEM TRADITION IN POETRY

Carpe diem is Latin for "seize the day." A long poetic tradition, it advocates making the most of time because it passes swiftly and life is short. It is found in multiple languages, including Latin, Torquato Tasso's Italian, Pierre de Ronsard's French, and Edmund Spenser's English, and is often used in seduction to argue for indulging in earthly pleasures. Roman poet Horace's Ode 1.11 tells a younger woman, Leuconoe, to enjoy the present, not worrying about inevitable aging. Two Renaissance Metaphysical Poets, Andrew Marvell and Robert Herrick, treated *carpe diem* more as a call to action. In "To His Coy Mistress," Marvell points out that time is fleeting, arguing for love, and concluding that because they cannot stop time, they may as well defy it, getting the most out of the short time they have. In "To the Virgins, to Make Much of Time," Herrick advises young women to take advantage of their good fortune in being young by getting married before they become too old to attract men and have babies.

"To His Coy Mistress" begins, "Had we but world enough, and time, / This coyness, lady, were no crime." Using imagery, Andrew Marvell describes leisure they could enjoy if time were unlimited. Arguing for seduction, he continues famously, "But at my back I always hear/Time's winged chariot hurrying near; / And yonder all before us lie / Deserts of vast eternity." He depicts time as turning beauty to death and decay. Contradictory images in "amorous birds of prey" and "tear our pleasures with rough strife / Through the iron gates of life" overshadow romance with impending death, linking present pleasure with mortality and spiritual values with moral considerations. Marvell's concluding couplet summarizes *carpe diem*: "Thus, though we cannot make our sun / Stand still, yet we will make him run." "To the Virgins, to Make Much of Time" begins with the famous "Gather ye rosebuds while ye may." Rather than seduction to live for the present, Robert Herrick's experienced persona advises young women's future planning: "Old time is still a-flying / And this same flower that smiles today, / Tomorrow will be dying."

EFFECT OF STRUCTURE ON MEANING IN POETRY

The way a poem is structured can affect its meaning. Different structural choices can change the way a reader understands a poem, so poets are careful to ensure that the form they use reflects the message they want to convey. The main structural elements in poetry include **lines** and **stanzas**. The number of lines within a stanza and the number of stanzas vary between different poems, but some poetic forms require a poem to have a certain number of lines and stanzas. Some of these forms also require each line to conform to a certain meter, or number and pattern of syllables. Many forms are associated with a certain topic or tone because of their meter. Poetic forms include sonnets, concrete poems, haiku, and villanelles. Another popular form of poetry is free verse, which is poetry that does not conform to a particular meter or rhyme scheme.

The arrangement of lines and stanzas determines the speed at which a poem is read. Long lines are generally read more quickly since the reader is often eager to reach the end of the line and does not have to stop to find the next word. Short lines cause the reader to briefly pause and look to the next line, so their reading is slowed. These effects often contribute to the meaning a reader gleans from a poem, so poets aim to make the line length compatible with the tone of their message.

For example, Edgar Allan Poe's poem "The Raven" is written with mostly long lines. The poem's speaker experiences troubling events and becomes paranoid throughout the poem, and he narrates his racing thoughts. Poe's use of long lines leads the reader to read each line quickly, allowing their reading experience to resemble the thoughts of the narrator:

> Deep into that darkness peering, long I stood there wondering, fearing,
> Doubting, dreaming dreams no mortal ever dared to dream before;
> But the silence was unbroken, and the stillness gave no token,
> And the only word there spoken was the whispered word, "Lenore?"
> This I whispered, and an echo murmured back the word, "Lenore!"—
> Merely this and nothing more.

The poem's meter also contributes to its tone, but consider the same stanza written using shorter lines:

> Deep into that darkness peering,
> long I stood there wondering, fearing,
> Doubting, dreaming dreams no mortal
> ever dared to dream before;
> But the silence was unbroken,
> and the stillness gave no token,
> And the only word there spoken
> was the whispered word, "Lenore?"
> This I whispered, and an echo
> murmured back the word, "Lenore!"—
> Merely this and nothing more.

Breaking the lines apart creates longer pauses and a slower, more suspenseful experience for the reader. While the tone of the poem is dark and suspense is appropriate, the longer lines allow Poe to emphasize and show the narrator's emotions. The narrator's emotions are more important to the poem's meaning than the creation of suspense, making longer lines more suitable in this case.

CONCRETE POETRY

A less common form of poetry is concrete poetry, also called shape poetry. **Concrete poems** are arranged so the full poem takes a shape that is relevant to the poem's message. For example, a concrete poem about the beach may be arranged to look like a palm tree. This contributes to a poem's meaning by influencing which aspect of the poem or message that the reader focuses on. In the beach poem example, the image of the palm tree leads the reader to focus on the poem's setting and visual imagery. The reader may also look for or anticipate the mention of a palm tree in the poem. This technique allows the poet to direct the reader's attention and emphasize a certain element of their work.

FREE VERSE

Free verse is a very common form of poetry. Because **free verse** poetry does not always incorporate meter or rhyme, it relies more heavily on punctuation and structure to influence the reader's experience and create emphasis. Free verse poetry makes strategic use of the length and number of both lines and stanzas. While meter and rhyme direct the flow and tone of other types of poems, poets of free verse pieces use the characteristics of lines and stanzas to establish flow and tone, instead.

Free verse also uses punctuation in each line to create flow and tone. The punctuation in each line directs the reader to pause after certain words, allowing the poet to emphasize specific ideas or images to clearly communicate their message. Similar to the effects of line length, the presence of punctuation at the end of a line can create pauses that affect a reader's pace. **End-stopped** lines, or lines with a punctuation mark at the end, create a pause that can contribute to the poem's flow or create emphasis. **Enjambed** lines, or lines that do not end with a punctuation mark, carry a sentence to the next line and create an effect similar to long lines. The use of enjambment can speed up a poem's flow and reflect an idea within the poem or contribute to tone.

POETIC STRUCTURE TO ENHANCE MEANING

The opening stanza of Romantic English poet, artist and printmaker William Blake's famous poem "The Tyger" demonstrates how a poet can create tension by using line length and punctuation independently of one another: "Tyger! Tyger! burning bright / In the forests of the night, / What immortal hand or eye / Could frame thy fearful symmetry?" The first three lines of this stanza are **trochaic** ($/\cup$), with "masculine" endings—that is, strongly stressed syllables at the ends of each of the lines. But Blake's punctuation contradicts this rhythmic regularity by not providing any divisions between the words "bright" and "In" or between "eye" and "Could." This irregular punctuation foreshadows how Blake disrupts the meter at the end of this first stanza by using a contrasting **dactyl** ($/\cup\cup$), with a "feminine" (unstressed) ending syllable in the last word, "symmetry." Thus, Blake uses structural contrasts to heighten the intrigue of his work.

In enjambment, one sentence or clause in a poem does not end at the end of its line or verse, but runs over into the next line or verse. Clause endings coinciding with line endings give readers a feeling of completion, but enjambment influences readers to hurry to the next line to finish and understand the sentence. In his blank-verse epic religious poem "Paradise Lost," John Milton wrote: "Anon out of the earth a fabric huge / Rose like an exhalation, with the sound / Of dulcet symphonies and voices sweet, / Built like a temple, where pilasters round / Were set, and Doric pillars overlaid / With golden architrave." Only the third line is end-stopped. Milton, describing the palace of Pandemonium bursting from Hell up through the ground, reinforced this idea through phrases and clauses bursting through the boundaries of the lines. A **caesura** is a pause in mid-verse. Milton's commas in the third and fourth lines signal caesuras. They interrupt flow, making the narration jerky to imply that Satan's glorious-seeming palace has a shaky and unsound foundation.

COUPLETS AND METER TO ENHANCE MEANING IN POETRY

When a poet uses a couplet—a stanza of two lines, rhymed or unrhymed—it can function as the answer to a question asked earlier in the poem, or the solution to a problem or riddle. Couplets can also enhance the establishment of a poem's mood, or clarify the development of a poem's theme. Another device to enhance thematic development is irony, which also communicates the poet's tone and draws the reader's attention to a point the poet is making. The use of meter gives a poem a rhythmic context, contributes to the poem's flow, makes it more appealing to the reader, can represent natural speech rhythms, and produces specific effects. For example, in "The Song of Hiawatha," Henry Wadsworth Longfellow uses trochaic (/ ◡) tetrameter (four beats per line) to evoke for readers the rhythms of Native American chanting: "*By* the *shores* of *Gitch*e *Gum*ee, / *By* the *shin*ing *Big*-Sea-*Wat*er / *Stood* the *wig*wam *of* No*kom*is." (Italicized syllables are stressed; non-italicized syllables are unstressed.)

REFLECTION OF CONTENT THROUGH STRUCTURE

Wallace Stevens' short yet profound poem "The Snow Man" is reductionist: the snow man is a figure without human biases or emotions. Stevens begins, "One must have a mind of winter," the criterion for realizing nature and life does not inherently possess subjective qualities; we only invest it with these. Things are not as we see them; they simply are. The entire poem is one long sentence of clauses connected by conjunctions and commas, and modified by relative clauses and phrases. The successive phrases lead readers continually to reconsider as they read. Stevens' construction of the poem mirrors the meaning he conveys. With a mind of winter, the snow man, Stevens concludes, "nothing himself, beholds nothing that is not there, and the nothing that is."

CONTRAST OF CONTENT AND STRUCTURE

Robert Frost's poem "Stopping by Woods on a Snowy Evening" (1923) is deceptively short and simple, with only four stanzas, each of only four lines, and short and simple words. Reinforcing this is Frost's use of regular rhyme and meter. The rhythm is iambic tetrameter throughout; the rhyme scheme is AABA in the first three stanzas and AAAA in the fourth. In an additional internal subtlety, B ending "here" in the first stanza is rhymed with A endings "queer," "near," and "year" of the second; B ending "lake" in the second is rhymed in A endings "shake," "mistake," and "flake" of the third. The final stanza's AAAA endings reinforce the ultimate darker theme. Though the first three stanzas seem to describe quietly watching snow fill the woods, the last stanza evokes the seductive pull of mysterious death: "The woods are lovely, dark and deep," countered by the obligations of living life: "But I have promises to keep, / And miles to go before I sleep, / And miles to go before I sleep." The last line's repetition strengthens Frost's message that despite death's temptation, life's course must precede it.

EFFECTS OF FIGURATIVE DEVICES ON MEANING IN POETRY

Through exaggeration, **hyperbole** communicates the strength of a poet's or persona's feelings and enhances the mood of the poem. **Imagery** appeals to the reader's senses, creating vivid mental pictures, evoking reader emotions and responses, and helping to develop themes. **Irony** also aids thematic development by drawing the reader's attention to the poet's point and communicating the poem's tone. Thematic development is additionally supported by the comparisons of **metaphors** and **similes**, which emphasize similarities, enhance imagery, and affect readers' perceptions. The use of **mood** communicates the atmosphere of a poem, builds a sense of tension, and evokes the reader's emotions. **Onomatopoeia** appeals to the reader's auditory sense and enhances sound imagery even when the poem is visual (read silently) rather than auditory (read aloud). **Rhyme** connects and unites verses, gives the rhyming words emphasis, and makes poems more fluent. **Symbolism** communicates themes, develops imagery, evokes readers' emotions, and elicits a response from the reader.

Review Video: What is Sensory Language?
Visit mometrix.com/academy and enter code: 177314

REPETITION TO ENHANCE MEANING

A **villanelle** is a nineteen-line poem composed of five tercets and one quatrain. The defining characteristic is the repetition: two lines appear repeatedly throughout the poem. In Theodore Roethke's "The Waking," the two repeated lines are "I wake to sleep, and take my waking slow," and "I learn by going where I have to go." At first these sound paradoxical, but the meaning is gradually revealed through the poem. The repetition also fits with the theme of cycle: the paradoxes of waking to sleep, learning by going, and thinking by feeling represent a constant cycle through life. They also symbolize abandoning conscious rationalism to embrace spiritual vision. We wake from the vision to "Great Nature," and "take the lively air." "This shaking keeps me steady"—another paradox—juxtaposes and balances fear of mortality with ecstasy in embracing experience. The transcendent vision of all life's interrelationship demonstrates, "What falls away is always. And is near." Readers experience the poem holistically, like music, through Roethke's integration of theme, motion, and sound.

Sylvia Plath's villanelle "Mad Girl's Love Song" narrows the scope from universal to personal but keeps the theme of cycle. The two repeated lines, "I shut my eyes and all the world drops dead" and "(I think I made you up inside my head.)" reflect the existential viewpoint that nothing exists in any absolute reality outside of our own perceptions. In the first stanza, the middle line, "I lift my lids and all is born again," in its recreating the world, bridges between the repeated refrain statements—one of obliterating reality, the other of having constructed her lover's existence. Unlike other villanelles wherein key lines are subtly altered in their repetitions, Plath repeats these exactly each time. This reflects the young woman's love, constant throughout the poem as it neither fades nor progresses.

Drama

EARLY DEVELOPMENT

English **drama** originally developed from religious ritual. Early Christians established traditions of presenting pageants or mystery plays, traveling on wagons and carts through the streets to depict Biblical events. Medieval tradition assigned responsibility for performing specific plays to the different guilds. In Middle English, "mystery" referred to craft, or trade, and religious ritual and truth. Historically, mystery plays were to be reproduced exactly the same every time they were performed, like religious rituals. However, some performers introduced individual interpretations of roles and even improvised. Thus, drama was born. Narrative detail and nuanced acting were evident in mystery cycles by the Middle Ages. As individualized performance evolved, plays on other subjects also developed. Middle English mystery plays that still exist include the York Cycle, Coventry Cycle, Chester Mystery Plays, N-Town Plays, and Towneley/Wakefield Plays. In recent times, these plays began to draw interest again, and several modern actors, such as Dame Judi Dench, began their careers with mystery plays.

> **Review Video: Dramas**
> Visit mometrix.com/academy and enter code: 216060

DEFINING CHARACTERISTICS

In the Middle Ages, plays were commonly composed in **verse**. By the time of the Renaissance, Shakespeare and other dramatists wrote plays that mixed **prose**, **rhymed verse**, and **blank verse**. The traditions of costumes and masks were seen in ancient Greek drama, medieval mystery plays, and Renaissance drama. Conventions like **asides**, in which actors make comments directly to the audience unheard by other characters, and **soliloquies** were also common during Shakespeare's Elizabethan dramatic period. **Monologues** date back to ancient Greek drama. Elizabethan dialogue tended to use colloquial prose for lower-class characters' speech and stylized verse for upper-class characters. Another Elizabethan convention was the play-within-a-play, as in *Hamlet.* As drama moved toward realism, dialogue became less poetic and more conversational, as in most modern English-language plays. Contemporary drama, both onstage and onscreen, includes a convention of **breaking the fourth wall**, as actors directly face and address audiences.

COMEDY

Today, most people equate the idea of **comedy** with something funny, and of **tragedy** with something sad. However, the ancient Greeks defined these differently. Comedy needed not be humorous or amusing; it needed only a happy ending. The classical definition of comedy, as included in Aristotle's works, is any work that tells the story of a sympathetic main character's rise in fortune. According to Aristotle, protagonists need not be heroic or exemplary, nor evil or worthless, but ordinary people of unremarkable morality. Comic figures who were sympathetic were usually of humble origins, proving their "natural nobility" through their actions as they were tested. Characters born into nobility were often satirized as self-important or pompous.

SHAKESPEAREAN COMEDY

William Shakespeare lived in England from 1564-1616. He was a poet and playwright of the Renaissance period in Western culture. He is generally considered the foremost dramatist in world literature and the greatest author to write in the English language. He wrote many poems, particularly sonnets, of which 154 survive today, and approximately 38 plays. Though his sonnets are greater in number and are very famous, he is best known for his plays, including comedies, tragedies, tragicomedies and historical plays. His play titles include: *All's Well That Ends Well, As You Like It, The Comedy of Errors, Love's Labour's Lost, Measure for Measure, The Merchant of Venice,*

The Merry Wives of Windsor, A Midsummer Night's Dream, Much Ado About Nothing, The Taming of the Shrew, The Tempest, Twelfth Night, The Two Gentlemen of Verona, The Winter's Tale, King John, Richard II, Henry IV, Henry V, Richard III, Romeo and Juliet, Coriolanus, Titus Andronicus, Julius Caesar, Macbeth, Hamlet, Troilus and Cressida, King Lear, Othello, Antony and Cleopatra, and *Cymbeline.* Some scholars have suggested that Christopher Marlowe wrote several of Shakespeare's works. While most scholars reject this theory, Shakespeare did pay homage to Marlowe, alluding to several of his characters, themes, or verbiage, as well as borrowing themes from several of his plays (e.g., Marlowe's *Jew of Malta* influenced Shakespeare's *Merchant of Venice*).

When Shakespeare was writing, during the Elizabethan period of the Renaissance, Aristotle's version of comedies was popular. While some of Shakespeare's comedies were humorous and others were not, all had happy endings. *A Comedy of Errors* is a farce. Based and expanding on a Classical Roman comedy, it is lighthearted and includes slapstick humor and mistaken identity. *Much Ado About Nothing* is a romantic comedy. It incorporates some more serious themes, including social mores, perceived infidelity, marriage's duality as both trap and ideal, honor and its loss, public shame, and deception, but also much witty dialogue and a happy ending.

DRAMATIC COMEDY

Three types of dramas classified as comedy include the farce, the romantic comedy, and the satirical comedy.

FARCE

The **farce** is a zany, goofy type of comedy that includes pratfalls and other forms of slapstick humor. The characters in a farce tend to be ridiculous or fantastical in nature. The plot also tends to contain highly improbable events, featuring complications and twists that continue throughout, and incredible coincidences that would likely never occur in reality. Mistaken identity, deceptions, and disguises are common devices used in farcical comedies. Shakespeare's play *The Comedy of Errors,* with its cases of accidental mistaken identity and slapstick, is an example of farce. Contemporary examples of farce include the Marx Brothers' movies, the Three Stooges movies and TV episodes, and the *Pink Panther* movie series.

ROMANTIC COMEDY

Romantic comedies are probably the most popular of the types of comedy, in both live theater performances and movies. They include not only humor and a happy ending, but also love. In the typical plot of a **romantic comedy**, two people well suited to one another are either brought together for the first time, or reconciled after being separated. They are usually both sympathetic characters and seem destined to be together, yet they are separated by some intervening complication, such as ex-lovers, interfering parents or friends, or differences in social class. The happy ending is achieved through the lovers overcoming all these obstacles. William Shakespeare's *Much Ado About Nothing,* Walt Disney's version of *Cinderella* (1950), and Broadway musical *Guys and Dolls* (1955) are example of romantic comedies. Many live-action movies are also examples of romantic comedies, such as *The Princess Bride* (1987), *Sleepless in Seattle* (1993), *You've Got Mail* (1998), and *Forget Paris* (1995).

SATIRICAL COMEDY AND BLACK COMEDY

Satires generally mock and lampoon human foolishness and vices. **Satirical comedies** fit the classical definition of comedy by depicting a main character's rise in fortune, but they also fit the definition of satire by making that main character either a fool, morally corrupt, or cynical in attitude. All or most of the other characters in the satirical comedy display similar foibles. These include gullible types, such as cuckolded spouses and dupes, and deceptive types, such as tricksters, con artists, criminals, hypocrites, and fortune seekers, who prey on the gullible. Some classical examples of satirical comedies include *The Birds* by ancient Greek comedic playwright Aristophanes, and *Volpone* by 17th-century poet and playwright Ben Jonson, who made the comedy of humors popular. When satirical comedy is extended to extremes, it becomes **black comedy**, wherein the comedic occurrences are grotesque or terrible.

TRAGEDY

The opposite of comedy is tragedy, portraying a hero's fall in fortune. While by classical definitions, tragedies could be sad, Aristotle went further, requiring that they depict suffering and pain to cause "terror and pity" in audiences. Additionally, he decreed that tragic heroes be basically good, admirable, or noble, and that their downfalls result from personal action, choice, or error, not by bad luck or accident.

ARISTOTLE'S CRITERIA FOR TRAGEDY

In his *Poetics,* Aristotle defined five critical terms relative to tragedy:

- *Anagnorisis*: Meaning tragic insight or recognition, this is a moment of realization by a tragic hero or heroine that he or she has become enmeshed in a "web of fate."
- *Hamartia*: This is often called a "tragic flaw," but is better described as a tragic error. *Hamartia* is an archery term meaning a shot missing the bull's eye, used here as a metaphor for a mistake—often a simple one—which results in catastrophe.
- *Hubris*: While often called "pride," this is actually translated as "violent transgression," and signifies an arrogant overstepping of moral or cultural bounds—the sin of the tragic hero who over-presumes or over-aspires.
- *Nemesis*: translated as "retribution," this represents the cosmic punishment or payback that the tragic hero ultimately receives for committing hubristic acts.
- *Peripateia*: Literally "turning," this is a plot reversal consisting of a tragic hero's pivotal action, which changes his or her status from safe to endangered.

HEGEL'S THEORY OF TRAGEDY

Georg Wilhelm Friedrich Hegel (1770-1831) proposed a different theory of tragedy than Aristotle (384-322 BC), which was also very influential. Whereas Aristotle's criteria involved character and plot, Hegel defined tragedy as a dynamic conflict of opposite forces or rights. For example, if an individual believes in the moral philosophy of the conscientious objector (i.e., that fighting in wars is morally wrong) but is confronted with being drafted into military service, this conflict would fit Hegel's definition of a tragic plot premise. Hegel theorized that a tragedy must involve some circumstance in which two values, or two rights, are fatally at odds with one another and conflict directly. Hegel did not view this as good triumphing over evil, or evil winning out over good, but rather as one good fighting against another good unto death. He saw this conflict of two goods as truly tragic. In ancient Greek playwright Sophocles' tragedy *Antigone,* the main character experiences this tragic conflict between her public duties and her family and religious responsibilities.

REVENGE TRAGEDY

Along with Aristotelian definitions of comedy and tragedy, ancient Greece was the origin of the **revenge tragedy**. This genre became highly popular in Renaissance England, and is still popular today in contemporary movies. In a revenge tragedy, the protagonist has suffered a serious wrong, such as the murder of a family member. However, the wrongdoer has not been punished. In contemporary plots, this often occurs when some legal technicality has interfered with the miscreant's conviction and sentencing, or when authorities are unable to locate and apprehend the criminal. The protagonist then faces the conflict of suffering this injustice, or exacting his or her own justice by seeking revenge. Greek revenge tragedies include *Agamemnon* and *Medea*. Playwright Thomas Kyd's *The Spanish Tragedy* (1582-1592) is credited with beginning the Elizabethan genre of revenge tragedies. Shakespearean revenge tragedies include *Hamlet* (1599-1602) and *Titus Andronicus* (1588-1593). A Jacobean example is Thomas Middleton's *The Revenger's Tragedy* (1606, 1607).

HAMLET'S "TRAGIC FLAW"

Despite virtually limitless interpretations, one way to view Hamlet's tragic error generally is as indecision. He suffers the classic revenge tragedy's conflict of whether to suffer with his knowledge of his mother's and uncle's assassination of his father, or to exact his own revenge and justice against Claudius, who has assumed the throne after his crime went unknown and unpunished. Hamlet's famous soliloquy, "To be or not to be" reflects this dilemma. Hamlet muses "Whether 'tis nobler in the mind to suffer the slings and arrows of outrageous fortune, / Or to take arms against a sea of troubles, / And by opposing end them?" Hamlet both longs for and fears death, as "the dread of something after death ... makes us rather bear those ills we have / Than fly to others that we know not ... Thus, conscience does make cowards of us all." For most of the play, Hamlet struggles with his responsibility to avenge his father, who was killed by Hamlet's uncle, Claudius. So, Hamlet's tragic error at first might be considered a lack of action. But he then makes several attempts at revenge, each of which end in worse tragedy, until his efforts are ended by the final tragedy—Hamlet's own death.

Informational Texts

TEXT FEATURES IN INFORMATIONAL TEXTS

The **title of a text** gives readers some idea of its content. The **table of contents** is a list near the beginning of a text, showing the book's sections and chapters and their coinciding page numbers. This gives readers an overview of the whole text and helps them find specific chapters easily. An **appendix**, at the back of the book or document, includes important information that is not present in the main text. Also at the back, an **index** lists the book's important topics alphabetically with their page numbers to help readers find them easily. **Glossaries**, usually found at the backs of books, list technical terms alphabetically with their definitions to aid vocabulary learning and comprehension. Boldface print is used to emphasize certain words, often identifying words included in the text's glossary where readers can look up their definitions. **Headings** separate sections of text and show the topic of each. **Subheadings** divide subject headings into smaller, more specific categories to help readers organize information. **Footnotes**, at the bottom of the page, give readers more information, such as citations or links. **Bullet points** list items separately, making facts and ideas easier to see and understand. A **sidebar** is a box of information to one side of the main text giving additional information, often on a more focused or in-depth example of a topic.

Illustrations and **photographs** are pictures that visually emphasize important points in text. The captions below the illustrations explain what those images show. Charts and tables are visual forms of information that make something easier to understand quickly. Diagrams are drawings that show relationships or explain a process. Graphs visually show the relationships among multiple sets of information plotted along vertical and horizontal axes. Maps show geographical information visually to help readers understand the relative locations of places covered in the text. Timelines are visual graphics that show historical events in chronological order to help readers see their sequence.

> **Review Video: Informative Text**
> Visit mometrix.com/academy and enter code: 924964

LANGUAGE USE
LITERAL AND FIGURATIVE LANGUAGE

As in fictional literature, informational text also uses both **literal language**, which means just what it says, and **figurative language**, which imparts more than literal meaning. For example, an informational text author might use a simile or direct comparison, such as writing that a racehorse "ran like the wind." Informational text authors also use metaphors or implied comparisons, such as "the cloud of the Great Depression." Imagery may also appear in informational texts to increase the reader's understanding of ideas and concepts discussed in the text.

EXPLICIT AND IMPLICIT INFORMATION

When informational text states something explicitly, the reader is told by the author exactly what is meant, which can include the author's interpretation or perspective of events. For example, a professor writes, "I have seen students go into an absolute panic just because they weren't able to complete the exam in the time they were allotted." This explicitly tells the reader that the students were afraid, and by using the words "just because," the writer indicates their fear was exaggerated out of proportion relative to what happened. However, another professor writes, "I have had students come to me, their faces drained of all color, saying 'We weren't able to finish the exam.'" This is an example of implicit meaning: the second writer did not state explicitly that the students were panicked. Instead, he wrote a description of their faces being "drained of all color." From this description, the reader can infer that the students were so frightened that their faces paled.

TECHNICAL LANGUAGE

Technical language is more impersonal than literary and vernacular language. Passive voice makes the tone impersonal. For example, instead of writing, "We found this a central component of protein metabolism," scientists write, "This was found a central component of protein metabolism." While science professors have traditionally instructed students to avoid active voice because it leads to first-person ("I" and "we") usage, science editors today find passive voice dull and weak. Many journal articles combine both. Tone in technical science writing should be detached, concise, and professional. While one may normally write, "This chemical has to be available for proteins to be digested," professionals write technically, "The presence of this chemical is required for the enzyme to break the covalent bonds of proteins." The use of technical language appeals to both technical and non-technical audiences by displaying the author or speaker's understanding of the subject and suggesting their credibility regarding the message they are communicating.

TECHNICAL MATERIAL FOR NON-TECHNICAL READERS

Writing about **technical subjects** for **non-technical readers** differs from writing for colleagues because authors place more importance on delivering a critical message than on imparting the maximum technical content possible. Technical authors also must assume that non-technical audiences do not have the expertise to comprehend extremely scientific or technical messages, concepts, and terminology. They must resist the temptation to impress audiences with their scientific knowledge and expertise and remember that their primary purpose is to communicate a message that non-technical readers will understand, feel, and respond to. Non-technical and technical styles include similarities. Both should formally cite any references or other authors' work utilized in the text. Both must follow intellectual property and copyright regulations. This includes the author's protecting his or her own rights, or a public domain statement, as he or she chooses.

NON-TECHNICAL AUDIENCES

Writers of technical or scientific material may need to write for many non-technical audiences. Some readers have no technical or scientific background, and those who do may not be in the same field as the authors. Government and corporate policymakers and budget managers need technical information they can understand for decision-making. Citizens affected by technology or science are a different audience. Non-governmental organizations can encompass many of the preceding groups. Elementary and secondary school programs also need non-technical language for presenting technical subject matter. Additionally, technical authors will need to use non-technical language when collecting consumer responses to surveys, presenting scientific or para-scientific material to the public, writing about the history of science, and writing about science and technology in developing countries.

USE OF EVERYDAY LANGUAGE

Authors of technical information sometimes must write using non-technical language that readers outside their disciplinary fields can comprehend. They should use not only non-technical terms, but also normal, everyday language to accommodate readers whose native language is different than the language the text is written in. For example, instead of writing that "eustatic changes like thermal expansion are causing hazardous conditions in the littoral zone," an author would do better to write that "a rising sea level is threatening the coast." When technical terms cannot be avoided, authors should also define or explain them using non-technical language. Although authors must cite references and acknowledge their use of others' work, they should avoid the kinds of references or citations that they would use in scientific journals—unless they reinforce author messages. They should not use endnotes, footnotes, or any other complicated referential techniques because non-technical journal publishers usually do not accept them. Including high-resolution illustrations, photos, maps, or satellite images and incorporating multimedia into digital publications will enhance non-technical writing about technical subjects. Technical authors may publish using non-technical language in e-journals, trade journals, specialty newsletters, and daily newspapers.

MAKING INFERENCES ABOUT INFORMATIONAL TEXT

With informational text, reader comprehension depends not only on recalling important statements and details, but also on reader inferences based on examples and details. Readers add information from the text to what they already know to draw inferences about the text. These inferences help the readers to fill in the information that the text does not explicitly state, enabling them to understand the text better. When reading a nonfictional autobiography or biography, for example, the most appropriate inferences might concern the events in the book, the actions of the subject of the autobiography or biography, and the message the author means to convey. When reading a nonfictional expository (informational) text, the reader would best draw inferences about problems and their solutions, and causes and their effects. When reading a nonfictional persuasive text, the reader will want to infer ideas supporting the author's message and intent.

STRUCTURES OR ORGANIZATIONAL PATTERNS IN INFORMATIONAL TEXTS

Informational text can be **descriptive**, appealing to the five senses and answering the questions what, who, when, where, and why. Another method of structuring informational text is sequence and order. **Chronological** texts relate events in the sequence that they occurred, from start to finish, while how-to texts organize information into a series of instructions in the sequence in which the steps should be followed. **Comparison-contrast** structures of informational text describe various ideas to their readers by pointing out how things or ideas are similar and how they are different. **Cause and effect** structures of informational text describe events that occurred and identify the causes or reasons that those events occurred. **Problem and solution** structures of informational texts introduce and describe problems and offer one or more solutions for each problem described.

DETERMINING AN INFORMATIONAL AUTHOR'S PURPOSE

Informational authors' purposes are why they write texts. Readers must determine authors' motivations and goals. Readers gain greater insight into a text by considering the author's motivation. This develops critical reading skills. Readers perceive writing as a person's voice, not simply printed words. Uncovering author motivations and purposes empowers readers to know what to expect from the text, read for relevant details, evaluate authors and their work critically, and respond effectively to the motivations and persuasions of the text. The main idea of a text is what the reader is supposed to understand from reading it; the purpose of the text is why the author has written it and what the author wants readers to do with its information. Authors state some purposes clearly, while other purposes may be unstated but equally significant. When stated purposes contradict other parts of a text, the author may have a hidden agenda. Readers can better evaluate a text's effectiveness, whether they agree or disagree with it, and why they agree or disagree through identifying unstated author purposes.

IDENTIFYING AUTHOR'S POINT OF VIEW OR PURPOSE

In some informational texts, readers find it easy to identify the author's point of view and purpose, such as when the author explicitly states his or her position and reason for writing. But other texts are more difficult, either because of the content or because the authors give neutral or balanced viewpoints. This is particularly true in scientific texts, in which authors may state the purpose of their research in the report, but never state their point of view except by interpreting evidence or data.

To analyze text and identify point of view or purpose, readers should ask themselves the following four questions:

1. With what main point or idea does this author want to persuade readers to agree?
2. How does this author's word choice affect the way that readers consider this subject?
3. How do this author's choices of examples and facts affect the way that readers consider this subject?
4. What is it that this author wants to accomplish by writing this text?

> **Review Video: Understanding the Author's Intent**
> Visit mometrix.com/academy and enter code: 511819
>
> **Review Video: Author's Position**
> Visit mometrix.com/academy and enter code: 827954

EVALUATING ARGUMENTS MADE BY INFORMATIONAL TEXT WRITERS

When evaluating an informational text, the first step is to identify the argument's conclusion. Then identify the author's premises that support the conclusion. Try to paraphrase premises for clarification and make the conclusion and premises fit. List all premises first, sequentially numbered, then finish with the conclusion. Identify any premises or assumptions not stated by the author but required for the stated premises to support the conclusion. Read word assumptions sympathetically, as the author might. Evaluate whether premises reasonably support the conclusion. For inductive reasoning, the reader should ask if the premises are true, if they support the conclusion, and if so, how strongly. For deductive reasoning, the reader should ask if the argument is valid or invalid. If all premises are true, then the argument is valid unless the conclusion can be false. If it can, then the argument is invalid. An invalid argument can be made valid through alterations such as the addition of needed premises.

USE OF RHETORIC IN INFORMATIONAL TEXTS

There are many ways authors can support their claims, arguments, beliefs, ideas, and reasons for writing in informational texts. For example, authors can appeal to readers' sense of **logic** by communicating their reasoning through a carefully sequenced series of logical steps to help "prove" the points made. Authors can appeal to readers' **emotions** by using descriptions and words that evoke feelings of sympathy, sadness, anger, righteous indignation, hope, happiness, or any other emotion to reinforce what they express and share with their audience. Authors may appeal to the **moral** or **ethical values** of readers by using words and descriptions that can convince readers that something is right or wrong. By relating personal anecdotes, authors can supply readers with more accessible, realistic examples of points they make, as well as appealing to their emotions. They can provide supporting evidence by reporting case studies. They can also illustrate their points by making analogies to which readers can better relate.

91

Vocabulary and Word Relationships

SYNONYMS AND ANTONYMS

When you understand how words relate to each other, you will discover more in a passage. This is explained by understanding **synonyms** (e.g., words that mean the same thing) and **antonyms** (e.g., words that mean the opposite of one another). As an example, *dry* and *arid* are synonyms, and *dry* and *wet* are antonyms.

There are many pairs of words in English that can be considered synonyms, despite having slightly different definitions. For instance, the words *friendly* and *collegial* can both be used to describe a warm interpersonal relationship, and one would be correct to call them synonyms. However, *collegial* (kin to *colleague*) is often used in reference to professional or academic relationships, and *friendly* has no such connotation.

If the difference between the two words is too great, then they should not be called synonyms. *Hot* and *warm* are not synonyms because their meanings are too distinct. A good way to determine whether two words are synonyms is to substitute one word for the other word and verify that the meaning of the sentence has not changed. Substituting *warm* for *hot* in a sentence would convey a different meaning. Although warm and hot may seem close in meaning, warm generally means that the temperature is moderate, and hot generally means that the temperature is excessively high.

Antonyms are words with opposite meanings. *Light* and *dark*, *up* and *down*, *right* and *left*, *good* and *bad*: these are all sets of antonyms. Be careful to distinguish between antonyms and pairs of words that are simply different. *Black* and *gray*, for instance, are not antonyms because gray is not the opposite of black. *Black* and *white*, on the other hand, are antonyms.

Not every word has an antonym. For instance, many nouns do not. What would be the antonym of *chair*? During your exam, the questions related to antonyms are more likely to concern adjectives. You will recall that adjectives are words that describe a noun. Some common adjectives include *purple*, *fast*, *skinny*, and *sweet*. From those four adjectives, *purple* is the item that lacks a group of obvious antonyms.

> **Review Video: What Are Synonyms and Antonyms?**
> Visit mometrix.com/academy and enter code: 105612

AFFIXES

Affixes in the English language are morphemes that are added to words to create related but different words. Derivational affixes form new words based on and related to the original words. For example, the affix *–ness* added to the end of the adjective *happy* forms the noun *happiness.* Inflectional affixes form different grammatical versions of words. For example, the plural affix *–s* changes the singular noun *book* to the plural noun *books*, and the past tense affix *–ed* changes the present tense verb *look* to the past tense *looked.* Prefixes are affixes placed in front of words. For example, *heat* means to make hot; *preheat* means to heat in advance. Suffixes are affixes placed at the ends of words. The *happiness* example above contains the suffix *–ness.* Circumfixes add parts both before and after words, such as how *light* becomes *enlighten* with the prefix *en-* and the suffix *–en.* Interfixes create compound words via central affixes: *speed* and *meter* become *speedometer* via the interfix *–o–*.

> **Review Video: Affixes**
> Visit mometrix.com/academy and enter code: 782422

WORD ROOTS, PREFIXES, AND SUFFIXES TO HELP DETERMINE MEANINGS OF WORDS

Many English words were formed from combining multiple sources. For example, the Latin *habēre* means "to have," and the prefixes *in-* and *im-* mean a lack or prevention of something, as in *insufficient* and *imperfect*. Latin combined *in-* with *habēre* to form *inhibēre,* whose past participle was *inhibitus*. This is the origin of the English word *inhibit,* meaning to prevent from having. Hence by knowing the meanings of both the prefix and the root, one can decipher the word meaning. In Greek, the root *enkephalo-* refers to the brain. Many medical terms are based on this root, such as encephalitis and hydrocephalus. Understanding the prefix and suffix meanings (*-itis* means inflammation; *hydro-* means water) allows a person to deduce that encephalitis refers to brain inflammation and hydrocephalus refers to water (or other fluid) in the brain.

> **Review Video: Determining Word Meanings**
> Visit mometrix.com/academy and enter code: 894894
>
> **Review Video: Root Words in English**
> Visit mometrix.com/academy and enter code: 896380

PREFIXES

While knowing prefix meanings helps ESL and beginning readers learn new words, other readers take for granted the meanings of known words. However, prefix knowledge will also benefit them for determining meanings or definitions of unfamiliar words. For example, native English speakers and readers familiar with recipes know what *preheat* means. Knowing that *pre-* means in advance can also inform them that *presume* means to assume in advance, that *prejudice* means advance judgment, and that this understanding can be applied to many other words beginning with *pre-*. Knowing that the prefix *dis-* indicates opposition informs the meanings of words like *disbar, disagree, disestablish,* and many more. Knowing *dys-* means bad, impaired, abnormal, or difficult informs *dyslogistic, dysfunctional, dysphagia,* and *dysplasia.*

SUFFIXES

In English, certain suffixes generally indicate both that a word is a noun, and that the noun represents a state of being or quality. For example, *-ness* is commonly used to change an adjective into its noun form, as with *happy* and *happiness, nice* and *niceness,* and so on. The suffix *–tion* is commonly used to transform a verb into its noun form, as with *converse* and *conversation or move* and *motion*. Thus, if readers are unfamiliar with the second form of a word, knowing the meaning of the transforming suffix can help them determine meaning.

PREFIXES FOR NUMBERS

Prefix	Definition	Examples
bi-	two	bisect, biennial
mono-	one, single	monogamy, monologue
poly-	many	polymorphous, polygamous
semi-	half, partly	semicircle, semicolon
uni-	one	uniform, unity

Prefixes for Time, Direction, and Space

Prefix	Definition	Examples
a-	in, on, of, up, to	abed, afoot
ab-	from, away, off	abdicate, abjure
ad-	to, toward	advance, adventure
ante-	before, previous	antecedent, antedate
anti-	against, opposing	antipathy, antidote
cata-	down, away, thoroughly	catastrophe, cataclysm
circum-	around	circumspect, circumference
com-	with, together, very	commotion, complicate
contra-	against, opposing	contradict, contravene
de-	from	depart
dia-	through, across, apart	diameter, diagnose
dis-	away, off, down, not	dissent, disappear
epi-	upon	epilogue
ex-	out	extract, excerpt
hypo-	under, beneath	hypodermic, hypothesis
inter-	among, between	intercede, interrupt
intra-	within	intramural, intrastate
ob-	against, opposing	objection
per-	through	perceive, permit
peri-	around	periscope, perimeter
post-	after, following	postpone, postscript
pre-	before, previous	prevent, preclude
pro-	forward, in place of	propel, pronoun
retro-	back, backward	retrospect, retrograde
sub-	under, beneath	subjugate, substitute
super-	above, extra	supersede, supernumerary
trans-	across, beyond, over	transact, transport
ultra-	beyond, excessively	ultramodern, ultrasonic

Negative Prefixes

Prefix	Definition	Examples
a-	without, lacking	atheist, agnostic
in-	not, opposing	incapable, ineligible
non-	not	nonentity, nonsense
un-	not, reverse of	unhappy, unlock

EXTRA PREFIXES

Prefix	Definition	Examples
belli-	war, warlike	bellicose
bene-	well, good	benefit, benefactor
equi-	equal	equivalent, equilibrium
for-	away, off, from	forget, forswear
fore-	previous	foretell, forefathers
homo-	same, equal	homogenized, homonym
hyper-	excessive, over	hypercritical, hypertension
in-	in, into	intrude, invade
magn-	large	magnitude, magnify
mal-	bad, poorly, not	malfunction, malpractice
mis-	bad, poorly, not	misspell, misfire
mor-	death	mortality, mortuary
neo-	new	Neolithic, neoconservative
omni-	all, everywhere	omniscient, omnivore
ortho-	right, straight	orthogonal, orthodox
over-	above	overbearing, oversight
pan-	all, entire	panorama, pandemonium
para-	beside, beyond	parallel, paradox
phil-	love, like	philosophy, philanthropic
prim-	first, early	primitive, primary
re-	backward, again	revoke, recur
sym-	with, together	sympathy, symphony
vis-	to see	visage, visible

Below is a list of common suffixes and their meanings:

ADJECTIVE SUFFIXES

Suffix	Definition	Examples
-able (-ible)	capable of being	toler*able*, ed*ible*
-esque	in the style of, like	picturesque, grotesque
-ful	filled with, marked by	thankful, zestful
-ific	make, cause	terrific, beatific
-ish	suggesting, like	churlish, childish
-less	lacking, without	hopeless, countless
-ous	marked by, given to	religious, riotous

NOUN SUFFIXES

Suffix	Definition	Examples
-acy	state, condition	accuracy, privacy
-ance	act, condition, fact	acceptance, vigilance
-ard	one that does excessively	drunkard, sluggard
-ation	action, state, result	occupation, starvation
-dom	state, rank, condition	serfdom, wisdom
-er (-or)	office, action	teacher, elevator, honor
-ess	feminine	waitress, duchess
-hood	state, condition	manhood, statehood
-ion	action, result, state	union, fusion
-ism	act, manner, doctrine	barbarism, socialism
-ist	worker, follower	monopolist, socialist
-ity (-ty)	state, quality, condition	acidity, civility, twenty
-ment	result, action	Refreshment
-ness	quality, state	greatness, tallness
-ship	position	internship, statesmanship
-sion (-tion)	state, result	revision, expedition
-th	act, state, quality	warmth, width
-tude	quality, state, result	magnitude, fortitude

VERB SUFFIXES

Suffix	Definition	Examples
-ate	having, showing	separate, desolate
-en	cause to be, become	deepen, strengthen
-fy	make, cause to have	glorify, fortify
-ize	cause to be, treat with	sterilize, mechanize

DENOTATIVE VS. CONNOTATIVE MEANING

The **denotative** meaning of a word is the literal meaning. The **connotative** meaning goes beyond the denotative meaning to include the emotional reaction that a word may invoke. The connotative meaning often takes the denotative meaning a step further due to associations the reader makes with the denotative meaning. Readers can differentiate between the denotative and connotative meanings by first recognizing how authors use each meaning. Most non-fiction, for example, is fact-based and authors do not use flowery, figurative language. The reader can assume that the writer is using the denotative meaning of words. In fiction, the author may use the connotative meaning. Readers can determine whether the author is using the denotative or connotative meaning of a word by implementing context clues.

> **Review Video: Connotation and Denotation**
> Visit mometrix.com/academy and enter code: 310092

NUANCES OF WORD MEANING RELATIVE TO CONNOTATION, DENOTATION, DICTION, AND USAGE

A word's denotation is simply its objective dictionary definition. However, its connotation refers to the subjective associations, often emotional, that specific words evoke in listeners and readers. Two or more words can have the same dictionary meaning, but very different connotations. Writers use diction (word choice) to convey various nuances of thought and emotion by selecting synonyms for other words that best communicate the associations they want to trigger for readers. For example, a car engine is naturally greasy; in this sense, "greasy" is a neutral term. But when a person's smile, appearance, or clothing is described as "greasy," it has a negative connotation. Some words have even gained additional or different meanings over time. For example, *awful* used to be used to describe things that evoked a sense of awe. When *awful* is separated into its root word, awe, and suffix, -ful, it can be understood to mean "full of awe." However, the word is now commonly used to describe things that evoke repulsion, terror, or another intense, negative reaction.

> **Review Video: Word Usage in Sentences**
> Visit mometrix.com/academy and enter code: 197863

CONTEXT CLUES

Readers of all levels will encounter words that they have either never seen or have encountered only on a limited basis. The best way to define a word in **context** is to look for nearby words that can assist in revealing the meaning of the word. For instance, unfamiliar nouns are often accompanied by examples that provide a definition. Consider the following sentence: *Dave arrived at the party in hilarious garb: a leopard-print shirt, buckskin trousers, and bright green sneakers.* If a reader was unfamiliar with the meaning of garb, he or she could read the examples (i.e., a leopard-print shirt, buckskin trousers, and high heels) and quickly determine that the word means *clothing*. Examples will not always be this obvious. Consider this sentence: *Parsley, lemon, and flowers were just a few of the items he used as garnishes.* Here, the word *garnishes* is exemplified by parsley, lemon, and flowers. Readers who have eaten in a variety of restaurants will probably be able to identify a garnish as something used to decorate a plate.

> **Review Video: Context Clues**
> Visit mometrix.com/academy and enter code: 613660

USING CONTRAST IN CONTEXT CLUES

In addition to looking at the context of a passage, readers can use contrast to define an unfamiliar word in context. In many sentences, the author will not describe the unfamiliar word directly; instead, he or she will describe the opposite of the unfamiliar word. Thus, you are provided with some information that will bring you closer to defining the word. Consider the following example: *Despite his intelligence, Hector's low brow and bad posture made him look obtuse.* The author writes that Hector's appearance does not convey intelligence. Therefore, *obtuse* must mean unintelligent. Here is another example: *Despite the horrible weather, we were beatific about our trip to Alaska.* The word *despite* indicates that the speaker's feelings were at odds with the weather. Since the weather is described as *horrible*, then *beatific* must mean something positive.

SUBSTITUTION TO FIND MEANING

In some cases, there will be very few contextual clues to help a reader define the meaning of an unfamiliar word. When this happens, one strategy that readers may employ is **substitution**. A good reader will brainstorm some possible synonyms for the given word, and he or she will substitute these words into the sentence. If the sentence and the surrounding passage continue to make sense, then the substitution has revealed at least some information about the unfamiliar word. Consider the sentence: *Frank's admonition rang in her ears as she climbed the mountain.* A reader unfamiliar with *admonition* might come up with some substitutions like *vow, promise, advice, complaint*, or *compliment*. All of these words make general sense of the sentence, though their meanings are diverse. However, this process has suggested that an admonition is some sort of message. The substitution strategy is rarely able to pinpoint a precise definition, but this process can be effective as a last resort.

Occasionally, you will be able to define an unfamiliar word by looking at the descriptive words in the context. Consider the following sentence: *Fred dragged the recalcitrant boy kicking and screaming up the stairs.* The words *dragged*, *kicking*, and *screaming* all suggest that the boy does not want to go up the stairs. The reader may assume that *recalcitrant* means something like unwilling or protesting. In this example, an unfamiliar adjective was identified.

Additionally, using description to define an unfamiliar noun is a common practice compared to unfamiliar adjectives, as in this sentence: *Don's wrinkled frown and constantly shaking fist identified him as a curmudgeon of the first order.* Don is described as having a *wrinkled frown and constantly shaking fist*, suggesting that a *curmudgeon* must be a grumpy person. Contrasts do not always provide detailed information about the unfamiliar word, but they at least give the reader some clues.

Words with Multiple Meanings

When a word has more than one meaning, readers can have difficulty determining how the word is being used in a given sentence. For instance, the verb *cleave*, can mean either *join* or *separate*. When readers come upon this word, they will have to select the definition that makes the most sense. Consider the following sentence: *Hermione's knife cleaved the bread cleanly.* Since a knife cannot join bread together, the word must indicate separation. A slightly more difficult example would be the sentence: *The birds cleaved to one another as they flew from the oak tree.* Immediately, the presence of the words *to one another* should suggest that in this sentence *cleave* is being used to mean *join*. Discovering the intent of a word with multiple meanings requires the same tricks as defining an unknown word: look for contextual clues and evaluate the substituted words.

Context Clues to Help Determine Meanings of Words

If readers simply bypass unknown words, they can reach unclear conclusions about what they read. However, looking for the definition of every unfamiliar word in the dictionary can slow their reading progress. Moreover, the dictionary may list multiple definitions for a word, so readers must search the word's context for meaning. Hence context is important to new vocabulary regardless of reader methods. Four types of context clues are examples, definitions, descriptive words, and opposites. Authors may use a certain word, and then follow it with several different examples of what it describes. Sometimes authors actually supply a definition of a word they use, which is especially true in informational and technical texts. Authors may use descriptive words that elaborate upon a vocabulary word they just used. Authors may also use opposites with negation that help define meaning.

Examples and Definitions

An author may use a word and then give examples that illustrate its meaning. Consider this text: "Teachers who do not know how to use sign language can help students who are deaf or hard of hearing understand certain instructions by using gestures instead, like pointing their fingers to indicate which direction to look or go; holding up a hand, palm outward, to indicate stopping; holding the hands flat, palms up, curling a finger toward oneself in a beckoning motion to indicate 'come here'; or curling all fingers toward oneself repeatedly to indicate 'come on', 'more', or 'continue.'" The author of this text has used the word "gestures" and then followed it with examples, so a reader unfamiliar with the word could deduce from the examples that "gestures" means "hand motions." Readers can find examples by looking for signal words "for example," "for instance," "like," "such as," and "e.g."

While readers sometimes have to look for definitions of unfamiliar words in a dictionary or do some work to determine a word's meaning from its surrounding context, at other times an author may make it easier for readers by defining certain words. For example, an author may write, "The company did not have sufficient capital, that is, available money, to continue operations." The author defined "capital" as "available money," and heralded the definition with the phrase "that is." Another way that authors supply word definitions is with appositives. Rather than being introduced by a signal phrase like "that is," "namely," or "meaning," an appositive comes after the vocabulary word it defines and is enclosed within two commas. For example, an author may write, "The Indians introduced the Pilgrims to pemmican, cakes they made of lean meat dried and mixed with fat, which proved greatly beneficial to keep settlers from starving while trapping." In this example, the appositive phrase following "pemmican" and preceding "which" defines the word "pemmican."

DESCRIPTIONS

When readers encounter a word they do not recognize in a text, the author may expand on that word to illustrate it better. While the author may do this to make the prose more picturesque and vivid, the reader can also take advantage of this description to provide context clues to the meaning of the unfamiliar word. For example, an author may write, "The man sitting next to me on the airplane was obese. His shirt stretched across his vast expanse of flesh, strained almost to bursting." The descriptive second sentence elaborates on and helps to define the previous sentence's word "obese" to mean extremely fat. A reader unfamiliar with the word "repugnant" can decipher its meaning through an author's accompanying description: "The way the child grimaced and shuddered as he swallowed the medicine showed that its taste was particularly repugnant."

OPPOSITES

Text authors sometimes introduce a contrasting or opposing idea before or after a concept they present. They may do this to emphasize or heighten the idea they present by contrasting it with something that is the reverse. However, readers can also use these context clues to understand familiar words. For example, an author may write, "Our conversation was not cheery. We sat and talked very solemnly about his experience and a number of similar events." The reader who is not familiar with the word "solemnly" can deduce by the author's preceding use of "not cheery" that "solemn" means the opposite of cheery or happy, so it must mean serious or sad. Or if someone writes, "Don't condemn his entire project because you couldn't find anything good to say about it," readers unfamiliar with "condemn" can understand from the sentence structure that it means the opposite of saying anything good, so it must mean reject, dismiss, or disapprove. "Entire" adds another context clue, meaning total or complete rejection.

SYNTAX TO DETERMINE PART OF SPEECH AND MEANINGS OF WORDS

Syntax refers to sentence structure and word order. Suppose that a reader encounters an unfamiliar word when reading a text. To illustrate, consider an invented word like "splunch." If this word is used in a sentence like "Please splunch that ball to me," the reader can assume from syntactic context that "splunch" is a verb. We would not use a noun, adjective, adverb, or preposition with the object "that ball," and the prepositional phrase "to me" further indicates "splunch" represents an action. However, in the sentence, "Please hand that splunch to me," the reader can assume that "splunch" is a noun. Demonstrative adjectives like "that" modify nouns. Also, we hand someone some*thing*—a thing being a noun; we do not hand someone a verb, adjective, or adverb. Some sentences contain further clues. For example, from the sentence, "The princess wore the glittering splunch on her head," the reader can deduce that it is a crown, tiara, or something similar from the syntactic context, without knowing the word.

SYNTAX TO INDICATE DIFFERENT MEANINGS OF SIMILAR SENTENCES

The syntax, or structure, of a sentence affords grammatical cues that aid readers in comprehending the meanings of words, phrases, and sentences in the texts that they read. Seemingly minor differences in how the words or phrases in a sentence are ordered can make major differences in meaning. For example, two sentences can use exactly the same words but have different meanings based on the word order:

- "The man with a broken arm sat in a chair."
- "The man sat in a chair with a broken arm."

While both sentences indicate that a man sat in a chair, differing syntax indicates whether the man's or chair's arm was broken.

DETERMINING MEANING OF PHRASES AND PARAGRAPHS

Like unknown words, the meanings of phrases, paragraphs, and entire works can also be difficult to discern. Each of these can be better understood with added context. However, for larger groups of words, more context is needed. Unclear phrases are similar to unclear words, and the same methods can be used to understand their meaning. However, it is also important to consider how the individual words in the phrase work together. Paragraphs are a bit more complicated. Just as words must be compared to other words in a sentence, paragraphs must be compared to other paragraphs in a composition or a section.

DETERMINING MEANING IN VARIOUS TYPES OF COMPOSITIONS

To understand the meaning of an entire composition, the type of composition must be considered. **Expository writing** is generally organized so that each paragraph focuses on explaining one idea, or part of an idea, and its relevance. **Persuasive writing** uses paragraphs for different purposes to organize the parts of the argument. **Unclear paragraphs** must be read in the context of the paragraphs around them for their meaning to be fully understood. The meaning of full texts can also be unclear at times. The purpose of composition is also important for understanding the meaning of a text. To quickly understand the broad meaning of a text, look to the introductory and concluding paragraphs. Fictional texts are different. Some fictional works have implicit meanings, but some do not. The target audience must be considered for understanding texts that do have an implicit meaning, as most children's fiction will clearly state any lessons or morals. For other fiction, the application of literary theories and criticism may be helpful for understanding the text.

ADDITIONAL RESOURCES FOR DETERMINING WORD MEANING AND USAGE

While these strategies are useful for determining the meaning of unknown words and phrases, sometimes additional resources are needed to properly use the terms in different contexts. Some words have multiple definitions, and some words are inappropriate in particular contexts or modes of writing. The following tools are helpful for understanding all meanings and proper uses for words and phrases.

- **Dictionaries** provide the meaning of a multitude of words in a language. Many dictionaries include additional information about each word, such as its etymology, its synonyms, or variations of the word.
- **Glossaries** are similar to dictionaries, as they provide the meanings of a variety of terms. However, while dictionaries typically feature an extensive list of words and comprise an entire publication, glossaries are often included at the end of a text and only include terms and definitions that are relevant to the text they follow.

- **Spell Checkers** are used to detect spelling errors in typed text. Some spell checkers may also detect the misuse of plural or singular nouns, verb tenses, or capitalization. While spell checkers are a helpful tool, they are not always reliable or attuned to the author's intent, so it is important to review the spell checker's suggestions before accepting them.
- **Style Manuals** are guidelines on the preferred punctuation, format, and grammar usage according to different fields or organizations. For example, the Associated Press Stylebook is a style guide often used for media writing. The guidelines within a style guide are not always applicable across different contexts and usages, as the guidelines often cover grammatical or formatting situations that are not objectively correct or incorrect.

Figurative Language

LITERAL AND FIGURATIVE MEANING

When language is used **literally**, the words mean exactly what they say and nothing more. When language is used **figuratively**, the words mean something beyond their literal meaning. For example, "The weeping willow tree has long, trailing branches and leaves" is a literal description. But "The weeping willow tree looks as if it is bending over and crying" is a figurative description—specifically, a **simile** or stated comparison. Another figurative language form is **metaphor**, or an implied comparison. A good example is the metaphor of a city, state, or city-state as a ship, and its governance as sailing that ship. Ancient Greek lyrical poet Alcaeus is credited with first using this metaphor, and ancient Greek tragedian Aeschylus then used it in *Seven Against Thebes,* and then Plato used it in the *Republic.*

FIGURES OF SPEECH

A **figure of speech** is a verbal expression whose meaning is figurative rather than literal. For example, the phrase "butterflies in the stomach" does not refer to actual butterflies in a person's stomach. It is a metaphor representing the fluttery feelings experienced when a person is nervous or excited—or when one "falls in love," which does not mean physically falling. "Hitting a sales target" does not mean physically hitting a target with arrows as in archery; it is a metaphor for meeting a sales quota. "Climbing the ladder of success" metaphorically likens advancing in one's career to ascending ladder rungs. Similes, such as "light as a feather" (meaning very light, not a feather's actual weight), and hyperbole, like "I'm starving/freezing/roasting," are also figures of speech. Figures of speech are often used and crafted for emphasis, freshness of expression, or clarity.

> **Review Video: Figures of Speech**
> Visit mometrix.com/academy and enter code: 111295

FIGURATIVE LANGUAGE

Figurative language extends past the literal meanings of words. It offers readers new insight into the people, things, events, and subjects covered in a work of literature. Figurative language also enables readers to feel they are sharing the authors' experiences. It can stimulate the reader's senses, make comparisons that readers find intriguing or even startling, and enable readers to view the world in different ways. When looking for figurative language, it is important to consider the context of the sentence or situation. Phrases that appear out of place or make little sense when read literally are likely instances of figurative language. Once figurative language has been recognized, context is also important to determining the type of figurative language being used and its function. For example, when a comparison is being made, a metaphor or simile is likely being used. This means the comparison may emphasize or create irony through the things being compared. Seven specific types of figurative language include: alliteration, onomatopoeia, personification, imagery, similes, metaphors, and hyperbole.

> **Review Video: Figurative Language**
> Visit mometrix.com/academy and enter code: 584902

ALLITERATION AND ONOMATOPOEIA

Alliteration describes a series of words beginning with the same sounds. **Onomatopoeia** uses words imitating the sounds of things they name or describe. For example, in his poem "Come Down, O Maid," Alfred Tennyson writes of "The moan of doves in immemorial elms, / And murmuring of innumerable bees." The word "moan" sounds like some sounds doves make, "murmuring" represents the sounds of bees buzzing. Onomatopoeia also includes words that are simply meant to represent sounds, such as "meow," "kaboom," and "whoosh."

PERSONIFICATION

Another type of figurative language is **personification**. This is describing a non-human thing, like an animal or an object, as if it were human. The general intent of personification is to describe things in a manner that will be comprehensible to readers. When an author states that a tree *groans* in the wind, he or she does not mean that the tree is emitting a low, pained sound from a mouth. Instead, the author means that the tree is making a noise similar to a human groan. Of course, this personification establishes a tone of sadness or suffering. A different tone would be established if the author said that the tree was *swaying* or *dancing*. Alfred Tennyson's poem "The Eagle" uses all of these types of figurative language: "He clasps the crag with crooked hands." Tennyson used alliteration, repeating /k/ and /kr/ sounds. These hard-sounding consonants reinforce the imagery, giving visual and tactile impressions of the eagle.

SIMILES AND METAPHORS

Similes are stated comparisons using "like" or "as." Similes can be used to stimulate readers' imaginations and appeal to their senses. Because a simile includes *like* or *as,* the device creates more space between the description and the thing being described than a metaphor does. If an author says that *a house was like a shoebox*, then the tone is different than the author saying that the house *was* a shoebox. Authors will choose between a metaphor and a simile depending on their intended tone.

Similes also help compare fictional characters to well-known objects or experiences, so the reader can better relate to them. William Wordsworth's poem about "Daffodils" begins, "I wandered lonely as a cloud." This simile compares his loneliness to that of a cloud. It is also personification, giving a cloud the human quality loneliness. In his novel *Lord Jim* (1900), Joseph Conrad writes in Chapter 33, "I would have given anything for the power to soothe her frail soul, tormenting itself in its invincible ignorance like a small bird beating about the cruel wires of a cage." Conrad uses the word "like" to compare the girl's soul to a small bird. His description of the bird beating at the cage shows the similar helplessness of the girl's soul to gain freedom.

A **metaphor** is a type of figurative language in which the writer equates something with another thing that is not particularly similar, instead of using *like* or *as.* For instance, *the bird was an arrow arcing through the sky.* In this sentence, the arrow is serving as a metaphor for the bird. The point of a metaphor is to encourage the reader to consider the item being described in a *different way.* Let's continue with this metaphor for a flying bird. You are asked to envision the bird's flight as being similar to the arc of an arrow. So, you imagine the flight to be swift and bending. Metaphors are a way for the author to describe an item *without being direct and obvious.* This literary device is a lyrical and suggestive way of providing information. Note that the reference for a metaphor will not always be mentioned explicitly by the author. Consider the following description of a forest in winter: *Swaying skeletons reached for the sky and groaned as the wind blew through them.* In this example, the author is using *skeletons* as a metaphor for leafless trees. This metaphor creates a spooky tone while inspiring the reader's imagination.

LITERARY EXAMPLES OF METAPHOR

A **metaphor** is an implied comparison, i.e., it compares something to something else without using "like", "as", or other comparative words. For example, in "The Tyger" (1794), William Blake writes, "Tyger Tyger, burning bright, / In the forests of the night." Blake compares the tiger to a flame not by saying it is like a fire, but by simply describing it as "burning." Henry Wadsworth Longfellow's poem "O Ship of State" (1850) uses an extended metaphor by referring consistently throughout the entire poem to the state, union, or republic as a seagoing vessel, referring to its keel, mast, sail, rope, anchors, and to its braving waves, rocks, gale, tempest, and "false lights on the shore." Within the extended metaphor, Wordsworth uses a specific metaphor: "the anchors of thy hope!"

TED HUGHES' ANIMAL METAPHORS

Ted Hughes frequently used animal metaphors in his poetry. In "The Thought Fox," a model of concise, structured beauty, Hughes characterizes the poet's creative process with succinct, striking imagery of an idea entering his head like a wild fox. Repeating "loneliness" in the first two stanzas emphasizes the poet's lonely work: "Something else is alive / Beside the clock's loneliness." He treats an idea's arrival as separate from himself. Three stanzas detail in vivid images a fox's approach from the outside winter forest at starless midnight—its nose, "Cold, delicately" touching twigs and leaves; "neat" paw prints in snow; "bold" body; brilliant green eyes; and self-contained, focused progress—"Till, with a sudden sharp hot stink of fox," he metaphorically depicts poetic inspiration as the fox's physical entry into "the dark hole of the head." Hughes ends by summarizing his vision of a poet as an interior, passive idea recipient, with the outside world unchanged: "The window is starless still; the clock ticks, / The page is printed."

> **Review Video: Metaphors in Writing**
> Visit mometrix.com/academy and enter code: 133295

HYPERBOLE

Hyperbole is excessive exaggeration used for humor or emphasis rather than for literal meaning. For example, in *To Kill a Mockingbird*, Harper Lee wrote, "People moved slowly then. There was no hurry, for there was nowhere to go, nothing to buy and no money to buy it with, nothing to see outside the boundaries of Maycomb County." This was not literally true; Lee exaggerates the scarcity of these things for emphasis. In "Old Times on the Mississippi," Mark Twain wrote, "I... could have hung my hat on my eyes, they stuck out so far." This is not literal, but makes his description vivid and funny. In his poem "As I Walked Out One Evening", W. H. Auden wrote, "I'll love you, dear, I'll love you / Till China and Africa meet, / And the river jumps over the mountain / And the salmon sing in the street." He used things not literally possible to emphasize the duration of his love.

> **Review Video: Hyperbole and Understatement**
> Visit mometrix.com/academy and enter code: 308470

LITERARY IRONY

In literature, irony demonstrates the opposite of what is said or done. The three types of irony are **verbal irony**, **situational irony**, and **dramatic irony**. Verbal irony uses words opposite to the meaning. Sarcasm may use verbal irony. One common example is describing something that is confusing as "clear as mud." For example, in his 1986 movie *Hannah and Her Sisters,* author, director, and actor Woody Allen says to his character's date, "I had a great evening; it was like the Nuremburg Trials." Notice these employ similes. In situational irony, what happens contrasts with what was expected. O. Henry's short story *The Gift of the Magi* uses situational irony: a husband and wife each sacrifice their most prized possession to buy each other a Christmas present. The irony is that she sells her long hair to buy him a watch fob, while he sells his heirloom pocket-watch to buy her the jeweled combs for her hair she had long wanted; in the end, neither of them can use their gifts. In dramatic irony, narrative informs audiences of more than its characters know. For example, in *Romeo and Juliet,* the audience is made aware that Juliet is only asleep, while Romeo believes her to be dead, which then leads to Romeo's death.

> **Review Video: What is the Definition of Irony?**
> Visit mometrix.com/academy and enter code: 374204

IDIOMS

Idioms create comparisons, and often take the form of similes or metaphors. Idioms are always phrases and are understood to have a meaning that is different from its individual words' literal meaning. For example, "break a leg" is a common idiom that is used to wish someone luck or tell them to perform well. Literally, the phrase "break a leg" means to injure a person's leg, but the phrase takes on a different meaning when used as an idiom. Another example is "call it a day," which means to temporarily stop working on a task, or find a stopping point, rather than literally referring to something as "a day." Many idioms are associated with a region or group. For example, an idiom commonly used in the American South is "'til the cows come home." This phrase is often used to indicate that something will take or may last for a very long time, but not that it will literally last until the cows return to where they reside.

Literary Elements

LITERARY TERMINOLOGY

- In works of prose such as novels, a group of connected sentences covering one main topic is termed a **paragraph**.
- In works of poetry, a group of verses similarly connected is called a **stanza**.
- In drama, when early works used verse, these were also divided into stanzas or **couplets**.
- Drama evolved to use predominantly prose. Overall, whether prose or verse, the conversation in a play is called **dialogue**.
- Large sections of dialogue spoken by one actor are called **soliloquies** or **monologues**.
- Dialogue that informs audiences but is unheard by other characters is called an **aside**.
- Novels and plays share certain common elements, such as:
  - **Characters** - the people in the story.
  - **Plot** - the action of the story.
  - **Climax** - when action or dramatic tension reaches its highest point.
  - **Denouement** - the resolution following the climax.
- Sections dividing novels are called **chapters**, while sections of plays are called **acts**.
- Subsections of plays' acts are called **scenes**. Novel chapters usually do not have subsections. However, some novels do include groups of chapters that form different sections.

LITERARY ANALYSIS

The best literary analysis shows special insight into at least one important aspect of a text. When analyzing literary texts, it can be difficult to find a starting place. Many texts can be analyzed several different ways, often leaving an overwhelming number of options for writers to consider. However, narrowing the focus to a particular element of literature can be helpful when preparing to analyze a text. Symbolism, themes, and motifs are common starting points for literary analysis. These three methods of analysis can lead to a holistic analysis of a text, since they involve elements that are often distributed throughout the text. However, not all texts feature these elements in a way that facilitates a strong analysis, if they are present at all. It is also common to focus on character or plot development for analysis. These elements are compatible with theme, symbolism, and allusion. Setting and imagery, figurative language, and any external contexts can also contribute to analysis or complement one of these other elements. The application of a critical, or literary, theory to a text can also provide a thorough and strong analysis.

SETTING AND TIME FRAME

A literary text has both a setting and time frame. A **setting** is the place in which the story as a whole is set. The **time frame** is the period in which the story is set. This may refer to the historical period the story takes place in or if the story takes place over a single day. Both setting and time frame are relevant to a text's meaning because they help the reader place the story in time and space. An author uses setting and time frame to anchor a text, create a mood, and enhance its meaning. This helps a reader understand why a character acts the way he does, or why certain events in the story are important. The setting impacts the **plot** and character **motivations**, while the time frame helps place the story in **chronological context**.

<u>EXAMPLE</u>

Read the following excerpt from The Adventures of Huckleberry Finn by Mark Twain and analyze the relevance of setting to the text's meaning:

> We said there warn't no home like a raft, after all. Other places do seem so cramped up and smothery, but a raft don't. You feel mighty free and easy and comfortable on a raft.

This excerpt from *The Adventures of Huckleberry Finn* by Mark Twain reveals information about the **setting** of the book. By understanding that the main character, Huckleberry Finn, lives on a raft, the reader can place the story on a river, in this case, the Mississippi River in the South before the Civil War. The information about the setting also gives the reader clues about the **character** of Huck Finn: he clearly values independence and freedom, and he likes the outdoors. The information about the setting in the quote helps the reader to better understand the rest of the text.

THEME

The **theme** of a passage is what the reader learns from the text or the passage. It is the lesson or **moral** contained in the passage. It also is a unifying idea that is used throughout the text; it can take the form of a common setting, idea, symbol, design, or recurring event. A passage can have two or more themes that convey its overall idea. The theme or themes of a passage are often based on **universal themes**. They can frequently be expressed using well-known sayings about life, society, or human nature, such as "Hard work pays off" or "Good triumphs over evil." Themes are not usually stated **explicitly**. The reader must figure them out by carefully reading the passage. Themes are often the reason why passages are written; they give a passage unity and meaning. Themes are created through **plot development**. The events of a story help shape the themes of a passage.

<u>EXAMPLE</u>

Explain why "Take care of what you care about" accurately describes the theme of the following excerpt.

> Luca collected baseball cards, but he wasn't very careful with them. He left them around the house. His dog liked to chew. One day, Luca and his friend Bart were looking at his collection. Then they went outside. When Luca got home, he saw his dog chewing on his cards. They were ruined.

This excerpt tells the story of a boy who is careless with his baseball cards and leaves them lying around. His dog ends up chewing them and ruining them. The lesson is that if you care about something, you need to take care of it. This is the theme, or point, of the story. Some stories have more than one theme, but this is not really true of this excerpt. The reader needs to figure out the theme based on what happens in the story. Sometimes, as in the case of fables, the theme is stated directly in the text. However, this is not usually the case.

> **Review Video: <u>Themes in Literature</u>**
> Visit mometrix.com/academy and enter code: 732074

PLOT AND STORY STRUCTURE

The **plot** includes the events that happen in a story and the order in which they are told to the reader. There are several types of plot structures, as stories can be told in many ways. The most common plot structure is the chronological plot, which presents the events to the reader in the same order they occur for the characters in the story. Chronological plots usually have five main parts, the **exposition**, **rising action**, the **climax**, **falling action**, and the **resolution**. This type of plot structure guides the reader through the story's events as the characters experience them and is the easiest structure to understand and identify. While this is the most common plot structure, many stories are nonlinear, which means the plot does not sequence events in the same order the characters experience them. Such stories might include elements like flashbacks that cause the story to be nonlinear.

> **Review Video: How to Make a Story Map**
> Visit mometrix.com/academy and enter code: 261719

EXPOSITION

The **exposition** is at the beginning of the story and generally takes place before the rising action begins. The purpose of the exposition is to give the reader context for the story, which the author may do by introducing one or more characters, describing the setting or world, or explaining the events leading up to the point where the story begins. The exposition may still include events that contribute to the plot, but the **rising action** and main conflict of the story are not part of the exposition. Some narratives skip the exposition and begin the story with the beginning of the rising action, which causes the reader to learn the context as the story intensifies.

CONFLICT

A **conflict** is a problem to be solved. Literary plots typically include one conflict or more. Characters' attempts to resolve conflicts drive the narrative's forward movement. **Conflict resolution** is often the protagonist's primary occupation. Physical conflicts like exploring, wars, and escapes tend to make plots most suspenseful and exciting. Emotional, mental, or moral conflicts tend to make stories more personally gratifying or rewarding for many audiences. Conflicts can be external or internal. A major type of internal conflict is some inner personal battle, or **man versus self**. Major types of external conflicts include **man versus nature**, **man versus man**, and **man versus society**. Readers can identify conflicts in literary plots by identifying the protagonist and antagonist and asking why they conflict, what events develop the conflict, where the climax occurs, and how they identify with the characters.

Read the following paragraph and discuss the type of conflict present:

> Timothy was shocked out of sleep by the appearance of a bear just outside his tent. After panicking for a moment, he remembered some advice he had read in preparation for this trip: he should make noise so the bear would not be startled. As Timothy started to hum and sing, the bear wandered away.

There are three main types of conflict in literature: **man versus man**, **man versus nature**, and **man versus self**. This paragraph is an example of man versus nature. Timothy is in conflict with the bear. Even though no physical conflict like an attack exists, Timothy is pitted against the bear. Timothy uses his knowledge to "defeat" the bear and keep himself safe. The solution to the conflict is that Timothy makes noise, the bear wanders away, and Timothy is safe.

> **Review Video: Conflict**
> Visit mometrix.com/academy and enter code: 559550
>
> **Review Video: Determining Relationships in a Story**
> Visit mometrix.com/academy and enter code: 929925

RISING ACTION

The **rising action** is the part of the story where conflict **intensifies**. The rising action begins with an event that prompts the main conflict of the story. This may also be called the **inciting incident**. The main conflict generally occurs between the protagonist and an antagonist, but this is not the only type of conflict that may occur in a narrative. After this event, the protagonist works to resolve the main conflict by preparing for an altercation, pursuing a goal, fleeing an antagonist, or doing some other action that will end the conflict. The rising action is composed of several additional events that increase the story's tension. Most often, other developments will occur alongside the growth of the main conflict, such as character development or the development of minor conflicts. The rising action ends with the **climax**, which is the point of highest tension in the story.

CLIMAX

The **climax** is the event in the narrative that marks the height of the story's conflict or tension. The event that takes place at the story's climax will end the rising action and bring about the results of the main conflict. If the conflict was between a good protagonist and an evil antagonist, the climax may be a final battle between the two characters. If the conflict is an adventurer looking for heavily guarded treasure, the climax may be the adventurer's encounter with the final obstacle that protects the treasure. The climax may be made of multiple scenes, but can usually be summarized as one event. Once the conflict and climax are complete, the **falling action** begins.

FALLING ACTION

The **falling action** shows what happens in the story between the climax and the resolution. The falling action often composes a much smaller portion of the story than the rising action does. While the climax includes the end of the main conflict, the falling action may show the results of any minor conflicts in the story. For example, if the protagonist encountered a troll on the way to find some treasure, and the troll demanded the protagonist share the treasure after retrieving it, the falling action would include the protagonist returning to share the treasure with the troll. Similarly, any unexplained major events are usually made clear during the falling action. Once all significant elements of the story are resolved or addressed, the story's resolution will occur. The **resolution** is the end of the story, which shows the final result of the plot's events and shows what life is like for the main characters once they are no longer experiencing the story's conflicts.

RESOLUTION

The way the conflict is **resolved** depends on the type of conflict. The plot of any book starts with the lead up to the conflict, then the conflict itself, and finally the solution, or **resolution**, to the conflict. In **man versus man** conflicts, the conflict is often resolved by two parties coming to some sort of agreement or by one party triumphing over the other party. In **man versus nature** conflicts, the conflict is often resolved by man coming to some realization about some aspect of nature. In **man versus self** conflicts, the conflict is often resolved by the character growing or coming to an understanding about part of himself.

SYNTAX AND WORD CHOICE

Authors use words and **syntax**, or sentence structure, to make their texts unique, convey their own writing style, and sometimes to make a point or emphasis. They know that word choice and syntax contribute to the reader's understanding of the text as well as to the tone and mood of a text.

> **Review Video: What is Syntax?**
> Visit mometrix.com/academy and enter code: 242280

109

ALLUSION

An allusion is an uncited but recognizable reference to something else. Authors use language to make allusions to places, events, artwork, and other books in order to make their own text richer. For example, an author may allude to a very important text in order to make his own text seem more important. Martin Luther King, Jr. started his "I Have a Dream" speech by saying "Five score years ago…" This is a clear allusion to President Abraham Lincoln's "Gettysburg Address" and served to remind people of the significance of the event. An author may allude to a place to ground his text or make a cultural reference to make readers feel included. There are many reasons that authors make allusions.

> **Review Video: Allusions**
> Visit mometrix.com/academy and enter code: 294065

COMIC RELIEF

Comic relief is the use of comedy by an author to break up a dramatic or tragic scene and infuse it with a bit of **lightheartedness**. In William Shakespeare's *Hamlet*, two gravediggers digging the grave for Ophelia share a joke while they work. The death and burial of Ophelia are tragic moments that directly follow each other. Shakespeare uses an instance of comedy to break up the tragedy and give his audience a bit of a break from the tragic drama. Authors sometimes use comic relief so that their work will be less depressing; other times they use it to create irony or contrast between the darkness of the situation and the lightness of the joke. Often, authors will use comedy to parallel what is happening in the tragic scenes.

> **Review Video: What is Comic Relief?**
> Visit mometrix.com/academy and enter code: 779604

MOOD AND TONE

Mood is a story's atmosphere, or the feelings the reader gets from reading it. The way authors set the mood in writing is comparable to the way filmmakers use music to set the mood in movies. Instead of music, though, writers judiciously select descriptive words to evoke certain **moods**. The mood of a work may convey joy, anger, bitterness, hope, gloom, fear, apprehension, or any other emotion the author wants the reader to feel. In addition to vocabulary choices, authors also use figurative expressions, particular sentence structures, and choices of diction that project and reinforce the moods they want to create. Whereas mood is the reader's emotions evoked by reading what is written, **tone** is the emotions and attitudes of the writer that she or he expresses in the writing. Authors use the same literary techniques to establish tone as they do to establish mood. An author may use a humorous tone, an angry or sad tone, a sentimental or unsentimental tone, or something else entirely.

MOOD AND TONE IN THE GREAT GATSBY

To understand the difference between mood and tone, look at this excerpt from F. Scott Fitzgerald's *The Great Gatsby*. In this passage, Nick Caraway, the novel's narrator, is describing his affordable house, which sits in a neighborhood full of expensive mansions.

> "I lived at West Egg, the—well the less fashionable of the two, though this is a most superficial tag to express the bizarre and not a little sinister contrast between them. My house was at the very tip of the egg, only fifty yard from the Sound, and squeezed between two huge places that rented for twelve or fifteen thousand a season … My own house was an eyesore, but it was a small eyesore, and it had been overlooked, so I had a view of the water,

a partial view of my neighbor's lawn, and the consoling proximity of millionaires—all for eighty dollars a month."

In this description, the mood created for the reader does not match the tone created through the narrator. The mood in this passage is one of dissatisfaction and inferiority. Nick compares his home to his neighbors', saying he lives in the "less fashionable" neighborhood and that his house is "overlooked," an "eyesore," and "squeezed between two huge" mansions. He also adds that his placement allows him the "consoling proximity of millionaires." A literal reading of these details leads the reader to have negative feelings toward Nick's house and his economic inferiority to his neighbors, creating the mood.

However, Fitzgerald also conveys an opposing attitude, or tone, through Nick's description. Nick calls the distinction between the neighborhoods "superficial," showing a suspicion of the value suggested by the neighborhoods' titles, properties, and residents. Nick also undermines his critique of his own home by calling it "a small eyesore" and claiming it has "been overlooked." However, he follows these statements with a description of his surroundings, claiming that he has "a view of the water" and can see some of his wealthy neighbor's property from his home, and a comparison between the properties' rent. While the mental image created for the reader depicts a small house shoved between looming mansions, the tone suggests that Nick enjoys these qualities about his home, or at least finds it charming. He acknowledges its shortcomings, but includes the benefits of his home's unassuming appearance.

> **Review Video: Style, Tone, and Mood**
> Visit mometrix.com/academy and enter code: 416961

CHARACTER DEVELOPMENT

When depicting characters or figures in a written text, authors generally use actions, dialogue, and descriptions as characterization techniques. Characterization can occur in both fiction and nonfiction and is used to show a character or figure's personality, demeanor, and thoughts. This helps create a more engaging experience for the reader by providing a more concrete picture of a character or figure's tendencies and features. Characterizations also gives authors the opportunity to integrate elements such as dialects, activities, attire, and attitudes into their writing.

To understand the meaning of a story, it is vital to understand the characters as the author describes them. We can look for contradictions in what a character thinks, says, and does. We can notice whether the author's observations about a character differ from what other characters in the story say about that character. A character may be dynamic, meaning they change significantly during the story, or static, meaning they remain the same from beginning to end. Characters may be two-dimensional, not fully developed, or may be well developed with characteristics that stand out vividly. Characters may also symbolize universal properties. Additionally, readers can compare and contrast characters to analyze how each one developed.

A well-known example of character development can be found in Charles Dickens's *Great Expectations*. The novel's main character, Pip, is introduced as a young boy, and he is depicted as innocent, kind, and humble. However, as Pip grows up and is confronted with the social hierarchy of Victorian England, he becomes arrogant and rejects his loved ones in pursuit of his own social advancement. Once he achieves his social goals, he realizes the merits of his former lifestyle, and lives with the wisdom he gained in both environments and life stages. Dickens shows Pip's ever-changing character through his interactions with others and his inner thoughts, which evolve as his personal values and personality shift.

DIALOGUE

Effectively written dialogue serves at least one, but usually several, purposes. It advances the story and moves the plot, develops the characters, sheds light on the work's theme or meaning, and can, often subtly, account for the passage of time not otherwise indicated. It can alter the direction that the plot is taking, typically by introducing some new conflict or changing existing ones. **Dialogue** can establish a work's narrative voice and the characters' voices and set the tone of the story or of particular characters. When fictional characters display enlightenment or realization, dialogue can give readers an understanding of what those characters have discovered and how. Dialogue can illuminate the motivations and wishes of the story's characters. By using consistent thoughts and syntax, dialogue can support character development. Skillfully created, it can also represent real-life speech rhythms in written form. Via conflicts and ensuing action, dialogue also provides drama.

DIALOGUE IN FICTION

In fictional works, effectively written dialogue does more than just break up or interrupt sections of narrative. While **dialogue** may supply exposition for readers, it must nonetheless be believable. Dialogue should be dynamic, not static, and it should not resemble regular prose. Authors should not use dialogue to write clever similes or metaphors, or to inject their own opinions. Nor should they use dialogue at all when narrative would be better. Most importantly, dialogue should not slow the plot movement. Dialogue must seem natural, which means careful construction of phrases rather than actually duplicating natural speech, which does not necessarily translate well to the written word. Finally, all dialogue must be pertinent to the story, rather than just added conversation.

FORESHADOWING

Foreshadowing is a device authors use to give readers **hints** about events that will take place later in a story. Foreshadowing most often takes place through a character's dialogue or actions. Sometimes the character will know what is going to happen and will purposefully allude to future events. For example, consider a protagonist who is about to embark on a journey through the woods. Just before the protagonist begins the trip, another character says, "Be careful, you never know what could be out in those woods!" This alerts the reader that the woods may be dangerous and prompts the reader to expect something to attack the protagonist in the woods. This is an example of foreshadowing through warning. Alternatively, a character may unknowingly foreshadow later events. For example, consider a story where a brother and sister run through their house and knock over a vase and break it. The brother says, "Don't worry, we'll clean it up! Mom will never know!" However, the reader knows that their mother will most likely find out what they have done, so the reader expects the siblings to later get in trouble for running, breaking the vase, and hiding it from their mother.

SYMBOLISM

Symbolism describes an author's use of a **symbol**, an element of the story that **represents** something else. Symbols can impact stories in many ways, including deepening the meaning of a story or its elements, comparing a story to another work, or foreshadowing later events in a story. Symbols can be objects, characters, colors, numbers, or anything else the author establishes as a symbol. Symbols can be clearly established through direct comparison or repetition, but they can also be established subtly or gradually over a large portion of the story. Another form of symbolism is **allusion**, which is when something in a story is used to prompt the reader to think about another work. Many well-known works use **Biblical allusions**, which are allusions to events or details in the Bible that inform a work or an element within it.

POINT OF VIEW

Another element that impacts a text is the author's point of view. The **point of view** of a text is the perspective from which a passage is told. An author will always have a point of view about a story before he or she draws up a plot line. The author will know what events they want to take place, how they want the characters to interact, and how they want the story to resolve. An author will also have an opinion on the topic or series of events which is presented in the story that is based on their prior experience and beliefs.

The two main points of view that authors use, especially in a work of fiction, are first person and third person. If the narrator of the story is also the main character, or *protagonist*, the text is written in first-person point of view. In first person, the author writes from the perspective of *I*. Third-person point of view is probably the most common that authors use in their passages. Using third person, authors refer to each character by using *he* or *she.* In third-person omniscient, the narrator is not a character in the story and tells the story of all of the characters at the same time.

> **Review Video: Point of View**
> Visit mometrix.com/academy and enter code: 383336

FIRST-PERSON NARRATION

First-person narratives let narrators express inner feelings and thoughts, especially when the narrator is the protagonist as Lemuel Gulliver is in Jonathan Swift's *Gulliver's Travels.* The narrator may be a close friend of the protagonist, like Dr. Watson in Sir Arthur Conan Doyle's *Sherlock Holmes.* Or, the narrator can be less involved with the main characters and plot, like Nick Carraway in F. Scott Fitzgerald's *The Great Gatsby.* When a narrator reports others' narratives, she or he is a "**frame narrator**," like the nameless narrator of Joseph Conrad's *Heart of Darkness* or Mr. Lockwood in Emily Brontë's *Wuthering Heights.* **First-person plural** is unusual but can be effective. Isaac Asimov's *I, Robot*, William Faulkner's *A Rose for Emily*, Maxim Gorky's *Twenty-Six Men and a Girl*, and Jeffrey Eugenides' *The Virgin Suicides* all use first-person plural narration. Author Kurt Vonnegut is the first-person narrator in his semi-autobiographical novel *Timequake.* Also unusual, but effective, is a **first-person omniscient** (rather than the more common third-person omniscient) narrator, like Death in Markus Zusak's *The Book Thief* and the ghost in Alice Sebold's *The Lovely Bones.*

SECOND-PERSON NARRATION

While **second-person** address is very commonplace in popular song lyrics, it is the least used form of narrative voice in literary works. Popular serial books of the 1980s like *Fighting Fantasy* or *Choose Your Own Adventure* employed second-person narratives. In some cases, a narrative combines both second-person and first-person voices, using the pronouns *you* and *I*. This can draw readers into the story, and it can also enable the authors to compare directly "your" and "my" feelings, thoughts, and actions. When the narrator is also a character in the story, as in Edgar Allan Poe's short story "The Tell-Tale Heart" or Jay McInerney's novel *Bright Lights, Big City,* the narrative is better defined as first-person despite it also addressing "you."

THIRD-PERSON NARRATION

Narration in the third person is the most prevalent type, as it allows authors the most flexibility. It is so common that readers simply assume without needing to be informed that the narrator is not a character in the story, or involved in its events. **Third-person singular** is used more frequently than **third-person plural**, though some authors have also effectively used plural. However, both singular and plural are most often included in stories according to which characters are being described. The third-person narrator may be either objective or subjective, and either omniscient or limited. **Objective third-person** narration does not include what the characters described are thinking or feeling, while **subjective third-person** narration does. The **third-person omniscient** narrator knows everything about all characters, including their thoughts and emotions, and all related places, times, and events. However, the **third-person limited** narrator may know everything about a particular character, but is limited to that character. In other words, the narrator cannot speak about anything that character does not know.

ALTERNATING-PERSON NARRATION

Although authors more commonly write stories from one point of view, there are also instances wherein they alternate the narrative voice within the same book. For example, they may sometimes use an omniscient third-person narrator and a more intimate first-person narrator at other times. In J. K. Rowling's series of *Harry Potter* novels, she often writes in a third-person limited narrative, but sometimes changes to narration by characters other than the protagonist. George R. R. Martin's series *A Song of Ice and Fire* changes the point of view to coincide with divisions between chapters. The same technique is used by Erin Hunter (a pseudonym for several authors of the *Warriors, Seekers,* and *Survivors* book series). Authors using first-person narrative sometimes switch to third-person to describe significant action scenes, especially those where the narrator was absent or uninvolved, as Barbara Kingsolver does in her novel *The Poisonwood Bible.*

HISTORICAL AND SOCIAL CONTEXT

Fiction that is heavily influenced by a historical or social context cannot be comprehended as the author intended if the reader does not keep this context in mind. Many important elements of the text will be influenced by any context, including symbols, allusions, settings, and plot events. These contexts, as well as the identity of the work's author, can help to inform the reader about the author's concerns and intended meanings. For example, George Orwell published his novel *1984* in the year 1949, soon after the end of World War II. At that time, following the defeat of the Nazis, the Cold War began between the Western Allied nations and the Eastern Soviet Communists. People were therefore concerned about the conflict between the freedoms afforded by Western democracies versus the oppression represented by Communism. Orwell had also previously fought in the Spanish Civil War against a Spanish regime that he and his fellows viewed as oppressive. From this information, readers can infer that Orwell was concerned about oppression by totalitarian governments. This informs *1984*'s story of Winston Smith's rebellion against the oppressive "Big Brother" government, of the fictional dictatorial state of Oceania, and his capture, torture, and ultimate conversion by that government. Some literary theories also seek to use historical and social contexts to reveal deeper meanings and implications in a text.

TEXTUAL EVIDENCE

No literary analysis is complete without textual evidence. Summaries, paraphrases, and quotes are all forms of textual evidence, but direct quotes from the text are the most effective form of evidence. The best textual evidence is relevant, accurate, and clearly supports the writer's claim. This can include pieces of descriptions, dialogue, or exposition that shows the applicability of the analysis to the text. Analysis that is average, or sufficient, shows an understanding of the text; contains supporting textual evidence that is relevant and accurate, if not strong; and shows a specific and clear response. Analysis that partially meets criteria also shows understanding, but the textual evidence is generalized, incomplete, only partly relevant or accurate, or connected only weakly. Inadequate analysis is vague, too general, or incorrect. It may give irrelevant or incomplete textual evidence, or may simply summarize the plot rather than analyzing the work. It is important to incorporate textual evidence from the work being analyzed and any supplemental materials and to provide appropriate attribution for these sources.

Themes and Plots in Literature

THEMES IN LITERATURE

When we read parables, their themes are the lessons they aim to teach. When we read fables, the moral of each story is its theme. When we read fictional works, the authors' perspectives regarding life and human behavior are their themes. Unlike in parables and fables, themes in literary fiction are usually not meant to preach or teach the readers a lesson. Hence, themes in fiction are not as explicit as they are in parables or fables. Instead, they are implicit, and the reader only infers them. By analyzing the fictional characters through thinking about their actions and behavior, understanding the setting of the story, and reflecting on how its plot develops, the reader comes to infer the main theme of the work. When writers succeed, they communicate with their readers such that common ground is established between author and audience. While a reader's individual experience may differ in its details from the author's written story, both may share universal underlying truths which allow author and audience to connect.

DETERMINING THEME

In well-crafted literature, theme, structure, and plot are interdependent and inextricable: each element informs and reflects the others. The structure of a work is how it is organized. The theme is the central idea or meaning found in it. The plot is what happens in the story. Titles can also inform us of a work's theme. For instance, the title of Edgar Allan Poe's "The Tell-Tale Heart" informs readers of the story's theme of guilt before they even read about the repeated heartbeat the protagonist hears immediately before and constantly after committing and hiding a murder. Repetitive patterns of events or behaviors also give clues to themes. The same is true of symbols. For example, in F. Scott Fitzgerald's *The Great Gatsby,* for Jay Gatsby the green light at the end of the dock symbolizes Daisy Buchanan and his own dreams for the future. More generally, it is also understood as a symbol of the American Dream, and narrator Nick Carraway explicitly compares it to early settlers' sight of America rising from the ocean.

THEMATIC DEVELOPMENT
THEME IN THE GREAT GATSBY

In *The Great Gatsby*, F. Scott Fitzgerald portrayed 1920s America as greedy, cynical, and rife with moral decay. Jay Gatsby's lavish weekly parties symbolize the reckless excesses of the Jazz Age. The growth of bootlegging and organized crime in reaction to Prohibition is symbolized by the character of Meyer Wolfsheim and by Gatsby's own ill-gotten wealth. Fitzgerald symbolized social divisions using geography. The "old money" aristocrats like the Buchanans lived on East Egg, while the "new money" bourgeois like Gatsby lived on West Egg. Fitzgerald also used weather, as many authors have, to reinforce narrative and emotional tones in the novel. Just as in *Romeo and Juliet*, where William Shakespeare set the confrontation of Tybalt and Mercutio and its deadly consequences on the hottest summer day under a burning sun, in *The Great Gatsby*, Fitzgerald did the same with Tom Wilson's deadly confrontation with Gatsby. Both works are ostensible love stories carrying socially critical themes about the destructiveness of pointless and misguided behaviors—family feuds in the former, pursuit of money in the latter.

> **Review Video: Thematic Development**
> Visit mometrix.com/academy and enter code: 576507

THEME IN LES MISÉRABLES

In Victor Hugo's novel *Les Misérables*, the overall metamorphosis of protagonist Jean Valjean from a cynical ex-convict into a noble benefactor demonstrates Hugo's theme of the importance of love and compassion for others. Hugo also reflects this in more specific plot events. For example, Valjean's love for Cosette sustains him through many difficult periods and trying events. Hugo illustrates how love and compassion for others beget the same in them: Bishop Myriel's kindness to Valjean eventually inspires him to become honest. Years later, Valjean, as M. Madeleine, has rescued Fauchelevent from under a fallen carriage, Fauchelevent returns the compassionate act by giving Valjean sanctuary in the convent. M. Myriel's kindness also ultimately enables Valjean to rescue Cosette from the Thénardiers. Receiving Valjean's father-like love enables Cosette to fall in love with and marry Marius, and the love between Cosette and Marius enables the couple to forgive Valjean for his past crimes when they are revealed.

THEME IN "THE TELL-TALE HEART"

In one of his shortest stories, "The Tell-Tale Heart," Poe used economy of language to emphasize the murderer-narrator's obsessive focus on bare details like the victim's cataract-milky eye, the sound of a heartbeat, and insistence he is sane. The narrator begins by denying he is crazy, even citing his extreme agitation as proof of sanity. Contradiction is then extended: the narrator loves the old man, yet kills him. His motives are irrational—not greed or revenge, but to relieve the victim of his "evil eye." Because "eye" and "I" are homonyms, readers may infer that eye/I symbolizes the old man's identity, contradicting the killer's delusion that he can separate them. The narrator distances himself from the old man by perceiving his eye as separate, and dismembering his dead body. This backfires when he imagines the victim's heartbeat, which is really his own, just before he kills him and frequently afterward. Guilty and paranoid, he gives himself away. Poe predated Freud in exploring the paradox of killing those we love and the concept of projecting our own processes onto others.

THEME IN THE WORKS OF WILLIAM FAULKNER AND CHARLES DICKENS

William Faulkner contrasts the traditions of the antebellum South with the rapid changes of post-Civil War industrialization in his short story "A Rose for Emily." Living inside the isolated world of her house, Emily Grierson denies the reality of modern progress. Contradictorily, she is both a testament to time-honored history and a mysterious, eccentric, unfathomable burden. Faulkner portrays her with deathlike imagery even in life, comparing her to a drowned woman and referring to her skeleton. Emily symbolizes the Old South; as her social status is degraded, so is the antebellum social order. Like Miss Havisham in Charles Dickens' *Great Expectations*, Emily preserves her bridal bedroom, denying change and time's passage. Emily tries to control death through denial, shown in her necrophilia with her father's corpse and her killing of Homer Barron to stop him from leaving her, then also denying his death. Faulkner uses the motif of dust throughout to represent not only the decay of Emily, her house, and Old Southern traditions, but also how her secrets are obscured from others.

THEME IN MOBY-DICK

The great White Whale in *Moby-Dick* plays various roles to different characters. In Captain Ahab's obsessive, monomaniacal quest to kill it, the whale represents all evil, and Ahab believes it his duty and destiny to rid the world of it. Ishmael attempts through multiple scientific disciplines to understand the whale objectively, but fails—it is hidden underwater and mysterious to humans— reinforcing Melville's theme that humans can never know everything; here the whale represents the unknowable. Melville reverses white's usual connotation of purity in Ishmael's dread of white, associated with crashing waves, polar animals, albinos—all frightening and unnatural. White is often viewed as an absence of color, yet white light is the sum total of all colors in the spectrum. In the same way, white can signify both absence of meaning, and totality of meaning incomprehensible to humans. As a creature of nature, the whale also symbolizes how 19th-century white men's exploitative expansionistic actions were destroying the natural environment.

THEME IN *THE OLD MAN AND THE SEA*

Because of the old fisherman Santiago's struggle to capture a giant marlin, some people characterize Ernest Hemingway's *The Old Man and the Sea* as telling of man against nature. However, it can more properly be interpreted as telling of man's role as part of nature. Both man and fish are portrayed as brave, proud, and honorable. In Hemingway's world, all creatures, including humans, must either kill or be killed. Santiago reflects, "man can be destroyed but not defeated," following this principle in his life. As heroes are often created through their own deaths, Hemingway seems to believe that while being destroyed is inevitable, destruction enables living beings to transcend it by fighting bravely with honor and dignity. Hemingway echoes Romantic poet John Keats' contention that only immediately before death can we understand beauty as it is about to be destroyed. He also echoes ancient Greek and Roman myths and the Old Testament with the tragic flaw of overweening pride or overreaching. Like Icarus, Prometheus, and Adam and Eve, the old man "went out too far."

UNIVERSAL THEMES

The Old Testament book of Genesis, the Quran, and the Epic of Gilgamesh all contain flood stories. Versions differ somewhat, yet marketed similarities also exist. Genesis describes a worldwide flood, attributing it to God's decision that mankind, his creation, had become incontrovertibly wicked in spirit and must be destroyed for the world to start anew. The Quran describes the flood as regional, caused by Allah after sending Nuh (notice the similarity in name to Noah) as a messenger to his people to cease their evil. The Quran stipulates that Allah only destroys those who deny or ignore messages from his messengers. In the Gilgamesh poems Utnapishtim, like Noah, is instructed to build a ship to survive the flood. Both men also send out birds afterward as tests, using doves and a raven, though with different outcomes. Many historians and archeologists believe a Middle Eastern tidal wave was a real basis for these stories. However, their universal themes remain the same: the flood was seen as God's way of wiping out humans whose behavior had become ungodly.

THEME OF OVERREACHING

A popular theme throughout literature is the human trait of **reaching too far** or **presuming too much**. In Greek mythology, Daedalus constructed wings of feathers and wax that men might fly like birds. He permitted his son Icarus to try them, but cautioned the boy not to fly too close to the sun. The impetuous youth (in what psychologist David Elkind later named adolescence's myth of invincibility) ignored this, flying too close to the sun. The wax melted, the wings disintegrated, and Icarus fell into the sea and perished. In the Old Testament, God warned Adam and Eve not to eat fruit from the tree of knowledge of good and evil. Because they ignored this command, they were banished from Eden's eternal perfection, condemning them to mortality and suffering. The Romans were themselves examples of overreaching in their conquest and assimilation of most of the then-known world and their ultimate demise. In Christopher Marlowe's *Dr. Faustus* and Johann Wolfgang von Goethe's *Faust,* the protagonist sells his soul to the Devil for unlimited knowledge and success, ultimately leading to his own tragic end.

STORY VS. DISCOURSE

In terms of plot, "story" is the characters, places, and events originating in the author's mind, while "discourse" is how the author arranges and sequences events—which may be chronological or not. Story is imaginary; discourse is words on the page. Discourse allows a story to be told in different ways. One element of plot structure is relating events differently from the order in which they occurred. This is easily done with cause-and-effect; for example, in the sentence, "He died following a long illness," we know the illness preceded the death, but the death precedes the illness in words. In Kate Chopin's short story "The Story of an Hour" (1894), she tells some of the events out of chronological order, which has the effect of amplifying the surprise of the ending for the reader. Another element of plot structure is selection. Chopin omits some details, such as Mr. Mallard's trip home; this allows readers to be as surprised at his arrival as Mrs. Mallard is.

PLOT AND MEANING

Novelist E. M. Forster has made the distinction between story as relating a series of events, such as a king dying and then his queen dying, versus plot as establishing motivations for actions and causes for events, such as a king dying and then his queen dying from grief over his death. Thus, plot fulfills the function of helping readers understand cause-and-effect in events and underlying motivations in characters' actions, which in turn helps them understand life. This affects a work's meaning by supporting its ability to explain why things happen, why people do things, and ultimately the meaning of life. Some authors find that while story events convey meaning, they do not tell readers there is any one meaning in life or way of living, but rather are mental experiments with various meanings, enabling readers to explore. Hence stories may not necessarily be constructed to impose one definitive meaning, but rather to find some shape, direction, and meaning within otherwise random events.

CLASSIC ANALYSIS OF PLOT STRUCTURE

In *Poetics,* Aristotle defined plot as "the arrangement of the incidents." He meant not the story, but how it is structured for presentation. In tragedies, Aristotle found results driven by chains of cause and effect preferable to those driven by the protagonist's personality or character. He identified "unity of action" as necessary for a plot's wholeness, meaning its events must be internally connected, not episodic or relying on *deus ex machina* or other external intervention. A plot must have a beginning, middle, and end. Gustav Freytag adapted Aristotle's ideas into his Pyramid (1863). The beginning, today called the exposition, incentive, or inciting moment, emphasizes causes and de-emphasizes effects. Aristotle called the ensuing cause and effect *desis*, or tying up, today called complications which occur during the rising action. These culminate in a crisis or climax, Aristotle's *peripateia.* This occurs at the plot's middle, where cause and effect are both emphasized. The falling action, which Aristotle called the *lusis* or unraveling, is today called the dénouement. The resolution comes at the catastrophe, outcome, or end, when causes are emphasized and effects de-emphasized.

> **Review Video: Plot line Definition**
> Visit mometrix.com/academy and enter code: 944011

ANALYSIS OF PLOT STRUCTURES THROUGH RECURRING PATTERNS

Authors of fiction select characters, places, and events from their imaginations and arrange them to create a story that will affect their readers. One way to analyze plot structure is to compare and contrast different events in a story. For example, in Kate Chopin's "The Story of an Hour," a very simple but key pattern of repetition is the husband's leaving and then returning. Such patterns fulfill the symmetrical aspect that Aristotle said was required of sound plot structure. In James Baldwin's short story, "Sonny's Blues," the narrator is Sonny's brother. In an encounter with one of Sonny's old friends early in the story, the brother initially disregards his communication. In a subsequent flashback, Baldwin informs us that this was the same way he had treated Sonny. In Nathaniel Hawthorne's "Young Goodman Brown," a pattern is created by the protagonist's recurrent efforts not to go farther into the wood. In Herman Melville's "Bartleby the Scrivener" and in William Faulkner's "Barn Burning," patterns are also created by repetition such as Bartleby's repeated refusals and the history of barn-burning episodes, respectively.

119

LITERARY THEORIES AND CRITICISM AND INTERPRETATION

Literary theory includes ideas that guide readers through the process of interpreting literature. Literary theory, as a subject, encompasses several specific, focused theories that lead readers to interpret or analyze literature through the context of the theory using the subjects and elements it involves. Some commonly used and discussed literary theories include **postcolonial theory**, **gender and feminist theory**, **structuralism**, **new historicism**, **reader-response theory**, and **sociological criticism**.

- **Postcolonial theory** involves the historical and geographical context of a work and leads readers to consider how colonization informs the plot, characters, setting, and other elements in the work.
- **Gender and feminist theory** invites readers to interpret a text by looking at its treatment of and suggestions about women and a culture's treatment of women. As with most literary theories, this information can be clearly stated or strongly implied in a work, but it may also be gleaned through looking closely at symbols, characters, and plot elements in a work.
- **Structuralism** uses the structure and organization of a work and the foundations of language to examine how and what a text conveys about the human experience and how those findings connect to common human experiences.
- **New historicism** heavily relies on the cultural and historical context of a work, including when it was written, where the author lives or lived, the culture and history of that location, and other works from the same culture. New historical readings seek to examine these details to expose the ideologies of the location and culture that influenced the work.
- **Reader-response theory** uses the individual reader's response to the text and experience while reading the text to examine the meaning of the reader's relationship with the text and what that relationship suggests about the reader or the factors impacting their experience.
- **Sociological criticism** considers the societies that are relevant to a text. The author's society and any reader's society are important to the text, as sociological criticism seeks to uncover what the text implies or reveals about those societies. This method of criticism can also involve studying the presentation of a society within the text and applying it to the author's society or their other writings.

Language and Dialect

DIVERSITY AND SITUATIONAL NATURE OF LANGUAGE

Language is a diverse tool that allows people to communicate. However, language is often impacted and molded by the culture that uses it. This can make it difficult to learn and use a new language, since not all native speakers of the language will use it or interpret it the same way. For example, English is spoken all over America, but Americans in various regions of the country speak using different **dialects**. Other differences in speech include **accents** and **rhythm of speech**. Language is also manipulated by situations. Some terms and phrases have multiple meanings. A word's meaning often depends on the **context** in which the word or phrase is used, meaning that non-native speakers must learn to interpret situations to understand messages.

FACTORS OF LANGUAGE AND COMMUNICATION

INFLUENCES ON LANGUAGE

While dialect and diction are heavily influenced by an individual's culture and the location and history of the place they live, other personal factors can also impact language. A person's ethnicity, religious beliefs or background, and gender can influence the way they use and understand language. **Ethnicity** impacts language by incorporating a group's communication norms into an individual's speech and behavior. These norms may affect a speaker's tone, volume, or pace. These factors may lead others outside of that group to misinterpret the speaker's message, depending on their understanding of how those factors are used in speech. A person's **religious beliefs** can also affect their use of language. Religious beliefs and practices may lead an individual to abstain from using certain terms and may change the context in which a speaker uses specific words, or change their understanding of the word's usage. Additionally, a person may use language differently depending on their gender. **Gender's** influence on communication varies by region and industry. A region or industry's treatment of gender roles often impacts language use among its members. This can lead members of one gender group to be more assertive or submissive or to use different terms and phrases.

CULTURE AND COMMUNICATION

Individuals from different countries and cultures communicate differently. Not only do many people speak different languages, but they also speak using different inflections, volumes, tones, and dialects. These factors can have a significant impact on communication, even if the communicators speak the same language. In different cultures, certain behaviors are associated with different meanings and implications. When communicators from different cultures have a conversation, these expectations and associations may lead to misunderstanding. For example, Americans are considered to be louder and more demonstrative than people from other countries. Someone from a country where people speak more quietly who is not aware of this characterization may perceive an American's volume or large gestures as an indication of anger, when in reality, the American speaker is calm. The American may similarly perceive the other person as sad or shy due to their quiet voice, when the speaker is actually happy and comfortable in the conversation. Awareness of these factors and effects promotes respect for others and helps speakers understand the reasons for differences in communication, rather than allowing these differences to create division or conflict.

LANGUAGE VS. DIALECT

Languages are distinct and structured forms of verbal communication. Languages have cohesive sets of rules and words that are shared between the majority of that language's users. The main identifier of a language is that members of one language group are incapable of communicating fluently with members of another language group. New languages are formed as different dialects grow further apart until the members of each dialect can no longer innately communicate with each other.

Dialects are subsets of languages that do not violate the rules of the language as a whole, but which vary from other dialects in vocabulary usage, grammar forms, pronunciation, and spelling. Two major groupings of dialects are American and British English. Most American English and British English speakers can communicate with relative ease with one another, though the pronunciation, vocabulary (torch vs. flashlight; trunk vs. boot), spelling (meter vs. metre; color vs. colour), and grammar (in American English, collective nouns are always considered singular, but can be singular or plural in British English).

DEVELOPMENT OF DIALECTS OVER TIME

Dialects are formed primarily through the influences of location and time, but can be the result of other elements of **social stratification** as well (economic, ethnic, religious, etc.). As one group of a language's speakers is separated from another, in British and American English speakers for example, the language develops in isolated locations at the same time, resulting in distinct dialects. Language changes continuously over time as new words and phrases are adopted and others are phased out. Eventually, these small changes result culminate into enough grammar and vocabulary changes that the speakers of the distinct dialects cannot easily communicate with one another. The dialects can then be recognized as distinct languages.

USE OF DIALECT IN MEDIA

Literary authors often use dialect when writing dialogue to illustrate the social and geographical backgrounds of specific characters, which supports character development. For example, in *The Adventures of Huckleberry Finn* (1885), Mark Twain's novel is written in the dialect of a young, uneducated, white, Southern character, opening with this sentence: "You don't know about me without you have read a book by the name of The Adventures of Tom Sawyer, but that ain't no matter." Twain uses a different and exaggerated dialect to represent the speech of the African-American slave Jim: "We's safe, Huck, we's safe! Jump up and crack yo' heels. Dat's de good ole Cairo at las', I jis knows it."

In *To Kill a Mockingbird,* author Harper Lee used dialect in the characters' dialogue to portray an uneducated boy in the American South: "Reckon I have. Almost died the first year I come to school and et them pecans—folks say he pizened 'em." Lee also uses many Southern regional expressions, such as "right stove up," "What in the sam holy hill?", "sit a spell," "fess" (meaning "confess"), "jim-dandy," and "hush your fussing." These contribute to Lee's characterization of the people she describes, who live in a small town in Alabama circa the 1930s. In *Wuthering Heights* (1847), Emily Bronte reproduces Britain's 18th–19th-century Yorkshire dialect in the speech of servant Joseph: "Running after t'lads, as usuald!... If I war yah, maister, I'd just slam t'boards i' their faces all on 'em, gentle and simple! Never a day ut yah're off, but yon cat o' Linton comes sneaking hither; and Miss Nelly, shoo's a fine lass!"

DIALECT VS. DICTION

When written as characters' dialogue in literary works, dialect represents the particular pronunciation, grammar, and figurative expressions used by certain groups of people based on their geographic region, social class, and cultural background. For example, when a character says, "There's gold up in them thar hills," the author is using dialect to add to the characterization of that individual. Diction is more related to individual characters than to groups of people. The way in which a specific character speaks, including his or her choice of words, manner of expressing

122

himself or herself, and use of grammar all represent individual types of diction. For example, two characters in the same novel might describe the same action or event using different diction: One says "I'm heading uptown for the evening," and the other says "I'm going out for a night on the town." These convey the same literal meaning, but due to their variations in diction, the speakers are expressing themselves in slightly different ways.

> **Review Video: <u>Dialogue, Paradox, and Dialect</u>**
> Visit mometrix.com/academy and enter code: 684341

INFLUENCES ON REGIONAL DIALECT

Linguistic researchers have identified regional variations in vocabulary choices, which have evolved because of differences in local climates and how they influence human behaviors. For example, in the Southern United States, the Linguistic Atlas of the Gulf States (LAGS) Project by Dr. Lee Pederson of Emory University discovered and documented that people living in the northern or Upland section of the Piedmont plateau region call the fungal infection commonly known as athlete's foot "toe itch," but people living in the southern or Lowland section call it "ground itch." The explanation for this difference is that in the north, temperatures are cooler and people wear shoes accordingly, so they associate the itching with the feet in their description, but in the south, temperatures are hotter and people often went barefoot, so they associated the itching with the ground that presumably transmitted the infection.

USING DIALECT IN WRITING

Dialect is most appropriate for informal or creative writing. Using dialectal writing when communicating casually or informally, such as in a text message or a quick email to a peer, is acceptable. However, in academic and professional contexts, writing using indications of dialect is inappropriate and often unacceptable. If the audience includes individuals who have a higher rank than the author, or authority over the author, it is best not to write in a way that suggests a dialect.

Media Types

MEDIA AND FORMAT CHOICES

Effective communication depends on choosing the correct method. Media and format choices are influenced by the target audience, the budget, and the needs of the audience.

INSTRUCTIONAL VIDEOS

Instructional videos have potential for excellent two-way communication because questions and feedback can be built in. Videos can be targeted to particular audiences, and they can be paused for discussion or replayed to reinforce concepts. Viewers can see processes, including "before," "during," and "after" phases. Videos are accessible because most communities have at least one DVD player or computer. Moreover, video players and computers are continually becoming less expensive to buy and use. Disadvantages include the necessity of editing software and equipment in some cases, as well as the need for support from other print materials. There is also danger of overuse, if other media or methods are more appropriate, and higher up-front costs. Producers of instructional videos must account for the costs of script development and hiring local performers as needed.

DVDs AND CDs

Interactive DVDs and CDs, such as games, give viewers the opportunity to actively participate as they learn information. Additionally, videos are considered to be a professional method of sharing information. Compared to many other media formats, discs are comparatively inexpensive to make and are easy to transport due to their small size and weight. They are more resistant to damage and aging than older videotape technology, making them more durable. Some disadvantages include needing access to technology to play what is stored on the disc and access to certain software programs to add new content to a disc, especially if the producer wants to include video animation or audio commentary. Producers must also consider expenses concerning paid staff and production and labeling expenses. Content that would appear on DVDs and CDs can alternatively be shared through streaming services or digital files stored on a computer or other compatible device.

TELEVISION AND RADIO

Both television and radio are forms of mass media that reach many people. TV has the broadest reach and can market to the general public or be customized for target audiences, while radio only tends to reach specific target audiences. TV has the advantage of video plus audio, while radio broadcasts only feature audio. However, access to television programs is more expensive than access to radio broadcasts. A shared disadvantage is that TV and radio audiences can only interact directly during call-in programs. Additionally, programming times may be inconvenient, but tape, digital sound, and digital video recording (DVR) can remedy this. Many streaming services also provide access to these programs. Both television and radio are useful for communicating simple slogans and messages, and both can generate awareness, interest, and excitement.

NEWSPAPERS

Except for the occasional community columns, news releases, and letters to the editor, newspaper pages and features afford little opportunity for audience input or participation. However, they do reach and appeal to the general public. Cost is an advantage: hiring a PR writer and paying for a news advertisement costs much less than a radio or TV spot. Additionally, newspaper features are high-status, and audiences can reread and review them as often as they like. However, newspaper ads may have difficulty affecting the reader as deeply without audio or video, and they require a literate audience. Their publication is also subject to editors' whims and biases. Newspaper pieces

124

combining advertising and editorial content—"advertorials"—provide inclusion of paid material, but are viewed as medium-status and cost more.

WEBSITES, BLOGS, MOBILE PHONES, AND TEXT MESSAGING

Computer literacy is required for online material, but participation potential is high via websites, e-networking, and blogging. Mobile phones and text messaging are used for enormous direct, public, two-way and one-on-one communication, with timely information and reminders. Web media need a literate public and can be tailored for specific audiences. They afford global information, are accessible by increasingly technology-literate populations, and are high-status. Web media disadvantages include the necessity of computers and people to design, manage, and supply content, as well as to provide technical support. Mobile and text media are globally popular, but appeal especially to certain demographics like teens and young adults. They are increasingly available, especially in rural regions, and are decreasing in cost. Mobile and text media disadvantages include required brevity in texts and provider messaging charges. Links to related websites and pages within existing sites are also advantages of digital media.

PUBLIC PRESENTATIONS AND SLIDESHOWS

Public presentations have great potential for audience participation and can directly target various audiences. They can encourage the establishment of partnerships and groups, stimulate local ownership of issues and projects, and make information public. A drawback to public presentations is that they are limited to nights, weekends, or whenever audiences are available and do not always attract the intended audience.

Another method of presentation is to use **slideshows**. These presentations are best for sophisticated audiences like professionals, civil servants, and service organizations. Well-designed slideshows are good for stimulating audience interest, selling ideas, and marketing products. Also, they are accessible online as well as in-person so they can reach a broader audience. Slideshow disadvantages include the necessity of projectors and other equipment. They are also limited to communicating more general points, outlines, and summaries rather than conveying a multitude of information in more detail.

POSTERS AND BROCHURES

Both **posters** and **brochures** can target audiences of the general public and more specific public sectors. Posters are better for communicating simple slogans and messages, while brochures can include more detail and are better for printing instructional information. Both can be inexpensive to produce, especially if printed only as needed and in-house. Posters can often be printed in-house without using outside printing companies. However, it is difficult to get feedback on both posters and brochures—unless they have been broadly tested, or if their publication is accompanied by workshops and other participatory events. A disadvantage of using posters is that they are designed to draw attention and communicate quickly, as they are mostly viewed in passing. This means that their messages must be simple and communicate efficiently. A disadvantage of using brochures is that they can only be distributed to a specific, limited group or area. Posters and brochures are also only understood when audiences are literate in both written language and visual elements.

FLYERS AND FACT SHEETS

Flyers and fact sheets have one-way communication potential because readers cannot give feedback. Their target audiences are general. Some advantages of using this form of media include flexibility: people can distribute them at meetings or events, put them on car windshields in parking lots, leave them in stores or on bulletin boards at community agencies and schools, hand them out from booths and other displays, or mail them. When printed in black and white, they can be very inexpensive. They afford recipients the convenience of being able to review them at their leisure. Organizations and individuals can produce flyers and fact sheets in-house, or even at home with desktop publishing software. Disadvantages include their limitation to single facts or tips and specific information on specified topics.

EVALUATING MEDIA INFORMATION SOURCES

With the wealth of media in different formats available today, users are more likely to take media at face value. However, to understand the content of media, consumers must **critically evaluate each source**.

Users should ask themselves the following questions about media sources:

- Who is delivering this message and why?
- What methods do a media source's publishers employ to gain and maintain users' attention?
- Which points of view is the media source representing?
- What are the various ways this message could be interpreted?
- What information is missing from the message?
- Is the source scholarly, i.e., peer-reviewed?
- Does it include author names and their credentials as they relate to the topic?
- Who publishes it and why?
- Who is the target audience?
- Is the language technically specific or non-technical?
- Are sources cited, research claims documented, conclusions based on furnished evidence, and references provided?
- Is the publication current?

OTHER CONSIDERATIONS FOR THE VALIDITY OF SOURCES

For books, consider whether information is **up-to-date** and whether **historical perspectives** apply. Content is more likely to be **scholarly** if publishers are universities, government, or professional organizations. Book reviews can also provide useful information. For articles, identify the author, publisher, frequency of the periodical's publication, and what kind of advertising, if any, is included. Looking for book reviews also informs users. For articles, look for biographical author information, publisher name, frequency of the periodical's publication, and whether advertising is included and, if so, whether it is for certain occupations or disciplines. For web pages, check their domain names, identify publishers or sponsors, look for the author or publisher's contact information, check dates of most recent page updates, be alert to biases, and verify the validity of the information on the webpage. The quality and accuracy of web pages located through search engines rather than library databases varies widely and requires careful user inspection. Web page recommendations from reliable sources like university faculties can help indicate quality and accuracy. Citations of websites by credible or scholarly sources also show reliability. Authors' names, relevant credentials, affiliations, and contact information support their authority. Site functionality, such as ease of navigation, ability to search, site maps, and indexes, is also a criterion to consider.

PERSUASIVE MEDIA

Advertising, public relations, and advocacy media all use **persuasion**. Advertisers use persuasion to sell goods and services. The public relations field uses persuasion to give good impressions of companies, governments, or organizations. Advocacy groups use persuasion to garner support or votes. Persuasion can come through commercials, public service announcements, speeches, websites, and newsletters, among other channels. Activists, lobbyists, government officials, and politicians use political rhetoric involving persuasive techniques. Basic techniques include using celebrity spokespersons, whom consumers admire or aspire to resemble, or conversely, "everyday people" (albeit often portrayed by actors) with whom consumers identify. Using expert testimonials lends credibility. Explicit claims of content, effectiveness, quality, and reliability—which often cannot be proven or disproven—are used to persuade. While news and advocacy messages mostly eschew humor for credibility's sake (except in political satire), advertising often persuades via humor, which gets consumer attention and associates its pleasure with advertised products and services. Qualifiers and other misleading terms, sometimes called "Weasel words," are often combined with exaggerated claims. Intensifiers, such as hyperboles, superlatives, repetitions, and sentimental appeals are also persuasive.

INTERMEDIATE TECHNIQUES

Dangerous propagandist Adolf Hitler said people suspect little lies more than big ones; hence the "Big Lie" is a persuasion method that cannot be identified without consumers' keen critical thinking. A related method is **charisma**, which can induce people to believe messages they would otherwise reject. **Euphemisms** substitute abstract, vague, or bland terms in place of more graphic, clear, and unpleasant ones. For example, the terms "layoffs" and "firing" are replaced by "downsizing," and "torture" is replaced with "intensive interrogation techniques." **Extrapolation** bases sweeping conclusions on small amounts of minor information to appeal to what consumers wish or hope. Flattery appeals to consumer self-esteem needs, such as L'Oréal's "You're worth it." Flattery is sometimes accomplished through contrast, like ads showing others' mistakes to make consumers feel superior and smarter. "Glittering generalities" refer to claims based on concepts such as beauty, love, health, democracy, freedom, and science. Persuaders use this tactic to gain consumer acceptance without consumers questioning what they mean. The opposite is name-calling to persuade consumers to reject someone or something.

American citizens love new ideas and technology. Persuaders exploit this by emphasizing the **newness** of products, services, and candidates. Conversely, they also use **nostalgia** to evoke consumers' happy memories, which they often remember more than unhappy ones. Citing "scientific evidence" is an intermediate version of the basic technique of expert testimonials. Consumers may accept this as proof, but some advertisers, politicians, and other persuaders may present inaccurate or misleading "evidence." Another intermediate technique is the "simple solution." Although the natures of people and life are complex, when consumers feel overwhelmed by complexity, persuaders exploit this by offering policies, products, or services they claim will solve complicated problems by simple means. Persuaders also use symbols, images, words, and names we associate with more general, emotional concepts like lifestyle, country, family, religion, and gender. While symbols have power, their significance also varies across individuals. For example, some consumers regard the Hummer SUV as a prestigious status symbol, while others regard it as environmentally harmful and irresponsible.

ADVANCED TECHNIQUES

Ad hominem, Latin for "against the man" attacks the person behind an idea rather than criticizing the idea itself. It operates by association: if a person is considered immoral or uneducated, then his or her ideas must be bad as well. **"Stacking the deck"** misleads by presenting only selected information that supports one position. **Apophasis**, or a false denial, allows the speaker or writer to indirectly bring attention to a flaw in an opponent's credibility. For example, a politician saying, "I won't mention my opponent's tax evasion issues" manages to mention them while seeming less accusatory. Persuaders may also use **majority belief**, making statements such as "Four out of five dentists recommend this brand" or "[insert number] people can't be wrong." In an intensified version, persuaders exploit group dynamics at rallies, speeches, and other live-audience events where people are vulnerable to surrounding crowd influences. **Scapegoating**, blaming one person or group for complex problems, is a form of the intermediate "simple solution" technique, a practice common in politics. **Timing** also persuades, like advertising flowers and candy in the weeks preceding Valentine's Day, ad campaigns preceding new technology rollouts, and politician speeches following big news events.

VISUAL MEDIA

Some images have the power to communicate more information than an entire paragraph. Images can contain several elements and be interpreted different ways, making them an effective vessel for abstract and emotionally appealing ideas. Humans are also able to understand images before they fully acquire language, meaning that images can reach more people than language can at any time. Images are also more quickly comprehended than text, making them a highly efficient method of communication. People can remember or memorize images more easily than text, also. Historically, images have been used for propaganda and subliminal messaging. Images are also used by different companies as an effective technique to entice customers to buy their products. Though images do not always contain text, they can still convey explicit and implicit meanings. An image's explicit meaning would be the most recognizable shape or concept in the image. The implicit meaning may be obscured within the image through the use of negative space, background images, or out-of-focus shapes.

INTERPRETING AND EVALUATING PERSUASIVE MEDIA

Most messages can be interpreted in different ways. They can be interpreted explicitly, where the literal meaning of the words in the message creates the meaning of the message, and no context is considered. Alternatively, other contexts can be considered alongside the explicit meaning of the message. These create alternative, not clearly stated meanings called **implicit meanings**. Politics, current events, regional norms, and even emotions are examples of contexts that can add implicit meanings to a message. These implicit meanings can change the effect a message has on its recipient. Many products have slogans with both implicit and explicit meanings. These implicit meanings must be considered to fully interpret a message.

Messages come in different forms, and each form has a unique way of communicating both explicit and implicit meanings. Images can come with captions that communicate a message, but some images carry subliminal messages. This means that their implicit meaning is received by the viewer, but the viewer is not aware of it. The term **propaganda** describes messages that advocate for a specific opinion or way of thinking. Most propaganda is politically driven and has been used during historical periods, most notably World War II. Unlike messages with hidden or veiled implicit meanings, most propaganda aggressively communicates its entire meaning and is difficult to misinterpret. Documentaries are another prominent form of communication. Documentaries are informational videos that focus on a specific figure, subject, phenomenon, or time period. While documentaries are primarily fact based and contain excerpts from interviews and testimonials, documentaries feature a limited view of their subject and sometimes attempt to persuade viewers to take action or embrace their central message. While some documentaries communicate this clearly, some hide an implicit meaning through the way they present each piece of information.

128

Skills and Processes

The Writing Process

BRAINSTORMING

Brainstorming is a technique that is used to find a creative approach to a subject. This can be accomplished by simple **free-association** with a topic. For example, with paper and pen, write every thought that you have about the topic in a word or phrase. This is done without critical thinking. You should put everything that comes to your mind about the topic on your scratch paper. Then, you need to read the list over a few times. Next, look for patterns, repetitions, and clusters of ideas. This allows a variety of fresh ideas to come as you think about the topic.

FREE WRITING

Free writing is a more structured form of brainstorming. The method involves taking a limited amount of time (e.g., 2 to 3 minutes) to write everything that comes to mind about the topic in complete sentences. When time expires, review everything that has been written down. Many of your sentences may make little or no sense, but the insights and observations that can come from free writing make this method a valuable approach. Usually, free writing results in a fuller expression of ideas than brainstorming because thoughts and associations are written in complete sentences. However, both techniques can be used to complement each other.

PLANNING

Planning is the process of organizing a piece of writing before composing a draft. Planning can include creating an outline or a graphic organizer, such as a Venn diagram, a spider-map, or a flowchart. These methods should help the writer identify their topic, main ideas, and the general organization of the composition. Preliminary research can also take place during this stage. Planning helps writers organize all of their ideas and decide if they have enough material to begin their first draft. However, writers should remember that the decisions they make during this step will likely change later in the process, so their plan does not have to be perfect.

DRAFTING

Writers may then use their plan, outline, or graphic organizer to compose their first draft. They may write subsequent drafts to improve their writing. Writing multiple drafts can help writers consider different ways to communicate their ideas and address errors that may be difficult to correct without rewriting a section or the whole composition. Most writers will vary in how many drafts they choose to write, as there is no "right" number of drafts. Writing drafts also takes away the pressure to write perfectly on the first try, as writers can improve with each draft they write.

REVISING, EDITING, AND PROOFREADING

Once a writer completes a draft, they can move on to the revising, editing, and proofreading steps to improve their draft. These steps begin with making broad changes that may apply to large sections of a composition and then making small, specific corrections. **Revising** is the first and broadest of these steps. Revising involves ensuring that the composition addresses an appropriate audience, includes all necessary material, maintains focus throughout, and is organized logically. Revising may occur after the first draft to ensure that the following drafts improve upon errors from the first draft. Some revision should occur between each draft to avoid repeating these errors. The **editing** phase of writing is narrower than the revising phase. Editing a composition should include steps such as improving transitions between paragraphs, ensuring each paragraph is on topic, and

129

improving the flow of the text. The editing phase may also include correcting grammatical errors that cannot be fixed without significantly altering the text. **Proofreading** involves fixing misspelled words, typos, other grammatical errors, and any remaining surface-level flaws in the composition.

RECURSIVE WRITING PROCESS

However you approach writing, you may find comfort in knowing that the revision process can occur in any order. The **recursive writing process** is not as difficult as the phrase may make it seem. Simply put, the recursive writing process means that you may need to revisit steps after completing other steps. It also implies that the steps are not required to take place in any certain order. Indeed, you may find that planning, drafting, and revising can all take place at about the same time. The writing process involves moving back and forth between planning, drafting, and revising, followed by more planning, more drafting, and more revising until the writing is satisfactory.

> **Review Video: Recursive Writing Process**
> Visit mometrix.com/academy and enter code: 951611

TECHNOLOGY IN THE WRITING PROCESS

Modern technology has yielded several tools that can be used to make the writing process more convenient and organized. Word processors and online tools, such as databases and plagiarism detectors, allow much of the writing process to be completed in one place, using one device.

TECHNOLOGY FOR PLANNING AND DRAFTING

For the planning and drafting stages of the writing process, word processors are a helpful tool. These programs also feature formatting tools, allowing users to create their own planning tools or create digital outlines that can be easily converted into sentences, paragraphs, or an entire essay draft. Online databases and references also complement the planning process by providing convenient access to information and sources for research. Word processors also allow users to keep up with their work and update it more easily than if they wrote their work by hand. Online word processors often allow users to collaborate, making group assignments more convenient. These programs also allow users to include illustrations or other supplemental media in their compositions.

TECHNOLOGY FOR REVISING, EDITING, AND PROOFREADING

Word processors also benefit the revising, editing, and proofreading stages of the writing process. Most of these programs indicate errors in spelling and grammar, allowing users to catch minor errors and correct them quickly. There are also websites designed to help writers by analyzing text for deeper errors, such as poor sentence structure, inappropriate complexity, lack of sentence variety, and style issues. These websites can help users fix errors they may not know to look for or may have simply missed. As writers finish these steps, they may benefit from checking their work for any plagiarism. There are several websites and programs that compare text to other documents and publications across the internet and detect any similarities within the text. These websites show the source of the similar information, so users know whether or not they referenced the source and unintentionally plagiarized its contents.

TECHNOLOGY FOR PUBLISHING

Technology also makes managing written work more convenient. Digitally storing documents keeps everything in one place and is easy to reference. Digital storage also makes sharing work easier, as documents can be attached to an email or stored online. This also allows writers to publish their work easily, as they can electronically submit it to other publications or freely post it to a personal blog, profile, or website.

Outlining and Organizing Ideas

MAIN IDEAS, SUPPORTING DETAILS, AND OUTLINING A TOPIC

A writer often begins the first paragraph of a paper by stating the **main idea** or point, also known as the **topic sentence**. The rest of the paragraph supplies particular details that develop and support the main point. One way to visualize the relationship between the main point and supporting information is by considering a table: the tabletop is the main point, and each of the table's legs is a supporting detail or group of details. Both professional authors and students can benefit from planning their writing by first making an outline of the topic. Outlines facilitate quick identification of the main point and supporting details without having to wade through the additional language that will exist in the fully developed essay, article, or paper. Outlining can also help readers to analyze a piece of existing writing for the same reason. The outline first summarizes the main idea in one sentence. Then, below that, it summarizes the supporting details in a numbered list. Writing the paper then consists of filling in the outline with detail, writing a paragraph for each supporting point, and adding an introduction and conclusion.

INTRODUCTION

The purpose of the introduction is to capture the reader's attention and announce the essay's main idea. Normally, the introduction contains 50-80 words, or 3-5 sentences. An introduction can begin with an interesting quote, a question, or a strong opinion—something that will **engage** the reader's interest and prompt them to keep reading. If you are writing your essay to a specific prompt, your introduction should include a **restatement or summarization** of the prompt so that the reader will have some context for your essay. Finally, your introduction should briefly state your **thesis or main idea**: the primary thing you hope to communicate to the reader through your essay. Don't try to include all of the details and nuances of your thesis, or all of your reasons for it, in the introduction. That's what the rest of the essay is for!

> **Review Video: Introduction**
> Visit mometrix.com/academy and enter code: 961328

THESIS STATEMENT

The thesis is the main idea of the essay. A temporary thesis, or working thesis, should be established early in the writing process because it will serve to keep the writer focused as ideas develop. This temporary thesis is subject to change as you continue to write.

The temporary thesis has two parts: a **topic** (i.e., the focus of your essay based on the prompt) and a **comment**. The comment makes an important point about the topic. A temporary thesis should be interesting and specific. Also, you need to limit the topic to a manageable scope. These three questions are useful tools to measure the effectiveness of any temporary thesis:

- Does the focus of my essay have enough interest to hold an audience?
- Is the focus of my essay specific enough to generate interest?
- Is the focus of my essay manageable for the time limit? Too broad? Too narrow?

The thesis should be a generalization rather than a fact because the thesis prepares readers for facts and details that support the thesis. The process of bringing the thesis into sharp focus may help in outlining major sections of the work. Once the thesis and introduction are complete, you can address the body of the work.

SUPPORTING THE THESIS

Throughout your essay, the thesis should be **explained clearly and supported** adequately by additional arguments. The thesis sentence needs to contain a clear statement of the purpose of your essay and a comment about the thesis. With the thesis statement, you have an opportunity to state what is noteworthy of this particular treatment of the prompt. Each sentence and paragraph should build on and support the thesis.

When you respond to the prompt, use parts of the passage to support your argument or defend your position. Using supporting evidence from the passage strengths your argument because readers can see your attention to the entire passage and your response to the details and facts within the passage. You can use facts, details, statistics, and direct quotations from the passage to uphold your position. Be sure to point out which information comes from the original passage and base your argument around that evidence.

BODY

In an essay's introduction, the writer establishes the thesis and may indicate how the rest of the piece will be structured. In the body of the piece, the writer **elaborates** upon, **illustrates**, and **explains** the **thesis statement**. How writers arrange supporting details and their choices of paragraph types are development techniques. Writers may give examples of the concept introduced in the thesis statement. If the subject includes a cause-and-effect relationship, the author may explain its causality. A writer will explain or analyze the main idea of the piece throughout the body, often by presenting arguments for the veracity or credibility of the thesis statement. Writers may use development to define or clarify ambiguous terms. Paragraphs within the body may be organized using natural sequences, like space and time. Writers may employ **inductive reasoning**, using multiple details to establish a generalization or causal relationship, or **deductive reasoning**, proving a generalized hypothesis or proposition through a specific example or case.

PARAGRAPHS

After the introduction of a passage, a series of body paragraphs will carry a message through to the conclusion. Each paragraph should be **unified around a main point**. Normally, a good topic sentence summarizes the paragraph's main point. A topic sentence is a general sentence that gives an introduction to the paragraph.

The sentences that follow support the topic sentence. However, though it is usually the first sentence, the topic sentence can come as the final sentence to the paragraph if the earlier sentences give a clear explanation of the paragraph's topic. This allows the topic sentence to function as a concluding sentence. Overall, the paragraphs need to stay true to the main point. This means that any unnecessary sentences that do not advance the main point should be removed.

The main point of a paragraph requires adequate development (i.e., a substantial paragraph that covers the main point). A paragraph of two or three sentences does not cover a main point. This is especially true when the main point of the paragraph gives strong support to the argument of the thesis. An occasional short paragraph is fine as a transitional device. However, a well-developed argument will have paragraphs with more than a few sentences.

METHODS OF DEVELOPING PARAGRAPHS

Common methods of adding substance to paragraphs include examples, illustrations, analogies, and cause and effect.

- **Examples** are supporting details to the main idea of a paragraph or a passage. When authors write about something that their audience may not understand, they can provide an example to show their point. When authors write about something that is not easily accepted, they can give examples to prove their point.
- **Illustrations** are extended examples that require several sentences. Well-selected illustrations can be a great way for authors to develop a point that may not be familiar to their audience.
- **Analogies** make comparisons between items that appear to have nothing in common. Analogies are employed by writers to provoke fresh thoughts about a subject. These comparisons may be used to explain the unfamiliar, to clarify an abstract point, or to argue a point. Although analogies are effective literary devices, they should be used carefully in arguments. Two things may be alike in some respects but completely different in others.
- **Cause and effect** is an excellent device to explain the connection between an action or situation and a particular result. One way that authors can use cause and effect is to state the effect in the topic sentence of a paragraph and add the causes in the body of the paragraph. This method can give an author's paragraphs structure, which always strengthens writing.

TYPES OF PARAGRAPHS

A **paragraph of narration** tells a story or a part of a story. Normally, the sentences are arranged in chronological order (i.e., the order that the events happened). However, flashbacks (i.e., an anecdote from an earlier time) can be included.

A **descriptive paragraph** makes a verbal portrait of a person, place, or thing. When specific details are used that appeal to one or more of the senses (i.e., sight, sound, smell, taste, and touch), authors give readers a sense of being present in the moment.

A **process paragraph** is related to time order (i.e., First, you open the bottle. Second, you pour the liquid, etc.). Usually, this describes a process or teaches readers how to perform a process.

Comparing two things draws attention to their similarities and indicates a number of differences. When authors contrast, they focus only on differences. Both comparing and contrasting may be done point-by-point, noting both the similarities and differences of each point, or in sequential paragraphs, where you discuss all the similarities and then all the differences, or vice versa.

BREAKING TEXT INTO PARAGRAPHS

For most forms of writing, you will need to use multiple paragraphs. As such, determining when to start a new paragraph is very important. Reasons for starting a new paragraph include:

- To mark off the introduction and concluding paragraphs
- To signal a shift to a new idea or topic
- To indicate an important shift in time or place
- To explain a point in additional detail
- To highlight a comparison, contrast, or cause and effect relationship

PARAGRAPH LENGTH

Most readers find that their comfort level for a paragraph is between 100 and 200 words. Shorter paragraphs cause too much starting and stopping and give a choppy effect. Paragraphs that are too long often test the attention span of readers. Two notable exceptions to this rule exist. In scientific or scholarly papers, longer paragraphs suggest seriousness and depth. In journalistic writing, constraints are placed on paragraph size by the narrow columns in a newspaper format.

The first and last paragraphs of a text will usually be the introduction and conclusion. These special-purpose paragraphs are likely to be shorter than paragraphs in the body of the work. Paragraphs in the body of the essay follow the subject's outline (e.g., one paragraph per point in short essays and a group of paragraphs per point in longer works). Some ideas require more development than others, so it is good for a writer to remain flexible. A paragraph of excessive length may be divided, and shorter ones may be combined.

COHERENT PARAGRAPHS

A smooth flow of sentences and paragraphs without gaps, shifts, or bumps will lead to paragraph **coherence**. Ties between old and new information can be smoothed using several methods:

- **Linking ideas clearly**, from the topic sentence to the body of the paragraph, is essential for a smooth transition. The topic sentence states the main point, and this should be followed by specific details, examples, and illustrations that support the topic sentence. The support may be direct or indirect. In **indirect support**, the illustrations and examples may support a sentence that in turn supports the topic directly.
- The **repetition of key words** adds coherence to a paragraph. To avoid dull language, variations of the key words may be used.
- **Parallel structures** are often used within sentences to emphasize the similarity of ideas and connect sentences giving similar information.
- Maintaining a **consistent verb tense** throughout the paragraph helps. Shifting tenses affects the smooth flow of words and can disrupt the coherence of the paragraph.

> **Review Video: How to Write a Good Paragraph**
> Visit mometrix.com/academy and enter code: 682127

SEQUENCE WORDS AND PHRASES

When a paragraph opens with the topic sentence, the second sentence may begin with a phrase like *first of all*, introducing the first supporting detail or example. The writer may introduce the second supporting item with words or phrases like *also, in addition*, and *besides*. The writer might introduce succeeding pieces of support with wording like, *another thing, moreover, furthermore*, or *not only that, but*. The writer may introduce the last piece of support with *lastly, finally*, or *last but not least*. Writers get off the point by presenting off-target items not supporting the main point. For

134

example, a main point *my dog is not smart* is supported by the statement, *he's six years old and still doesn't answer to his name*. But *he cries when I leave for school* is not supportive, as it does not indicate lack of intelligence. Writers stay on point by presenting only supportive statements that are directly relevant to and illustrative of their main point.

Review Video: <u>Sequence</u>
Visit mometrix.com/academy and enter code: 489027

TRANSITIONS

Transitions between sentences and paragraphs guide readers from idea to idea and indicate relationships between sentences and paragraphs. Writers should be judicious in their use of transitions, inserting them sparingly. They should also be selected to fit the author's purpose—transitions can indicate time, comparison, and conclusion, among other purposes. Tone is also important to consider when using transitional phrases, varying the tone for different audiences. For example, in a scholarly essay, *in summary* would be preferable to the more informal *in short*.

When working with transitional words and phrases, writers usually find a natural flow that indicates when a transition is needed. In reading a draft of the text, it should become apparent where the flow is disrupted. At this point, the writer can add transitional elements during the revision process. Revising can also afford an opportunity to delete transitional devices that seem heavy handed or unnecessary.

Review Video: <u>Transitions in Writing</u>
Visit mometrix.com/academy and enter code: 233246

TYPES OF TRANSITIONAL WORDS

Time	Afterward, immediately, earlier, meanwhile, recently, lately, now, since, soon, when, then, until, before, etc.
Sequence	too, first, second, further, moreover, also, again, and, next, still, besides, finally
Comparison	similarly, in the same way, likewise, also, again, once more
Contrasting	but, although, despite, however, instead, nevertheless, on the one hand... on the other hand, regardless, yet, in contrast.
Cause and Effect	because, consequently, thus, therefore, then, to this end, since, so, as a result, if... then, accordingly
Examples	for example, for instance, such as, to illustrate, indeed, in fact, specifically
Place	near, far, here, there, to the left/right, next to, above, below, beyond, opposite, beside
Concession	granted that, naturally, of course, it may appear, although it is true that
Repetition, Summary, or Conclusion	as mentioned earlier, as noted, in other words, in short, on the whole, to summarize, therefore, as a result, to conclude, in conclusion
Addition	and, also, furthermore, moreover
Generalization	in broad terms, broadly speaking, in general

> **Review Video: Transitional Words and Phrases**
> Visit mometrix.com/academy and enter code: 197796
>
> **Review Video: What are Transition Words?**
> Visit mometrix.com/academy and enter code: 707563
>
> **Review Video: How to Effectively Connect Sentences**
> Visit mometrix.com/academy and enter code: 948325

CONCLUSION

Two important principles to consider when writing a conclusion are strength and closure. A strong conclusion gives the reader a sense that the author's main points are meaningful and important, and that the supporting facts and arguments are convincing, solid, and well developed. When a conclusion achieves closure, it gives the impression that the writer has stated all necessary information and points and completed the work, rather than simply stopping after a specified length. Some things to avoid when writing concluding paragraphs include:

- Introducing a completely new idea
- Beginning with obvious or unoriginal phrases like "In conclusion" or "To summarize"
- Apologizing for one's opinions or writing
- Repeating the thesis word for word rather than rephrasing it
- Believing that the conclusion must always summarize the piece

> **Review Video: Drafting Conclusions**
> Visit mometrix.com/academy and enter code: 209408

Writing Style and Form

WRITING STYLE AND LINGUISTIC FORM

Linguistic form encodes the literal meanings of words and sentences. It comes from the phonological, morphological, syntactic, and semantic parts of a language. **Writing style** consists of different ways of encoding the meaning and indicating figurative and stylistic meanings. An author's writing style can also be referred to as his or her **voice**.

Writers' stylistic choices accomplish three basic effects on their audiences:

- They **communicate meanings** beyond linguistically dictated meanings,
- They communicate the **author's attitude**, such as persuasive or argumentative effects accomplished through style, and
- They communicate or **express feelings**.

Within style, component areas include:

- Narrative structure
- Viewpoint
- Focus
- Sound patterns
- Meter and rhythm
- Lexical and syntactic repetition and parallelism
- Writing genre
- Representational, realistic, and mimetic effects
- Representation of thought and speech
- Meta-representation (representing representation)
- Irony
- Metaphor and other indirect meanings
- Representation and use of historical and dialectal variations
- Gender-specific and other group-specific speech styles, both real and fictitious
- Analysis of the processes for inferring meaning from writing

LEVEL OF FORMALITY

The relationship between writer and reader is important in choosing a **level of formality** as most writing requires some degree of formality. **Formal writing** is for addressing a superior in a school or work environment. Business letters, textbooks, and newspapers use a moderate to high level of formality. **Informal writing** is appropriate for private letters, personal emails, and business correspondence between close associates.

For your exam, you will want to be aware of informal and formal writing. One way that this can be accomplished is to watch for shifts in point of view in the essay. For example, unless writers are using a personal example, they will rarely refer to themselves (e.g., "*I* think that *my* point is very clear.") to avoid being informal when they need to be formal.

Also, be mindful of an author who addresses his or her audience **directly** in their writing (e.g., "Readers, *like you*, will understand this argument.") as this can be a sign of informal writing. Good writers understand the need to be consistent with their level of formality. Shifts in levels of formality or point of view can confuse readers and cause them to discount the message.

CLICHÉS

Clichés are phrases that have been **overused** to the point that the phrase has no importance or has lost the original meaning. These phrases have no originality and add very little to a passage. Therefore, most writers will avoid the use of clichés. Another option is to make changes to a cliché so that it is not predictable and empty of meaning.

Examples:

When life gives you lemons, make lemonade.

Every cloud has a silver lining.

JARGON

Jargon is **specialized vocabulary** that is used among members of a certain trade or profession. Since jargon is understood by only a small audience, writers will use jargon in passages that will only be read by a specialized audience. For example, medical jargon should be used in a medical journal but not in a New York Times article. Jargon includes exaggerated language that tries to impress rather than inform. Sentences filled with jargon are not precise and are difficult to understand.

Examples:

"He is going to *toenail* these frames for us." (Toenail is construction jargon for nailing at an angle.)

"They brought in a *kip* of material today." (Kip refers to 1000 pounds in architecture and engineering.)

SLANG

Slang is an **informal** and sometimes private language that is understood by some individuals. Slang terms have some usefulness, but they can have a small audience. So, most formal writing will not include this kind of language.

Examples:

"Yes, the event was a blast!" (In this sentence, *blast* means that the event was a great experience.)

"That attempt was an epic fail." (By *epic fail*, the speaker means that his or her attempt was not a success.)

COLLOQUIALISM

A colloquialism is a word or phrase that is found in informal writing. Unlike slang, **colloquial language** will be familiar to a greater range of people. However, colloquialisms are still considered inappropriate for formal writing. Colloquial language can include some slang, but these are limited to contractions for the most part.

Examples:

> "Can *y'all* come back another time?" (Y'all is a contraction of "you all.")

> "Will you stop him from building this *castle in the air*?" (A "castle in the air" is an improbable or unlikely event.)

ACADEMIC LANGUAGE

In educational settings, students are often expected to use academic language in their schoolwork. Academic language is also commonly found in dissertations and theses, texts published by academic journals, and other forms of academic research. Academic language conventions may vary between fields, but general academic language is free of slang, regional terminology, and noticeable grammatical errors. Specific terms may also be used in academic language, and it is important to understand their proper usage. A writer's command of academic language impacts their ability to communicate in an academic or professional context. While it is acceptable to use colloquialisms, slang, improper grammar, or other forms of informal speech in social settings or at home, it is inappropriate to practice non-academic language in academic contexts.

TONE

Tone may be defined as the writer's **attitude** toward the topic, and to the audience. This attitude is reflected in the language used in the writing. The tone of a work should be **appropriate to the topic** and to the intended audience. While it may be fine to use slang or jargon in some pieces, other texts should not contain such terms. Tone can range from humorous to serious and any level in between. It may be more or less formal, depending on the purpose of the writing and its intended audience. All these nuances in tone can flavor the entire writing and should be kept in mind as the work evolves.

WORD SELECTION

A writer's choice of words is a signature of their style. Careful thought about the use of words can improve a piece of writing. A passage can be an exciting piece to read when attention is given to the use of vivid or specific nouns rather than general ones.

Example:

> General: His kindness will never be forgotten.

> Specific: His thoughtful gifts and bear hugs will never be forgotten.

Attention should also be given to the kind of verbs that are used in sentences. Active verbs (e.g., run, swim) are about an action. Whenever possible, an **active verb should replace a linking verb** to provide clear examples for arguments and to strengthen a passage overall. When using an active verb, one should be sure that the verb is used in the active voice instead of the passive voice. Verbs are in the active voice when the subject is the one doing the action. A verb is in the passive voice when the subject is the recipient of an action.

Example:

> Passive: The winners were called to the stage by the judges.

> Active: The judges called the winners to the stage.

CONCISENESS

Conciseness is writing that communicates a message in the fewest words possible. Writing concisely is valuable because short, uncluttered messages allow the reader to understand the author's message more easily and efficiently. Planning is important in writing concise messages. If you have in mind what you need to write beforehand, it will be easier to make a message short and to the point. Do not state the obvious.

Revising is also important. After the message is written, make sure you have effective, pithy sentences that efficiently get your point across. When reviewing the information, imagine a conversation taking place, and concise writing will likely result.

APPROPRIATE KINDS OF WRITING FOR DIFFERENT TASKS, PURPOSES, AND AUDIENCES

When preparing to write a composition, consider the audience and purpose to choose the best type of writing. Three common types of writing are persuasive, expository, and narrative. **Persuasive**, or argumentative writing, is used to convince the audience to take action or agree with the author's claims. **Expository** writing is meant to inform the audience of the author's observations or research on a topic. **Narrative** writing is used to tell the audience a story and often allows more room for creativity. While task, purpose, and audience inform a writer's mode of writing, these factors also impact elements such as tone, vocabulary, and formality.

For example, students who are writing to persuade their parents to grant them some additional privilege, such as permission for a more independent activity, should use more sophisticated vocabulary and diction that sounds more mature and serious to appeal to the parental audience. However, students who are writing for younger children should use simpler vocabulary and sentence structure, as well as choose words that are more vivid and entertaining. They should treat their topics more lightly, and include humor when appropriate. Students who are writing for their classmates may use language that is more informal, as well as age-appropriate.

> **Review Video: Writing Purpose and Audience**
> Visit mometrix.com/academy and enter code: 146627

Modes of Writing

ESSAYS

Essays usually focus on one topic, subject, or goal. There are several types of essays, including informative, persuasive, and narrative. An essay's structure and level of formality depend on the type of essay and its goal. While narrative essays typically do not include outside sources, other types of essays often require some research and the integration of primary and secondary sources.

The basic format of an essay typically has three major parts: the introduction, the body, and the conclusion. The body is further divided into the writer's main points. Short and simple essays may have three main points, while essays covering broader ranges and going into more depth can have almost any number of main points, depending on length.

An essay's introduction should answer three questions:

1. What is the **subject** of the essay?

    If a student writes an essay about a book, the answer would include the title and author of the book and any additional information needed—such as the subject or argument of the book.

2. How does the essay **address** the subject?

    To answer this, the writer identifies the essay's organization by briefly summarizing main points and the evidence supporting them.

3. What will the essay **prove**?

    This is the thesis statement, usually the opening paragraph's last sentence, clearly stating the writer's message.

The body elaborates on all the main points related to the thesis, introducing one main point at a time, and includes supporting evidence with each main point. Each body paragraph should state the point in a topic sentence, which is usually the first sentence in the paragraph. The paragraph should then explain the point's meaning, support it with quotations or other evidence, and then explain how this point and the evidence are related to the thesis. The writer should then repeat this procedure in a new paragraph for each additional main point.

The conclusion reiterates the content of the introduction, including the thesis, to remind the reader of the essay's main argument or subject. The essay writer may also summarize the highlights of the argument or description contained in the body of the essay, following the same sequence originally used in the body. For example, a conclusion might look like: Point 1 + Point 2 + Point 3 = Thesis, or Point 1 → Point 2 → Point 3 → Thesis Proof. Good organization makes essays easier for writers to compose and provides a guide for readers to follow. Well-organized essays hold attention better and are more likely to get readers to accept their theses as valid.

INFORMATIVE VS. PERSUASIVE WRITING

Informative writing, also called explanatory or expository writing, begins with the basis that something is true or factual, while **persuasive** writing strives to prove something that may or may not be true or factual. Whereas argumentative text is written to **persuade** readers to agree with the author's position, informative text merely **provides information and insight** to readers. Informative writing concentrates on **informing** readers about why or how something is as it is. This can include offering new information, explaining how a process works, and developing a concept for readers. To accomplish these objectives, the essay may name and distinguish various things within a category, provide definitions, provide details about the parts of something, explain a particular function or behavior, and give readers explanations for why a fact, object, event, or process exists or occurs.

NARRATIVE WRITING

Put simply, **narrative** writing tells a story. The most common examples of literary narratives are novels. Non-fictional biographies, autobiographies, memoirs, and histories are also narratives. Narratives should tell stories in such a way that the readers learn something or gain insight or understanding. Students can write more interesting narratives by describing events or experiences that were meaningful to them. Narratives should start with the story's actions or events, rather than long descriptions or introductions. Students should ensure that there is a point to each story by describing what they learned from the experience they narrate. To write an effective description, students should include sensory details, asking themselves what they saw, heard, felt or touched, smelled, and tasted during the experiences they describe. In narrative writing, the details should be **concrete** rather than **abstract**. Using concrete details enables readers to imagine everything that the writer describes.

> **Review Video: Narratives**
> Visit mometrix.com/academy and enter code: 280100

SENSORY DETAILS

Students need to use vivid descriptions when writing descriptive essays. Narratives should also include descriptions of characters, things, and events. Students should remember to describe not only the visual detail of what someone or something looks like, but details from other senses, as well. For example, they can contrast the feeling of a sea breeze to that of a mountain breeze, describe how they think something inedible would taste, and compare sounds they hear in the same location at different times of day and night. Readers have trouble visualizing images or imagining sensory impressions and feelings from abstract descriptions, so concrete descriptions make these more real.

CONCRETE VS. ABSTRACT DESCRIPTIONS IN NARRATIVE

Concrete language provides information that readers can grasp and may empathize with, while **abstract language**, which is more general, can leave readers feeling disconnected, empty, or even confused. "It was a lovely day" is abstract, but "The sun shone brightly, the sky was blue, the air felt warm, and a gentle breeze wafted across my skin" is concrete. "Ms. Couch was a good teacher" uses abstract language, giving only a general idea of the writer's opinion. But "Ms. Couch is excellent at helping us take our ideas and turn them into good essays and stories" uses concrete language, giving more specific examples of what makes Ms. Couch a good teacher. "I like writing poems but not essays" gives readers a general idea that the student prefers one genre over another, but not why. But when reading, "I like writing short poems with rhythm and rhyme, but I hate writing five-page essays that go on and on about the same ideas," readers understand that the student prefers the brevity, rhyme, and meter of short poetry over the length and redundancy of longer prose.

AUTOBIOGRAPHICAL NARRATIVES

Autobiographical narratives are narratives written by an author about an event or period in their life. Autobiographical narratives are written from one person's perspective, in first person, and often include the author's thoughts and feelings alongside their description of the event or period. Structure, style, or theme varies between different autobiographical narratives, since each narrative is personal and specific to its author and his or her experience.

REFLECTIVE ESSAY

A less common type of essay is the reflective essay. **Reflective essays** allow the author to reflect, or think back, on an experience and analyze what they recall. They should consider what they learned from the experience, what they could have done differently, what would have helped them during the experience, or anything else that they have realized from looking back on the experience. Reflection essays incorporate both objective reflection on one's own actions and subjective explanation of thoughts and feelings. These essays can be written for a number of experiences in a formal or informal context.

JOURNALS AND DIARIES

A **journal** is a personal account of events, experiences, feelings, and thoughts. Many people write journals to express their feelings and thoughts or to help them process experiences they have had. Since journals are **private documents** not meant to be shared with others, writers may not be concerned with grammar, spelling, or other mechanics. However, authors may write journals that they expect or hope to publish someday; in this case, they not only express their thoughts and feelings and process their experiences, but they also attend to their craft in writing them. Some authors compose journals to record a particular time period or a series of related events, such as a cancer diagnosis, treatment, surviving the disease, and how these experiences have changed or affected them. Other experiences someone might include in a journal are recovering from addiction, journeys of spiritual exploration and discovery, time spent in another country, or anything else someone wants to personally document. Journaling can also be therapeutic, as some people use journals to work through feelings of grief over loss or to wrestle with big decisions.

EXAMPLES OF DIARIES IN LITERATURE

The Diary of a Young Girl by Dutch Jew Anne Frank (1947) contains her life-affirming, nonfictional diary entries from 1942-1944 while her family hid in an attic from World War II's genocidal Nazis. *Go Ask Alice* (1971) by Beatrice Sparks is a cautionary, fictional novel in the form of diary entries by Alice, an unhappy, rebellious teen who takes LSD, runs away from home and lives with hippies, and eventually returns home. Frank's writing reveals an intelligent, sensitive, insightful girl, raised by intellectual European parents—a girl who believes in the goodness of human nature despite surrounding atrocities. Alice, influenced by early 1970s counterculture, becomes less optimistic. However, similarities can be found between them: Frank dies in a Nazi concentration camp while the fictitious Alice dies from a drug overdose. Both young women are also unable to escape their surroundings. Additionally, adolescent searches for personal identity are evident in both books.

> **Review Video: Journals, Diaries, Letters, and Blogs**
> Visit mometrix.com/academy and enter code: 432845

LETTERS

Letters are messages written to other people. In addition to letters written between individuals, some writers compose letters to the editors of newspapers, magazines, and other publications, while some write "Open Letters" to be published and read by the general public. Open letters, while intended for everyone to read, may also identify a group of people or a single person whom the letter directly addresses. In everyday use, the most-used forms are business letters and personal or friendly letters. Both kinds share common elements: business or personal letterhead stationery; the writer's return address at the top; the addressee's address next; a salutation, such as "Dear [name]" or some similar opening greeting, followed by a colon in business letters or a comma in personal letters; the body of the letter, with paragraphs as indicated; and a closing, like "Sincerely/Cordially/Best regards/etc." or "Love," in intimate personal letters.

EARLY LETTERS

The Greek word for "letter" is *epistolē*, which became the English word "epistle." The earliest letters were called epistles, including the New Testament's epistles from the apostles to the Christians. In ancient Egypt, the writing curriculum in scribal schools included the epistolary genre. Epistolary novels frame a story in the form of letters. Examples of noteworthy epistolary novels include:

- *Pamela* (1740), by 18th-century English novelist Samuel Richardson
- *Shamela* (1741), Henry Fielding's satire of *Pamela* that mocked epistolary writing.
- *Lettres persanes* (1721) by French author Montesquieu
- *The Sorrows of Young Werther* (1774) by German author Johann Wolfgang von Goethe
- *The History of Emily Montague* (1769), the first Canadian novel, by Frances Brooke
- *Dracula* (1897) by Bram Stoker
- *Frankenstein* (1818) by Mary Shelley
- *The Color Purple* (1982) by Alice Walker

BLOGS

The word "blog" is derived from "weblog" and refers to writing done exclusively on the internet. Readers of reputable newspapers expect quality content and layouts that enable easy reading. These expectations also apply to blogs. For example, readers can easily move visually from line to line when columns are narrow, while overly wide columns cause readers to lose their places. Blogs must also be posted with layouts enabling online readers to follow them easily. However, because the way people read on computer, tablet, and smartphone screens differs from how they read print on paper, formatting and writing blog content is more complex than writing newspaper articles. Two major principles are the bases for blog-writing rules: The first is while readers of print articles skim to estimate their length, online they must scroll down to scan; therefore, blog layouts need more subheadings, graphics, and other indications of what information follows. The second is onscreen reading can be harder on the eyes than reading printed paper, so legibility is crucial in blogs.

RULES AND RATIONALES FOR WRITING BLOGS

1. Format all posts for smooth page layout and easy scanning.
2. Column width should not be too wide, as larger lines of text can be difficult to read
3. Headings and subheadings separate text visually, enable scanning or skimming, and encourage continued reading.
4. Bullet-pointed or numbered lists enable quick information location and scanning.
5. Punctuation is critical, so beginners should use shorter sentences until confident in their knowledge of punctuation rules.
6. Blog paragraphs should be far shorter—two to six sentences each—than paragraphs written on paper to enable "chunking" because reading onscreen is more difficult.
7. Sans-serif fonts are usually clearer than serif fonts, and larger font sizes are better.
8. Highlight important material and draw attention with **boldface**, but avoid overuse. Avoid hard-to-read *italics* and ALL CAPITALS.
9. Include enough blank spaces: overly busy blogs tire eyes and brains. Images not only break up text but also emphasize and enhance text and can attract initial reader attention.
10. Use background colors judiciously to avoid distracting the eye or making it difficult to read.
11. Be consistent throughout posts, since people read them in different orders.
12. Tell a story with a beginning, middle, and end.

SPECIALIZED MODES OF WRITING

EDITORIALS

Editorials are articles in newspapers, magazines, and other serial publications. Editorials express an opinion or belief belonging to the majority of the publication's leadership. This opinion or belief generally refers to a specific issue, topic, or event. These articles are authored by a member, or a small number of members, of the publication's leadership and are often written to affect their readers, such as persuading them to adopt a stance or take a particular action.

RESUMES

Resumes are brief, but formal, documents that outline an individual's experience in a certain area. Resumes are most often used for job applications. Such resumes will list the applicant's work experience, certification, and achievements or qualifications related to the position. Resumes should only include the most pertinent information. They should also use strategic formatting to highlight the applicant's most impressive experiences and achievements, to ensure the document can be read quickly and easily, and to eliminate both visual clutter and excessive negative space.

REPORTS

Reports summarize the results of research, new methodology, or other developments in an academic or professional context. Reports often include details about methodology and outside influences and factors. However, a report should focus primarily on the results of the research or development. Reports are objective and deliver information efficiently, sacrificing style for clear and effective communication.

MEMORANDA

A memorandum, also called a memo, is a formal method of communication used in professional settings. Memoranda are printed documents that include a heading listing the sender and their job title, the recipient and their job title, the date, and a specific subject line. Memoranda often include an introductory section explaining the reason and context for the memorandum. Next, a memorandum includes a section with details relevant to the topic. Finally, the memorandum will conclude with a paragraph that politely and clearly defines the sender's expectations of the recipient.

Research Writing

RESEARCH WRITING

Writing for research is essentially writing to answer a question or a problem about a particular **research topic**. A **problem statement** is written to clearly define the problem with a topic before asking about how to solve the problem. A **research question** serves to ask what can be done to address the problem. Before a researcher should try to solve a problem, the researcher should spend significant time performing a **literature review** to find out what has already been learned about the topic and if there are already solutions in place. The literature review can help to re-evaluate the research question as well. If the question has not been thoroughly answered, then it is proper to do broader research to learn about the topic and build up the body of literature. If the literature review provides plenty of background, but no practical solutions to the problem, then the research question should be targeted at solving a problem more directly. After the research has been performed, a **thesis** can act as a proposal for a solution or as a recommendation to future researchers to continue to learn more about the topic. The thesis should then be supported by significant contributing evidence to help support the proposed solution.

EXAMPLE OF RESEARCH WRITING ELEMENTS

Topic	The general idea the research is about. This is usually broader than the problem itself. Example: Clean Water
Problem Statement	A problem statement is a brief, clear description of a problem with the topic. Example: Not all villages in third-world countries have ready access to clean water.
Research Question	A research question asks a specific question about what needs to be learned or done about the problem statement. Example: What can local governments do to improve access to clean water?
Literature Review	A review of the body of literature by the researcher to show what is already known about the topic and the problem. If the literature review shows that the research question has already been thoroughly answered, the researcher should consider changing problem statements to something that has not been solved.
Thesis	A brief proposal of a solution to a problem. Theses do not include their own support, but are supported by later evidence. Example: Local governments can improve access to clean water by installing sealed rain-water collection units.
Body Paragraphs	Paragraphs focused on the primary supporting evidence for the main idea of the thesis. There are usually three body paragraphs, but there can be more if needed.
Conclusion	A final wrap-up of the research project. The conclusion should reiterate the problem, question, thesis, and briefly mention how the main evidences support the thesis.

THE RESEARCH PROCESS

Researchers should prepare some information before gathering sources. Researchers who have chosen a **research question** should choose key words or names that pertain to their question. They should also identify what type of information and sources they are looking for. Researchers should consider whether secondary or primary sources will be most appropriate for their research project. As researchers find credible and appropriate sources, they should be prepared to adjust the scope of their research question or topic in response to the information and insights they gather.

USING SOURCES AND SYNTHESIZING INFORMATION

As researchers find potential sources for their research project, it is important to keep a **record** of the material they find and note how each source may impact their work. When taking these notes, researchers should keep their research question or outline in mind and consider how their chosen references would complement their discussion. **Literature reviews** and **annotated bibliographies** are helpful tools for evaluating sources, as they require the researcher to consider the qualities and offerings of the sources they choose to use. These tools also help researchers synthesize the information they find.

SYNTHESIZING INFORMATION

Synthesizing information requires the researcher to integrate sources and their own thoughts by quoting, paraphrasing, or summarizing outside information in their research project. Synthesizing information indicates that the research complements the writer's claims, ensures that the ideas in the composition flow logically, and makes including small details and quotes easier. Paraphrasing is one of the simplest ways to integrate a source. **Paraphrasing** allows the writer to support their ideas with research while presenting the information in their own words, rather than using the source's original wording. Paraphrasing also allows the writer to reference the source's main ideas instead of specific details. While paraphrasing does not require the writer to quote the source, it still entails a direct reference to the source, meaning that any paraphrased material still requires a citation.

CITING SOURCES

While researchers should combine research with their own ideas, the information and ideas that come from outside sources should be attributed to the author of the source. When conducting research, it is helpful to record the publication information for each source so that **citations** can be easily added within the composition. Keeping a close record of the source of each idea in a composition or project is helpful for avoiding plagiarism, as both direct and indirect references require documentation.

PLAGIARISM

Understanding what is considered to be plagiarism is important to preventing unintentional plagiarism. Using another person's work in any way without proper attribution is **plagiarism**. However, it is easy to mistakenly commit plagiarism by improperly citing a source or creating a citation that is not intended for the way the source was used. Even when an honest attempt to attribute information is made, small errors can still result in plagiarized content. For this reason, it is important to create citations carefully and review citations before submitting or publishing research. It is also possible to plagiarize one's own work. This occurs when a writer has published work with one title and purpose and then attempts to publish it again as new material under a new title or purpose.

LITERATURE REVIEW

One of the two main parts of a literature review is searching through existing literature. The other is actually writing the review. Researchers must take care not to get lost in the information and inhibit progress toward their research goal. A good precaution is to write out the research question and keep it nearby. It is also wise to make a search plan and establish a time limit in advance. Finding a seemingly endless number of references indicates a need to revisit the research question because the topic is too broad. Finding too little material means that the research topic is too narrow. With new or cutting-edge research, one may find that nobody has investigated this particular question. This requires systematic searching, using abstracts in periodicals for an overview of available literature, research papers or other specific sources to explore its reference, and references in books and other sources.

When searching published literature on a research topic, one must take thorough notes. It is common to find a reference that could be useful later in the research project, but is not needed yet. In situations like this, it is helpful to make a note of the reference so it will be easy to find later. These notes can be grouped in a word processing document, which also allows for easy compiling of links and quotes from internet research. Researchers should explore the internet regularly, view resources for their research often, learn how to use resources correctly and efficiently, experiment with resources available within the disciplines, open and examine databases, become familiar with reference desk materials, find publications with abstracts of articles and books on one's topic, use papers' references to locate the most useful journals and important authors, identify keywords for refining and narrowing database searches, and peruse library catalogues online for available sources—all while taking notes.

As one searches for references, one will gradually develop an overview of the body of literature available for his or her subject. This signals the time to prepare for writing the literature review. The researcher should assemble his or her notes along with copies of all the journal articles and all the books he or she has acquired. Then one should write the research question again at the top of a page and list below it all of the author names and keywords discovered while searching. It is also helpful to observe whether any groups or pairs of these stand out. These activities are parts of structuring one's literature review—the first step for writing a thesis, dissertation, or research paper. Writers should rewrite their work as necessary rather than expecting to write only one draft. However, stopping to edit along the way can distract from the momentum of writing the first draft. If the writer is dissatisfied with a certain part of the draft, it may be better to skip to a later portion of the paper and revisit the problem section at another time.

BODY AND CONCLUSION IN LITERATURE REVIEW

The first step of a literature review paper is to create a rough draft. The next step is to edit: rewrite for clarity, eliminate unnecessary verbiage, and change terminology that could confuse readers. After editing, a writer should ask others to read and give feedback. Additionally, the writer should read the paper aloud to hear how it sounds, editing as needed. Throughout a literature review, the writer should not only summarize and comment on each source reviewed, but should also relate these findings to the original research question. The writer should explicitly state in the conclusion how the research question and pertinent literature interaction is developed throughout the body, reflecting on insights gained through the process.

SUMMARIES AND ABSTRACTS

When preparing to submit or otherwise publish research, it may be necessary to compose a summary or abstract to accompany the research composition.

A summary is a brief description of the contents of a longer work that provides an overview of the work and may include its most important details. One common type of summary is an abstract. Abstracts are specialized summaries that are most commonly used in the context of research. Abstracts may include details such as the purpose for the research, the researcher's methodology, and the most significant results of the research. Abstracts sometimes include sections and headings, where most summaries are limited to one or a few paragraphs with no special groupings.

EDITING AND REVISING

After composing a rough draft of a research paper, the writer should **edit** it. The purpose of the paper is to communicate the answer to one's research question in an efficient and effective manner. The writing should be as **concise** and **clear** as possible, and the style should also be consistent. Editing is often easier to do after writing the first draft rather than during it, as taking time between writing and editing allows writers to be more objective. If the paper includes an abstract and an introduction, the writer should compose these after writing the rest, when he or she will have a better grasp of the theme and arguments. Not all readers understand technical terminology or long words, so writers should use these sparingly. Finally, writers should consult a writing and style guide to address any industry- or institution-specific issues that may arise as they edit.

Review Video: <u>Revising and Editing</u>
Visit mometrix.com/academy and enter code: 674181

Information Sources

PRIMARY SOURCES

In literature review, one may examine both primary and secondary sources. Primary sources contain original information that was witnessed, gathered, or otherwise produced by the source's author. **Primary sources** can include firsthand accounts, found in sources such as books, autobiographies, transcripts, speeches, videos, photos, and personal journals or diaries. Primary sources may also include records of information, such as government documents, or personally-conducted research in sources like reports and essays. They may be found in academic books, journals and other periodicals, and authoritative databases. Using primary sources allows researchers to develop their own conclusions about the subject. Primary sources are also reliable for finding information about a person or their personal accounts and experiences. Primary sources such as photos, videos, audio recordings, transcripts, and government documents are often reliable, as they are usually objective and can be used to confirm information from other sources.

SECONDARY SOURCES

Secondary sources are sources that reference information originally provided by another source. The original source may be cited, quoted, paraphrased, or described in a secondary source. **Secondary sources** may be articles, essays, videos, or books found in periodicals, magazines, newspapers, films, databases, or websites. A secondary source can be used to reference another researcher's analysis or conclusion from a primary source. This information can inform the researcher of the existing discussions regarding their subject. These types of sources may also support the researcher's claims by providing a credible argument that contributes to the researcher's argument. Secondary sources may also highlight connections between primary sources or criticize both primary and other secondary sources. These types of secondary sources are valuable because they provide information and conclusions the researcher may not have considered or found, otherwise.

> **Review Video: Primary and Secondary Sources**
> Visit mometrix.com/academy and enter code: 383328

TYPES OF SOURCES

- **Textbooks** are specialized materials that are designed to thoroughly instruct readers on a particular topic. Textbooks often include features such as a table of contents, visuals, an index, a glossary, headings, and practice questions and exercises.
- **Newspapers** are collections of several written pieces and are primarily used to distribute news stories to their audience. In addition to news articles, newspapers may also include advertisements or pieces meant to entertain their audience, such as comic strips, columns, and letters from readers. Newspapers are written for a variety of audiences, as they are published on both the local and national levels.
- **Manuals** are instructional documents that accompany a product or explain an important procedure. Manuals include a table of contents, guidelines, and instructional content. Instructional manuals often include information about safe practices, risks, and product warranty. The instructions in manuals are often presented as step-by-step instructions, as they are meant to help users properly use a product or complete a task.

- **Electronic texts** are written documents that are read digitally and are primarily accessed online or through a network. Many electronic texts have characteristics similar to printed texts, such as a table of contents, publication information, a main text, and supplemental materials. However, electronic texts are more interactive and can be navigated more quickly. Electronic texts can also provide more accessibility, as they can be easily resized or narrated by text-to-speech software.

FINDING SOURCES

Finding sources for a research project may be intimidating or difficult. There are numerous sources available, and several research tools to help researchers find them. Starting with one of these tools can help narrow down the number of sources a researcher is working with at one time.

- **Libraries** house independent, printed publications that are organized by subject. This makes finding sources easy, since researchers can visit sections with sources relevant to their topic and immediately see what sources are available. Many libraries also offer printed journals and collections that include sources related to a common subject or written by the same author.
- **Databases** offer digital access to sources from a wide variety of libraries and online containers. To use a database, users search for keywords related to their topic or the type of source they want to use. The database then lists results related to or featuring those key words. Users can narrow their results using filters that will limit their results based on factors such as publication year, source type, or whether the sources are peer-reviewed. Database search results also list individual articles and methods of accessing the article directly. While databases help users find sources, they do not guarantee users access to each source.
- **Academic Journals** are collections of articles that cover a particular topic or fit within a certain category. These journals are often offered both online and in print. Academic journals typically contain peer-reviewed works or works that have undergone another type of reviewing process.

CREDIBILITY

There are innumerable primary and secondary sources available in print and online. However, not every published or posted source is appropriate for a research project. When finding sources, the researcher must know how to evaluate each source for credibility and relevance. Not only must the sources be reliable and relevant to the research subject, but they must also be appropriate and help form an answer to the research question. As researchers progress in their research and composition, the relevance of each source will become clear. Appropriate sources will contribute valuable information and arguments to the researcher's own thoughts and conclusions, providing useful evidence to bolster the researcher's claims. The researcher has the freedom to choose which sources they reference or even change their research topic and question in response to the sources they find. However, the researcher should not use unreliable sources, and determining a source's credibility is not always easy.

CONSIDERATIONS FOR EVALUATING THE CREDIBILITY OF A SOURCE
- The author and their purpose for writing the source
- The author's qualifications to write on the topic
- Whether the source is peer-reviewed or included in a scholarly publication
- The publisher
- The target audience

- The jargon or dialect the source is written in (e.g., academic, technical)
- The presence of bias or manipulation of information
- The date of publication
- The author's use of other sources to support their claims
- Whether any outside sources are cited appropriately in the source
- The accuracy of information presented

AUTHOR'S PURPOSE AND CREDIBILITY

Knowing who wrote a source and why they wrote it is important to determine whether a source is appropriate for a research project. The author should be qualified to write on the subject of the material. Their purpose may be to inform their audience of information, to present and defend an analysis, or even to criticize a work or other argument. The researcher must decide whether the author's purpose makes the source appropriate to use. The source's container and publisher are important to note because they indicate the source's reputability and whether other qualified individuals have reviewed the information in the source. Credible secondary sources should also reference other sources, primary or secondary, that support or inform the source's content. Evaluating the accuracy of the information or the presence of bias in a source will require careful reading and critical thinking on the part of the researcher. However, a source with excellent credentials may still contain pieces of inaccurate information or bias, so it is the researcher's responsibility to be careful in their use of each source.

INTEGRATING REFERENCES AND QUOTATIONS

In research papers, one can include studies whose conclusions agree with one's position (Reed 284; Becker and Fagen 93), as well as studies that disagree (Limbaugh 442, Beck 69) by including parenthetical citations as demonstrated in this sentence. Quotations should be selective: writers should compose an original sentence and incorporate only a few words from a research source. If students cannot use more original words than quotation, they are likely padding their compositions. However, including quotations appropriately increases the credibility of the writer and their argument.

PROPERLY INTEGRATING QUOTATIONS

When using sources in a research paper, it is important to integrate information so that the flow of the composition is not interrupted as the two compositions are combined. When quoting outside sources, it is necessary to lead into the quote and ensure that the whole sentence is logical, is grammatically correct, and flows well. Below is an example of an incorrectly integrated quote.

> During the Industrial Revolution, many unions organized labor strikes "child labor, unregulated working conditions, and excessive working hours" in America.

Below is the same sentence with a properly integrated quote.

> During the Industrial Revolution, many unions organized labor strikes to protest the presence of "child labor, unregulated working conditions, and excessive working hours" in America.

In the first example, the connection between "strikes" and the quoted list is unclear. In the second example, the phrase "to protest the presence of" link the ideas together and successfully creates a suitable place for the quotation.

When quoting sources, writers should work quotations and references seamlessly into their sentences instead of interrupting the flow of their own argument to summarize a source.

152

Summarizing others' content is often a ploy to bolster word counts. Writing that analyzes the content, evaluates it, and synthesizes material from various sources demonstrates critical thinking skills and is thus more valuable.

PROPERLY INCORPORATING OUTSIDE SOURCES

Writers do better to include short quotations rather than long. For example, quoting six to eight long passages in a 10-page paper is excessive. It is also better to avoid wording like "This quotation shows," "As you can see from this quotation," or "It talks about." These are amateur, feeble efforts to interact with other authors' ideas. Also, writing about sources and quotations wastes words that should be used to develop one's own ideas. Quotations should be used to stimulate discussion rather than taking its place. Ending a paragraph, section, or paper with a quotation is not incorrect per se, but using it to prove a point, without including anything more in one's own words regarding the point or subject, suggests a lack of critical thinking about the topic and consideration of multiple alternatives. It can also be a tactic to dissuade readers from challenging one's propositions. Writers should include references and quotations that challenge as well as support their thesis statements. Presenting evidence on both sides of an issue makes it easier for reasonably skeptical readers to agree with a writer's viewpoint.

CITING SOURCES

Formal research writers must **cite all sources used**—books, articles, interviews, conversations, and anything else that contributed to the research. One reason is to **avoid plagiarism** and give others credit for their ideas. Another reason is to help readers find the sources consulted in the research and access more information about the subject for further reading and research. Additionally, citing sources helps to make a paper academically authoritative. To prepare, research writers should keep a running list of sources consulted, in an electronic file or on file cards. For every source used, the writer needs specific information. For books, a writer needs to record the author's and editor's names, book title, publication date, city, and publisher name. For articles, one needs the author's name, article title, journal (or magazine or newspaper) name, volume and issue number, publication date, and page numbers. For electronic resources, a writer will need the author's name, article information plus the URL, database name, name of the database's publisher, and the date of access.

COMMON REFERENCE STYLES

Three common reference styles are **MLA** (Modern Language Association), **APA** (American Psychological Association), and **Turabian** (created by author Kate Turabian, also known as the Chicago Manual of Style). Each style formats citation information differently. Professors and instructors often specify that students use one of these. Generally, APA style is used in psychology and sociology papers, and MLA style is used in English literature papers and similar scholarly projects. To understand how these styles differ, consider an imaginary article cited in each of these styles. This article is titled "Ten Things You Won't Believe Dragons Do," written by author Andra Gaines, included in the journal *Studies in Fantasy Fiction*, and published by Quest for Knowledge Publishing.

MLA:

Gaines, Andra. "Ten Things You Won't Believe Dragons Do." Studies in Fantasy Fiction, vol. 3, no. 8, Quest for Knowledge Publishing, 21 Aug. 2019.

APA:

Gaines, A. (2019). Ten Things You Won't Believe Dragons Do. *Studies in Fantasy Fiction*, *3(8)*, 42-65.

Gaines, Andra. "Ten Things You Won't Believe Dragons Do," *Studies in Fantasy Fiction* 3, no. 8 (2019): 42-65.

Within each of these styles, citations, though they vary according to the type of source and how its used, generally follow a structure and format similar to those above. For example, citations for whole books will probably not include a container title or a volume number, but will otherwise look very similar.

> **Review Video: <u>Citing Sources</u>**
> Visit mometrix.com/academy and enter code: 993637

Copyright © Mometrix Media. You have been licensed one copy of this document for personal use only. Any other reproduction or redistribution is strictly prohibited. All rights reserved. This content is provided for test preparation purposes only and does not imply an endorsement by Mometrix of any particular political, scientific, or religious point of view.

MTTC Practice Test

Want to take this practice test in an online interactive format?
Check out the bonus page, which includes interactive practice questions and
much more: **mometrix.com/bonus948/mttclanartelem**

1. Which of the following students may need extra instruction and evaluation with respect to oral language skills?

   a. Rosa: whose first language is Spanish. Rosa speaks with a distinct accent and can be difficult to understand when speaking about a new or unfamiliar topic.
   b. Greer: who avoids oral assignments when possible. He avoids speaking up in class and only responds when called upon.
   c. Ashley: who often has trouble answering questions in class. Her responses are often off-topic. She also struggles with oral presentations, seeming to present a string of unrelated facts.
   d. Brett: who frequently becomes loud and disruptive whenever group work is assigned. He often becomes involved in heated discussions with classmates when discussing ideas.

2. Mr. Callas is introducing a unit on oral traditions from around the world. He wants his seventh-grade students to gain a better understanding of the relationship between written text and oral language, as well as increase their multi-cultural understanding. Which of the following assignments would be the most relevant?

   a. "Read Chapter 12 on Oral Traditions and complete the end-of-chapter review."
   b. "Select a poem or song from a culture around the world and recite it for the class."
   c. "Conduct a poll of twenty fellow students, asking about their family's country of origin. Present a graph or diagram of your results in class."
   d. "Choose a country to research and write a first-person narrative about a typical day in the life of one of its citizens. The narratives will be read in class."

3. Which of the following exercises would be the most appropriate tool for helping students evaluate the effectiveness of their own spoken messages?

   a. Discuss written and oral assignments in class before completing them. Once the assignments are completed, the teacher meets individually with each student to discuss the content and effectiveness of each student's work.
   b. Instruct students to present oral reports in class, which are then "graded" by classmates. A score of 1-10 is assigned based on students' perception of the reports' clarity. The student's average score determines his report's effectiveness.
   c. Ask each student to prepare an oral report and a content quiz that highlights the report's main idea. The student then uses classmates' scores on the reviews to determine his report's effectiveness.
   d. Put students into groups of three. Two students complete a role-playing assignment based on prompts provided by the teacher. The third student gives constructive feedback on how the other two can refine and clarify their speech.

155

Use the following information to answer the next two questions.

> Mr. Gilbert teaches fourth graders whose reading skills range from emergent to advanced. He introduces an activity called "Book Buddies" in which his students are paired with emerging Kindergarten readers to practice reading beginner-level short books. He hopes they will gain confidence and increase their own reading skills through these visits. Mr. Gilbert's students pick their Book Buddies up once a week and read together for about half an hour.

4. What aspect of this program is most likely to increase all of the fourth-graders' oral language skills?
   a. Finding opportunities to explain unfamiliar ideas or sound out new words with the younger students.
   b. Spending time with younger students and being reminded of how much they have learned in the past three years.
   c. Being exposed to different kinds of reading texts.
   d. Practicing their decoding skills and increasing their vocabulary.

5. What might be the best way to adapt the Book Buddy program for fourth grade students who are still learning English?
   a. Exempt ESOL students from the program altogether so that they can practice reading with their primary teacher.
   b. Create some groups that have three Book Buddies: a skilled reader, an ESOL student, and a Kindergartener; this will allow the English language learner to listen, learn, and give guidance when he is able.
   c. Make no changes to the program and simply allow the younger students and the English language learner to help each other decode and compare ideas in their own way.
   d. Allow English language learners to listen to books on tape read by native English speakers with their Kindergarten partners.

6. Mr. Campbell begins each Language Arts lesson with the "Phrase of the Day." This phrase ranges from analogies to idioms to snippets of figurative language. His students use their journals to explain what they think the phrase means and to draw a picture, also. Mr. Campbell then reveals the phrase's true meaning, which the children record on the same page as their own interpretations. When he reviews these pages in the students' journals, Mr. Campbell is most likely to:
   a. Check to ensure that each student is diligently recording both their own interpretations and the correct interpretations.
   b. Use the mechanics and spelling errors within to help him design test questions and worksheets.
   c. Grade the pages for originality and humor.
   d. Use them to informally assess students' oral language skills.

7. Which of the following activities would incorporate the best use of technology to increase students' oral language skills?

    a. Students visit the school computer lab to work on math and science activities with software that utilizes voice-recognition technology in an interactive process.

    b. Students use an internet program and computer camera to converse with English-speaking students in other countries.

    c. Students can visit the classroom's Language Lab, in which there are tape recorders and CD players. Students can use these players to listen to novels, poetry, and other literary works on tape.

    d. A teacher videotapes a class discussion about a story and replays it for the students to watch and discuss.

8. Every year, students prepare with excitement for Historical Characters Day. Each student is expected to choose a character who was influential in years past and compose a report on why he was important. The students are permitted to dress up as their respective characters on the day on which the reports are turned in. This year, the teachers want to incorporate an aspect of this anticipated event that will more directly increase their students' oral communication skills. Of the options they have brainstormed, which of the following would be most helpful?

    a. Ask the students to read their reports aloud to the class.

    b. Require that the reports be memorized so that students can make better use of voice modulation and eye contact while presenting.

    c. Require the students to write why they chose their character and three interesting things they learned on a set note cards, and present what they have written to the class.

    d. Hold an election for the student with the most realistic costume and require students to give supporting evidence for their votes.

Use the information below to answer the questions 9 and 10:

A middle school teacher consistently includes "the Daily Chat" in her lesson plans, several times a week. Students are placed into pairs, with the occasional group of three. The teacher chooses one student during each chat with whom she will partner. During these conversations, students can pick a topic and discuss it for five to ten minutes. They are asked to use the following log sheet:

Date:

Name:

Partner's Name:

☐ My partner looked at me most of the time while we were speaking.

☐ My partner listened while I was speaking.

☐ My partner waited until I finished before taking his turn to speak.

☐ My partner enunciated while speaking (I understood the words he was saying).

☐ My partner explained himself well (I understood the ideas behind what he was saying).

9. Which skill is least likely to be improved by this activity?
   a. Active listening; students listen for the purpose of understanding and responding appropriately.
   b. Speaking clearly; students practice speaking in ways that can be easily heard and understood.
   c. Nonverbal communication skills; students communicate engagement in conversation through body language, etc.
   d. Oral conflict resolution; students can resolve disagreements using their verbal skills.

10. What is the most likely purpose for the teacher to partner with a new student during each Daily Chat?
   a. She wants to make sure that the students get positive feedback on a regular basis during skill-building exercises.
   b. She has found that there are almost always absent students, creating a space for her to function as a partner during days where one student lacks a partner.
   c. She recognizes the value of building oral communication skills with adults as well as peers.
   d. She wants to demonstrate how to resolve conflicts or common problems that students often face when attempting to communicate effectively.

11. The eighth-grade class will be holding class elections in the fall as part of an integrated Social Studies and English unit. The students will be studying government elections and modeling their process based on their studies. The candidates for Vice President and President will debate pre-determined issues in front of their class using modified rules found in formal debates (i.e. they are timed and will use a moderator). Which of the following exercises would be most beneficial to introduce in English class to help prepare each student for the debates?

    a. Watch recordings of Presidential and Vice Presidential debates from years past and model their speech from what they have heard.

    b. Create multiple opportunities for students to discuss the pre-determined issues in class, allowing for free-flowing dialogue and differing opinions.

    c. Students write their thoughts in short-essay format so that each section can be read aloud during the appropriate part of the debate.

    d. Students determine a position on each selected issue and assign it to a note card or small piece of paper. On each card, they record two to three reasons or supporting ideas for the opinion.

12. A teacher wants to work on her students' listening comprehension in addition to their reading comprehension, since she understands that the skills are interrelated. She has a series of short stories that she thinks the students will enjoy. Which of the following would be the best supplement to typical written comprehension exercises?

    a. Preview content and then read the stories aloud to the students. Assess listening comprehension through verbal and written questions.

    b. Ask the students to choose one story each to read aloud to a small group. Encourage the students to discuss what they have learned afterward.

    c. Assign each student a story to read and require them to write a report on it. Each student should then present his report based on what he has learned to the class.

    d. Have the students read stories aloud to the class, and create mock tests based upon the main ideas which they identify.

13. Ms. Walters wants to help her brand-new group of still-emergent fourth-grade students build comprehension skills. Which of the following exercises would be the best way to quickly gauge the students' current comprehension levels during the first week of class?

    a. Provide the students with instruction-level text to be read independently. Hold an in-class discussion about what happened in the story.

    b. Read a story aloud to the class and then ask each student to draw three pictures representing the beginning, middle and end of the story.

    c. Put students into group or pairs to read the story aloud. Each group then collaborates to answer the story review questions.

    d. Have each student re-tell the story to the class in his own words.

14. Which of the following strategies would not be helpful in building the word-identification skills of emergent readers?

    a. Allowing for invented spelling in written assignments or in-class work

    b. Reinforcing phonemic awareness while reading aloud

    c. Using dictionaries to look up unfamiliar words

    d. Studying and reviewing commonly used sight words at the students' ability level

15. Mrs. Harris is pleased that her fifth-graders are showing progress in their reading comprehension and writing skills. The students are performing very well on their written tests, evaluations, and homework. After the holiday break, she wants to design lessons that increase the students' literacy skills by incorporating multiple contexts. Which of the following might be the best way to do this?

a. Read their next book aloud and discuss it in class.
b. Have the students quiz one another in small groups on the content of their textbooks and other reading assignments.
c. Read a play in class and allow the students to act it out for their peers following their unit test.
d. Administer spelling and vocabulary tests orally to determine students' verbal skills.

16. Which of the following would be most useful in assessing and documenting students' language progress throughout a school year?

a. An audio/video recording of each student reading the same text at the beginning of the year and again at the end of the year
b. A portfolio including pre-tests, post-tests, vocabulary work, journal entries, writing assignments, group projects and other relevant work from throughout the year
c. Score composites and details from state- and national-referenced exams or other standardized tests.
d. A detailed narrative composed by the student's teacher, detailing strengths, weaknesses, and descriptions of the student's work.

17. Valeria is a bright sixth-grader who struggles with reading fluency. She comes from a predominantly Spanish-speaking home and has only lived in the United States for two years. Her teacher plans to use the guided oral reading strategy to help increase Valeria's reading skills. Which of the following would not be a part of this strategy?

a. Valeria is partnered with another student who is also struggling with language fluency in class.
b. Valeria's partner reads a given text aloud and then gives her a chance to read the text silently several times.
c. Valeria reads the text aloud three to four times.
d. Valeria's partner gives encouragement and feedback.

18. Mr. Waleran requires his students of all ability levels to write freely in their journals twice a week. While students are encouraged to use proper spelling and mechanics as much as possible, the purpose behind this activity is to encourage students to express themselves through writing without concern for grading parameters. How should he adapt this activity for Dimitri, who has several academic delays that keep him from reading and writing in legible or coherent ways?

a. Allow Dimitri to dictate his thoughts to another student or teacher who will then record them into his journal in writing.
b. Encourage Dimitri to draw pictures in his journal that represent his thoughts, and encourage him to use the words he knows to label or describe the pictures.
c. Tell Dimitri to keep an audio journal at home, using a personal tape recorder.
d. Require Dimitri to attempt to write in complete sentences as much as he can, and then edit the journal together for spelling and mechanical errors.

19. A teacher reads to her students at least once a week. This month, she plans to read poetry to her class. The students will then discuss what they have heard for the rest of each class period. What is this teacher's most likely purpose in designing these lessons?

    a. To give students a break from extensive reading requirements.
    b. To build phonological awareness, specifically of rhyming words.
    c. To teach students that there is more to literature than prose.
    d. To increase students' listening skills while exposing them to new kinds of literature.

20. Mrs. Taylor is working with a diverse group of fifth-graders. She introduces a lesson and project that students can work on once they have finished their regular class work. Students may visit a section of the classroom where they can listen to a lesson via headphones on ancient Egyptian hieroglyphics and look at various library books on the subject. Students are then expected to create their own hieroglyphics that they can use to tell a short story. Which of the following skills is not built with this project?

    a. Understanding of various kinds of written expression, including non-alphabetic languages.
    b. Building multi-cultural awareness that will increase understanding between students of different backgrounds.
    c. Reading for purposes of information or new knowledge (i.e. 'reading to learn').
    d. Exposure to various media to build literacy skills across all levels of reading ability.

21. Each week, a teacher asks one student to bring in a recording of his favorite song and a written version of the lyrics. The students listen to the song and receive a copy of the lyrics. They discuss these words as either one large group or in small groups. What are these students probably learning from this exercise?

    a. Students are learning about the lives of their peers indirectly by listening to each student's favorite song; they can begin to understand each other by the meaning behind the song lyrics.
    b. Students are learning that they are very diverse in many ways: they have different musical tastes and prefer many different styles of music and expression.
    c. Students are learning that it is very difficult to communicate freely when bound by various musical traits such as rhyming, rhythm, and phrasing.
    d. Students are learning that literacy skills do not just pertain to schoolwork. These skills allow students to understand and communicate meanings through a variety of ways, including music and lyrics.

22. A teacher notices that one of her students is inconsistent with recalling his letter-sounds. He may remember a particular sound or blend one day and read it correctly; however, the next day, he may not be able to produce the same sound. What should she do?

    a. Immediately refer the student to the appropriate professional for educational testing since it is likely that he is exhibiting early signs of a learning difference or disability.
    b. Recognize that children all learn at different rates and that learning and producing letter-sounds involve multiple mental processes. Give the student as much time as he needs to internalize the sounds and produce them correctly.
    c. Provide the student with targeted instruction in letter-sound correspondence, using a schema such as Alphabet Action, in which letter-sounds are associated with physical actions (e.g., C is for Catch). Set a time frame after which, if the student does not improve, to begin the procedure for special-needs testing.
    d. Hold a conference with the child's parents and encourage them to seek outside tutoring or professional assistance with his reading skills.

23. Mrs. Bundy has three groups of students in her fifth-grade English class: those who want to answer every question, those who only speak when spoken to, and those who never speak at all. She is making plans for upcoming lessons and thinks about the last group of children who never speak up in class. What is important for Mrs. Bundy to know and do with respect to these students?

a. Know that some students are simply quiet and do not feel comfortable speaking up in class. As long as the children are completing their work accurately, do not be concerned about them.

b. Speak with those students after or before class. Let them know how important it is to express themselves in class, because that is part of what building literacy is all about.

c. Make a point to speak directly to those students who talk less in class. Limit the amount of time the more verbal students can speak in class and require the quieter students to answer more direct questions and prompts.

d. Place students who don't speak up in class together for group work. Make a point to spend time with those groups to give guidance and encouragement as they express their ideas verbally.

24. Some of the students in Mr. Smith's fourth-grade class cannot decode words well enough to read fluently in class. He knows they are well behind grade level and that he needs to provide them with activities that will allow them to be successful, building skills and confidence at the same time. Which activity would be best for this purpose?

a. Enlist the parents' help by sending home a weekly list of sight words that the students can practice and memorize, decreasing the need to decode when they read.

b. Show the students how to create words out of movable alphabet tiles or magnetic letters, building (encoding) words as they sound them out.

c. Provide the children with early childhood readers that contain only very simple words so that the children will not feel badly as they read.

d. Allow those children having trouble to stop each time they reach a challenging word and sound it out carefully, recording it to a list that will be studied for homework.

25. Which of the following statements is true regarding the relationship of reading fluency to reading comprehension?

a. Reading fluency and reading comprehension should be considered separate, equally valuable skills that can be taught independently of one another.

b. Reading comprehension is an important component of achieving a level of overall reading fluency.

c. Reading fluency refers to a set of skills that should be continually improved upon, so that students can consistently comprehend that which they read.

d. Reading comprehension and reading fluency are so intertwined that a child struggling in one area is often incapable of making progress in the other.

26. Abi, a fifth-grader, is reading aloud to his teacher during one-on-one reading time. His teacher uses this time to evaluate ongoing fluency and comprehension skills. Following today's reading, Abi's teacher determines that he needs practice with words that begin with digraphs. Which of the following sets of words would most likely be part of this assignment?

a. Chicken, Shells, That

b. Were, Frame, Click

c. Sponge, Think, Blank

d. Packed, Blistered, Smoothed

27. Which of the following generally would not be expected of an eighth-grader?

a. Identify grade-level vocabulary words and be able to decode their roots, prefixes, and suffixes, as well as non-English words that are commonly used in English writing (e.g. phenomenon, charisma, etc.).

b. Analyze literary works and identify common themes in various pieces of literature.

c. Understand different points of view in literature (e.g. omniscient, subjective)

d. Explain how media messages are reflective of the literature in cultures from which they originate.

28. Which of the following reading skills might be most helpful for Susannah?

Susannah wrote the following journal entry on her happiest memory during journal time:

I lov going on picnics with my mom and dad. We et sandwitches and lemanad and somtyms mom and dad drink coffee. we play gams and haf fun.

a. Decoding work focusing on silent ending phonemes.

b. Sight word drills and practice.

c. Reading aloud to a partner who gives constructive feedback.

d. More spelling practice using original sentences.

29. A teacher writes four sentences on the board and instructs his students to copy the sentences from the board into their notebooks. They must capitalize words with suffixes. Which sentence is correct?

a. The PRINCE declared his undying love for the PRINCESS.

b. Television is a form of MULTIMEDIA.

c. This loud, loud noise is very DISPLEASING.

d. The BOOKKEEPER examined every page of the rare play.

30. Which of the following computer activities/games would be most beneficial during media time for students who are working on reading fluency?

a. Students can select from a variety of high-interest texts and read aloud what they see on the screen.

b. Students hear high-frequency sight and vocabulary words in their headphones and get points for "zapping" (clicking) the correct matching word on their screen.

c. Students practice typing in a keyboarding program to build their speed and accuracy in writing reports and papers.

d. Students can surf a limited and pre-approved number of internet sites to read on subjects of their choosing.

31. A teacher is fortunate to have many parent volunteers for the current school year, giving him parental help at least three times a week. He wants to utilize these volunteers in a way that will not only take into account their limited training, but will most benefit students. Which option should he choose?

a. Ask each parent to speak to the class about what kinds of literacy skills they use each day in their careers.

b. Enlist parents to help grade papers and presentations using a rubric.

c. Ask parents to listen to his students read challenging but manageable texts, one at a time, helping students identify and sound out unfamiliar words.

d. Primarily utilize parents' for non-instructional tasks, such as making copies, organizing the class library, monitoring the classroom during test time, etc.

32. Which of the following aspects of oral reading is the most important accompaniment to speed and accuracy?

    a. Vocal expression based on punctuation and content.
    b. Volume of the reader's/speaker's voice.
    c. Interest level of the text to be read aloud.
    d. Consistently increasing the number of words read aloud per minute.

33. Which of the following activities is widely used in building students' reading fluency?

    a. Sole focus on phonetic instruction.
    b. Repeated oral readings combined with feedback.
    c. Participation in vocabulary-building activities.
    d. Utilizing speed-reading techniques often used in adult literacy courses.

34. In monitoring a group of elementary-age students' reading fluency, which of the following students may need extra or specialized instruction?

    a. A student who reads an unfamiliar text more slowly than he reads a familiar text.
    b. A student reading an independent-level text, finding approximately 1 in 25 words difficult to read.
    c. A student reading an instructional-level text, finding approximately 1 in 5 words difficult to read.
    d. A student who scores a 70% on a comprehension test.

35. Which of the following reading assignments would be most appropriate as a context for teaching students how to preview information to improve comprehension?

    a. A written version of a popular movie that most of the students have seen outside of class.
    b. A reading assignment from the students' science class that they will be tested on next month.
    c. A novel the students read in English class last year.
    d. A set of poems that will be studied next month during Poetry Week.

36. A sixth-grade teacher is preparing to begin a unit in which students will be reading a novel in class. She plans to use the novel to teach her students specific strategies to improve and monitor their reading comprehension. Which of the following techniques would likely be taught during class?

    a. Discuss story elements such as exposition, climax and resolution.
    b. Demonstrate the practice of stopping at the end of chapters to summarize and review the content.
    c. Ask students to complete a review sheet before taking the unit test.
    d. Practice decoding unfamiliar words throughout the book by using knowledge of frequently-used root words.

37. A teacher notices that her new student, Carl, has a hard time answering questions related to comprehension during class and has scored low on comprehension quizzes and worksheets. What would be the most logical first step in determining how to help Carl?

a. Encourage Carl to read all assigned texts at least twice before class to help him understand what he has read.

b. Provide Carl with story maps of what he will be reading to assist his comprehension visually.

c. Ask Carl to read aloud with his teacher individually so that she can ensure that he is reading with expected accuracy and speed (i.e., fluently).

d. Modify Carl's class work so that he is able to work on easier comprehension material until his skills are brought up to speed.

38. Which of the following would be the best strategy for helping eighth-grade students choose books that they will read independently and use to write book reports?

a. Provide two choices from which the students can pick that you know everybody can understand.

b. Allow students to freely pick their books, but require that they read a few pages aloud to you in order to ensure that the reading level is neither too easy nor too difficult based on their abilities.

c. Encourage the students to read a book that contains unfamiliar words and idioms so that they will be challenged to use context clues, dictionaries and other sources to build comprehension.

d. Establish no parameters on book selection to encourage free choice and promote students' excitement about the project.

39. Which of the following students is not performing "at grade level" and may warrant academic support or testing?

a. Karishma, seventh grade, looks panicked and becomes very quiet when asked to state her opinion about a particular subject in class discussions and rarely raises her hand when a question about text comprehension is posed.

b. Lynne, fifth grade, is able to comprehend most of what she reads in plays and in fiction, but sometimes has trouble understanding poetry.

c. Barron, sixth grade, can read fluently aloud and often recall concrete facts, but is rarely able to draw conclusions, make inferences, or understand figurative language.

d. Sebastien, eighth grade, lacks motivation to read much of what is assigned in class and frequently fails to complete his homework; he often contributes intelligently to class discussions.

Use the following information to answer questions 40 and 41:

> Autumn must be the most enchanting season of all. The wind takes on a _____ chill that, when inhaled, ____ with the scent of ____ wood to lightly and_____singe your throat! Statuesque ___ seem to erupt into ___ blooms of colors seen ____ no other time, except _____ inside boxes of children's ____. For many people, the ____of camping, cookouts, sports, ___school creates warm, tingling ___ of security as the _____ slowly turns from Summer _____Fall. There is no other day in the year like the first day of Autumn.

40. The passage above is an example of what kind of reading comprehension assessment?
   a. Vocabulary Memorization Test
   b. Cloze Individual Assessment
   c. Student Response Form
   d. Figurative Language Assessment

41. In determining his students' reading comprehension levels, a teacher uses the above passage. He finds that about half of Anne's answers make sense in the blanks. Which answer choice describes the level at which Anne is reading the text?
   a. instructional level
   b. independent level
   c. frustration level
   d. novice level

42. Which of the following practices would assist students in constructing meaning from a fictional text written long before the students were born?
   a. After the text is read for homework, students discuss any aspects of the story that they did not understand or that were unfamiliar to them.
   b. Students individually visualize scenery and events in the text as they read.
   c. The class makes a list of unfamiliar words in the text and looks them up in the dictionary as the text is read.
   d. Before the text is assigned, students learn about pertinent historical events or aspects of culture that informed the writing of the text.

43. Which of the following strategies would be most appropriate for increasing comprehension before reading a chapter book without pictures?
   a. Previewing the chapter titles and identifying questions that would be answered by reading.
   b. Predicting the ending of the story after reading the introduction and first chapter of the book.
   c. Discussing what the students have heard from other individuals about the story.
   d. Researching and reading book reviews to get an idea of what experts have said about the story.

44. Which of these sets of factors would most greatly affect a student's reading comprehension in class and on tests?
   a. Oral language development, written language development and eating a healthy breakfast.
   b. Word analysis skills, sight word knowledge and ability to monitor understanding.
   c. Vocabulary development, sight word knowledge and reference skills.
   d. Prior knowledge, good classroom participation and academic performance in other subjects.

45. A teacher assigns a project in which students must compare excerpts from the Charles Dickens novel they are reading in class and an article from the week's newspaper. The teacher has chosen a specific passage from the novel. The students can choose the newspaper excerpts, as long as they are of similar lengths. The students must then write a short essay comparing the two. What is this teacher hoping to show her students?

    a. That Dickens' writing style is journalistic and that he informed much of what is considered to be current journalistic philosophy.

    b. That there are links between the students' lives and what they read in class; the relationships are there if they make an effort to see them.

    c. That you can compare even two unlike things.

    d. That there are distinct differences between the way meaning is constructed in daily life and in literature; different processes must be applied.

46. A seventh-grade teacher wants to encourage her students to read more for pleasure. She knows that the students' comprehension, vocabulary and writing skills will also be improved by reading more frequently. What is the best way to increase the amount of time students spend reading for pleasure?

    a. Assign "extra-credit" in which students can write a book report on a favorite book they read as a child.

    b. Increase the number of books and poems included in each unit of study.

    c. Ask the students to read a text of their choosing (e.g., a magazine, comic book, internet source, novel) each week and present to the class what they enjoyed about it.

    d. Have each student make a list of books they would like to read someday and then create a timeline for when they want to complete each one.

47. Students in Mr. Carmen's class receive a list of words each month that make up their spelling and vocabulary work. They are expected to write the words in original sentences to help them remember spellings and meanings of each one. Mr. Carmen also, however, wants to build the students' vocabulary using indirect learning styles. Which of the following would not contribute to learning vocabulary indirectly?

    a. Assigning more complex "bonus words" each month that can be written and defined for extra credit.

    b. Expecting students to read a weekly newspaper.

    c. Watching an instructional-level video in class and discussing any unknown words.

    d. Asking students to complete a series of short interviews with adults in their lives.

48. Which of the following vocabulary activities would best prepare students for a unit on imagery and figurative language?

    a. A class discussion on the difference between literal and inferential comprehension.

    b. A worksheet on synonyms and antonyms.

    c. A set of word games (e.g., crosswords, word searches) involving adjectives and adverbs.

    d. A vocabulary quiz

Use the following information to answer questions 49 and 50:

A class considers the paragraph below:

Sarah and Kelly grinned at one another conspiratorially as they approached Dad, who was quietly reading his paper in the living room. "Dad, we'd like to ride our bikes down to Emil's house today," giggled Kelly. She glanced at her sister and shifted her weight from foot to foot. Dad appeared to think this over for a moment and replied, "Sure, that's fine with me!" The girls scampered to get their bikes and were soon on their way. With the children gone, Dad noticed how peaceful and quiet the house sounded. His reverie was quickly interrupted as he heard Mom calling from upstairs, "okay, everybody, I told you at breakfast that I need as much help as I can get to help me give the dog a bath, clean the house and finish the laundry today!" Dad groaned, knowing that he had been conned!

49. Which method would be best for helping students determine the meaning of the word "reverie" in the next to last sentence?

    a. Using context clues
    b. Making an educated guess
    c. Decoding the prefix, root, and suffix of the word
    d. Previewing and reviewing

50. Which of the following questions, when assigned as an in-class writing topic, would allow the teacher to monitor the children's inferential comprehension?

    a. What do you think the girls plan to do at Emil's once they arrive?
    b. What does it mean to say that Dad had been "conned?"
    c. Why is it important for everyone to help Mom with the chores?
    d. What did Dad enjoy so much while he was reading?

51. Which of the following choices shows the correct type of text matched with an appropriate strategy for increasing reading comprehension?

    a. Popular magazine: critical analysis/deconstruction
    b. Literary novel: key concept synthesis
    c. Persuasive essay: journaling over time, recording personal thoughts about the reading
    d. Chapter from science textbook: text outlining with vocabulary and main ideas

52. Students in an eighth grade class examine this vocabulary list on Monday. Which literary genre is likely to be introduced this week?

Vocabulary:
Narrative
Heroism
Ancient
Martyr
Duality
Supernatural
Deity
Culture

a. Historical Fiction
b. Poetry
c. Mythology
d. Drama

53. Which question below applies most closely to data analysis skills for Mrs. Layton's fifth-graders?

Our Hobbies	
Reading	8
Soccer	4
Dance	3
Art	10
Music	9
Video Games	2

a. How many students in all reported their hobbies in this chart?
b. Which of these hobbies is the best use of time for students?
c. What kind of activities do the students enjoy most: physical or artistic?
d. What is the numeric difference between the most popular and least popular hobby?

54. Which of the following practices is the best use of technology to increase reading comprehension and literacy skills?

a. Encourage the use of tape recorders in class, by which students can record classroom conversations and lessons to be reviewed during homework and study time.
b. Accessing a specific website online that shows children how to use graphic organizers for the stories and texts which they are reading in class.
c. Allowing students who have completed their class work to play games or spend monitored time online.
d. Asking students to read articles on various comprehension skills and provide a post-test to measure how well they can apply specific skills.

55. **Which of the following approaches would be best for scaffolding students' peer interactions regarding classroom and independent reading?**
   a. Incorporating debates into class time in which students are assigned an argument and must debate its merits with another student.
   b. Encourage students to form book groups outside of the classroom in which they select and discuss books of interest.
   c. Free discussion across the entire classroom in which students raise their hands to share thoughts and are called upon by the teacher.
   d. Dividing students into small groups of three or four and discussing comprehension/opinion questions, monitored by the teacher.

56. **Examine the following excerpt from a worksheet assigned to a group of sixth graders.**

   Match the numbers to the corresponding letter.

1. Victor spends about an hour every day helping his grandmother around the house.	___a. He does not see or learn as much as he could.
2. Stella is always quick to smile and talk with new students at school.	___b. They have grown much closer and have a stronger relationship.
3. Jorge did not read the directions that came with his brand new telescope.	___c. She has begun to teach her little sister some of the things she has learned.
4. Faye has been enjoying the weekend art classes she just began.	___d. She is well-respected among all the students.

56. **What particular skill does this set of questions address?**
   a. Distinguishing fact from opinion
   b. Relationship of main and supporting ideas
   c. Understanding cause and effect
   d. Sequencing in a story

57. **Mr. Garson's sixth-grade class is working on a creative writing assignment in which they imagine themselves living a "day in the life" of a person from another country. This project is intended to help his students understand different points of view. Mr. Garson is surprised that Kim, who moved to Houston from China last year, is struggling to complete the assignment. She is composing very slowly compared to her classmates. How should he help Kim?**
   a. Allow Kim to write freely in her first language and then ask her English as a Second Language teacher help her translate the assignment into English.
   b. Suggest that Kim simply write about a day in her own life, since she probably understands the lives of those different from her.
   c. Allow Kim to choose another topic that she is more comfortable with to write creatively about.
   d. Pair Kim with another English-language learner to assist her with completing the assignment.

58. Ms. Carroll teaches Social Studies to sixth- and seventh-grade students. She recently assigned a written report for homework. Many of the students turned in reports that were difficult to read due to phonetic and incorrect spelling. When Ms. Carroll speaks with the Language Arts teachers on her team, they tell her that the same students typically achieve very high scores on their spelling tests. Students are given a word list at the beginning of each week to be studied, and then tested on some of the words each week (the teacher reads words aloud to be recorded on an answer sheet). Which of the following is most likely to be the reason for discrepancy in spelling skills between tests and assignments?

    a. When they must concentrate on other grammar and writing skills, the students forget what they have learned for their spelling tests.
    b. The students' handwriting skills are poor, leading to unclear words and inadvertent spelling mistakes.
    c. The students have determined a way to cheat on spelling tests, knowing exactly which words to study beforehand, and do not learn the entire list.
    d. The students memorize only specific words for the week; they have not had the opportunity to develop their spelling skills within the context of writing assignments.

59. What might be the best method for informally assessing students' writing development and skills?

    a. Create a rule that mistakes on class work can always be corrected for extra credit.
    b. Make time for journaling in class during which students can write freely without being graded on mechanics, spelling, or structure.
    c. Create a class website upon which students can write content and post comments to one another.
    d. Occasionally ask the students' other teachers how they are doing with writing assignments.

Use the following information to answer questions 60 and 61:

Dear Grandma,

Hello, how are you doing? How are grandpa and Daisy? Daisy is such a cute Dog she is growing up really fast. I just started Middle School last month, I stay late on Tusdays and Thursdays so I can practice with the Team and go to meetings. I wasn't too sure how it would work out for me when I started. there is a lot more homework and lots of new, older kids. but I am starting to get used to the homework and have met some cool, new friends. I am really looking forward to visting you and grandpa during Thanksgiving. I also joined the soccer team and the drama club. thank you so much for the art set you sent me for my birthday. I have already used it to do some skeches and some sculpting! Please make the Pumpkin Pie that I like so much! Okay, that's about all I have to say right now. Write me back if you can I'll see you soon!
Love, Chris

60. A sixth-grade class is instructed to write letters to family members describing daily life that will be sent out via the post office. The teacher notices several writing errors that are common across the writing samples. If this letter is a primary example of these writing errors, which set is most salient?

    a. Organization of ideas, capitalization and punctuation
    b. Contractions, punctuation, and writing style
    c. Capitalization, spelling and use of passive voice
    d. Writing style, organization of ideas, and use of active voice

61. Which lesson would not be helpful in addressing the primary issues in the students' writing?

a. Direct instruction on organizing ideas.
b. Practice with peer-editing for punctuation and capitalization errors.
c. Correcting sentences that incorrectly use passive voice.
d. Review of commonly-made spelling and capitalization mistakes.

62. Ms. Trent plans to create a rubric that will help her grade her middle-schoolers' writing samples. She wants to make sure that she is consistent across time and between various students who write with different styles. Which of the following would be most important for her to do in order to help build her students' writing skills?

a. Be sure to include every possible aspect of the writing process so that no detail is left out, as different students have different strengths.
b. Share the rubric with students so that they can monitor their own understanding of the writing process as they complete their assignments.
c. Use clear, simple language so that there is no confusion at a later date about what was intended.
d. Divide each segment of the rubric into its own category and assign equal point values—the purpose of which will be to help students understand that each aspect of the writing process is of equal value.

63. All of the following approaches are important for building students' writing skills in conjunction with one another, except:

a. Discussing the various purposes for writing, including self-expression, narration, story-telling, persuasion and explanation.
b. Exercises and activities that isolate and build students' writing skills, including grammar, spelling, mechanics, etc.
c. Creating multiple and various opportunities for students to feel more at ease with the process, diminishing fear or discomfort with it.
d. Maintaining a sequential approach to teaching writing, allowing all students to excel at one level or in one context before moving on to another.

64. What is the primary grammatical problem with this student's paragraph?

Each of the kids in our class love to play games. Our favorite game, Hide and Go Seek, are fun and easy to play anywhere you go. The people in our class really enjoys getting to spend time with friends.

a. punctuation
b. subject-verb agreement
c. word choice
d. split infinitives

65. A teacher provides some guidelines for her students who are having trouble with the Revision step of the writing process:

> Take your time
> Read very carefully, line by line
> Use the proper symbols for specific revisions

What should she add to this list for students who are struggling with writing?

a. If you find a mistake, re-write the whole sentence again.
b. Ask a family member or friend to read your writing and suggest any revisions you ought to make.
c. Read the paper once to correct only one convention at a time; re-reading multiple times helps eliminate mistakes.
d. Write your paper carefully the first time around so that you do not have to spend much time in revision.

66. What activity would be most helpful to the students in the Revision step of the writing process?

a. Provide extra direct instruction or lectures in the specific areas with which the students are struggling.
b. Correct the students' writing and then require them to re-write their original pieces using proper grammar, spelling, etc.
c. Place the students into pairs and have them correct each other's essays or papers to vary instruction and alleviate aversion to revision.
d. Pull sentences from older students' writing and project it on the overhead. Use these samples to guide students in correcting them as a group.

67. All of the following are standard expectations of a child upon entering sixth grade (middle school), except for one. Which one is not a standard expectation of a child entering sixth grade?

a. Identify and correctly spell words that are known as "commonly misspelled words," such as their/they're/there.
b. Identify various points of view in a text, including first-person, third-person, etc.
c. Compose poetry employing techniques such as figurative language, alliteration, onomatopoeia, etc.
d. Understands the meanings and uses of various parts of speech in reading and writing: verbs, nouns, adjectives, pronouns, conjunctions, adverbs, prepositions, etc.

68. For students who have access to word processors in class, which phase of the writing process would be most appropriate to require the use of pencil and paper?

a. Prewriting
b. Drafting
c. Publishing
d. Presenting

Use the following information to answer questions 69 and 70:

The following conversation took place after class as a sixth-grade teacher handed Alex his most recent book report.

Mrs. Blaine: "Alex, I think you did an excellent job on the first part of your book report. You really picked up on a lot of the details in the plot—what a great memory

173

you have! But what about the second part of the assignment? I didn't see anything about whether or not you liked the book with reasons for your opinion?"

Alex: "Yea...I just wasn't really sure what to write on that part, so I left it blank."

Mrs. Blaine: "Can you tell me now how you felt about the book?"

Alex: "It was alright, I guess. It was pretty good. It was boring at first, but I liked the way it ended."

Mrs. Blaine: "And why is that?"

Alex: "It was cool how the burglar was someone you knew all along; the author gave you clues and stuff throughout the story and you could try to solve the mystery while you were reading it."

Mrs. Blaine: "I understand. I liked that part of the story, too. Getting started on work like this can be challenging at first. <u>But it is important that you begin to learn this skill because you will use it over and over again in school and in your eventual career</u>. Let's talk about some ways to help you get going."

Alex: "Okay...sounds good."

69. What skill is Mrs. Blaine referring to in the underlined sentence?
   a. Understanding his feelings.
   b. Completing assignments thoroughly without leaving any information out.
   c. Stating an opinion or thesis and supplying supporting evidence.
   d. Writing even when you are unsure about the topic or instructions.

70. What would be the best way for Mrs. Blaine to help Alex build his skills in this area?
   a. Have Alex write his opinions and each supporting idea on paper plates or pieces of cardstock and show him how to move them around and arrange them in logical order on a large table or the floor.
   b. Have Alex explain his opinions and supporting ideas to her while she writes them down for him; he can then re-write them into the body of his report.
   c. Have Alex participate in extra lessons that let him explore his feelings about or reactions to various media, including books.
   d. Have Alex review each assignment with her before he turns it in to ensure that he has not left anything out.

71. Mr. Benton is in the process of grading the first writing assignments of the year for his eighth-grade students. He is a bit overwhelmed at the volume of errors in grammar, usage and overall composition he finds in almost every student's writing. Mr. Benton wants to use a systematic approach to building his students' writing skills, beginning by giving the students a clear and simple method to apply to their work. His goal is that the students can take part in analyzing and monitoring their own progress. What should he do?

a. Show his students an outline of the six common writing traits and ask the students to evaluate their own skills within each trait. Teacher and student can use this evaluation to establish a plan for working on the skills that need the most help.

b. Assign each student a writing buddy. The students can meet during writing assignments to edit one another's work. They can then separate to make the suggested revisions.

c. Encourage the students to grade their own work using a rubric provided to them. Meet with the student to determine where they believe they need the most help and focus class work around those areas.

d. Teach the students that most writing assignments can be composed using the five-paragraph essay model. Invest class time and homework in perfecting the model that includes thesis, evidence, and conclusions.

72. Mrs. Matson's 6th graders are chatting during snack time and she overhears the following conversation:

Ellie: I hate how my mom always asks me how my day was, every single day! And then she gets mad when I say it's fine. But it really IS fine almost every day!
Brynn: Oh, I know! My dad always wants to know what my reading is about, but sometimes I just don't feel like talking about it. It takes long enough to read it without talking about it.
Jon: You have it easy. My mom AND dad help me with my homework every night, and then they give me extra work to do!

Mrs. Matson would like to not only give students a chance to voice their feelings about the changing communications with their parents, but also help them find a way to channel those feelings into something positive. Which project would be best for allowing students a positive way to communicate with their parents about what is happening in school?

a. Encourage the students to talk to their parents about everything that is happening in school; after all, their parents only want to help them.

b. After talking about this issue, ask the students to write short pieces about their schoolwork and experiences during the day and compile them into a newsletter to be sent home every two weeks.

c. Help the students write letters to their parents, telling them how they feel about the issue

d. Tell students to keep a log of their activities in the classroom and throughout the day to be shown to parents on a daily or weekly basis.

73. A middle-school teacher has written several questions on the chalk board to assist students in revising their most recent essays.

> Do you know the meanings of all the vocabulary in your essay?
>
> Did you use any major words (besides articles like a, an, and, the) more than three times?
>
> Do you like the way your writing sounds when you read it aloud?
>
> Does all the language used make sense?

Judging by the questions above, which writing trait is this teacher encouraging her students to work on today?

- a. sentence fluency
- b. ideas and development
- c. writing conventions
- d. word choice

74. Read the persuasive writing excerpt below:

> "Why Peace is Important"
>
> Peace is important to our lives. We have to have peace because we can't be fighting all the time. When people fight, they can't do anything else. It also makes everybody else feel upset and angry because they have to listen to the fighting. If you want to have peace you can talk to the person and try to get them to agree with you and say you are sorry if you do something wrong.

How could a teacher help this student develop his persuasive writing skills, based on this initial attempt?

- a. Continue to give positive reinforcement; this student has a good understanding of the persuasive structure.
- b. Introduce the use of a graphic organizer or flow chart to help the student organize his main idea and supporting evidence in a logical way.
- c. Encourage the student to include more details in his writing to make it more interesting and more personal.
- d. Focus primarily on the editing and revising processes to correct writing conventions, usage, and grammar.

75. A Language teacher is introducing a new writing topic to her class. She asks them to pretend that the person they are writing to or for is "an alien from outer space." What type of writing is she probably introducing?

- a. Fantasy/fiction
- b. Poetry
- c. Persuasive essay
- d. How-to article

76. **Ms. Burns' fourth-graders are working very hard at building writing skills on many levels. They have come a long way with their knowledge of the six traits of writing, as well as their confidence in their own abilities. Some of the students have trouble finding their own unique "voices" when writing, probably because they are working so hard to maintain accurate grammar, spelling, organization, and continuity of ideas. How can Ms. Burns help the students inject their own personalities and voices into their writing without sacrificing correctness?**

   a. Explain that they should always be sure to include personal opinions and insights to make the writing interesting.
   b. Project overhead examples of good writing that appropriately utilizes personal voice and lead a discussion about them in class.
   c. Guide students to select only topics with which they are very knowledgeable and explain that it is never a good idea to write about something that is unfamiliar to them.
   d. Teach students to imagine themselves as a new character every time they write--they should write from the point of view of that individual, phrasing things the way that person or character would if they were speaking.

77. **Read the excerpt below:**

   I like sweets. Cookies, cake and ice cream are very sweet and good. I like to eat these things after school or after I eat. Sweet tastes are the best for me and I do not like salty food. When I eat dessert, I feel so good and happy. My mom says that I should not eat too many sweets or I will get cavities, so I have to brush my teeth after eating them.

   Which activity would benefit this student's writing skills the most?

   a. Make "word bulletin boards" with the student to help her build vocabulary to make her writing more interesting.
   b. Practice with editing other students' writing to familiarize her with writing conventions.
   c. Grammar exercises, specifically subject-verb agreement.
   d. Encouraging her to select a more challenging writing topic to stretch her skill level.

78. **Mr. Talbot's class has an opportunity to begin writing letters to students in France who are learning English, just as Mr. Talbot's class is learning French. He knows that this will be an excellent opportunity for the students to work on letter-writing as well as build their language skills. What other writing skill can he use this opportunity to strengthen in his students?**

   a. He can help them work through the five-step writing process and the six traits of writing; letter-writing is an excellent exercise for bringing all of those traits and steps together.
   b. He can teach them the proper formatting of letters and the etiquette of writing a good letter.
   c. He can teach them to consider their audience when writing by talking about what they know of their pen pals' lives, what they would find interesting, and how to communicate effectively with others who are not like themselves.
   d. He can teach his students about the importance of proper writing conventions like punctuation, grammar, and spelling, because their pen pals are still learning English.

79. An eighth-grade teacher assigns an end-of-the-year project for her English students. The students are placed into groups and instructed to make an "ad campaign" that includes a print ad, a television/radio commercial, and a persuasive essay. What is the teacher's most likely primary objective?

    a. To equip students with practical, real-life job experience in a competitive world.
    b. To allow students to apply concepts they have learned about audience, point of view, media messages, etc.
    c. To incorporate the use of technology into a unit of study.
    d. To encourage students to work cooperatively in groups.

80. A sixth-grade teacher begins class by showing a series of inkblot images, one by one, on pieces of cardstock. She asks her students to number their papers from 1-20 and write down what they think each image depicts. After the exercise, she asks for a few volunteers to explain what they saw in each inkblot. What do you think this teacher is attempting to convey?

    a. That visual images can be interpreted differently, depending on the individual viewer.
    b. That cultural symbols are typically universal and are inherent in our cultural mindset.
    c. That psychological differences are often misconstrued as mental illness.
    d. That it is important not to confirm understandings of visual images with peers before determining their meaning.

81. After reading Shakespeare's Romeo and Juliet in class, students watch the most recent Hollywood film version, starring Leonardo DiCaprio. Their teacher leads a class discussion after the film. Which of the following essay topics would be most helpful in challenging students to analyze how visual media affects their perceptions of a piece of literature?

    a. Discuss your favorite character in the film version of Romeo and Juliet, and give at least three reasons to back up your opinion.
    b. Which version of Romeo and Juliet did you like better, and why?
    c. Compare the film with the play and point out at least four instances in which portions of the play were left out of the film version.
    d. Describe the setting of the film and discuss why you think the film's director chose to portray the play in modern times.

82. Mr. James created a poster featuring this chart to accompany his class instruction for the day. He will be showing students how to organize information into text organizers to help themselves understand what they have read. What other skill might this kind of organizer build as well?

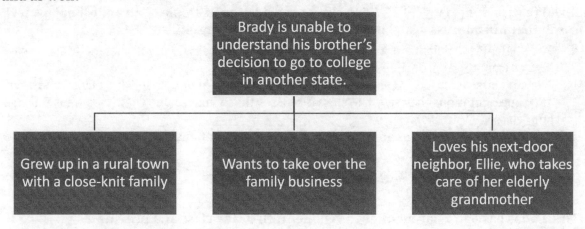

a. Constructing a paragraph
b. Answering literature-based multiple-choice questions
c. Character analysis
d. Writing conventions

83. Mr. Ank has a game he plans to play with his middle school English students today. He has recorded several commercials from television and will play them without sound for the students. After each silent commercial, the students will share their ideas about what product the commercial is advertising. Following this game, the class will participate in a follow-up discussion and exercise. What is the likely purpose of Mr. Ank's game?

a. To turn his students into savvy consumers.
b. To help students understand how visual images affect meaning and understanding.
c. To demonstrate how students can use visual images in their own schoolwork.
d. To introduce variation into his instruction and give the kids a fun activity.

84. A teacher plans to use the drawing below to explain story elements. Each point on the line represents an element of the story. Which choice matches the point on the chart with the smiling face above it?

a. Rising Action
b. Exposition
c. Resolution
d. Climax

85. Mrs. Gilbert, an English teacher, and Ms. Dudley, an Art teacher, are working together to create an integrated unit of study for their common students. The students will be studying King Tut, reading various accounts of his life, both fiction and non-fiction. Ms. Dudley will be guiding the students through various art projects related to the time period in which King Tut lived (e.g., making papyrus). Which choice provides an example of an additional project or lesson that will address visual interpretation and decoding skills?

a. The students participate in Ancient Egypt Day and can dress up as characters or historical figures from the appropriate time period.

b. The students visit a local museum exhibit on Ancient Egypt and keep a log of visual images and representations they see. The class discusses those images and their meanings during both classes.

c. The students write stories about the lives of Ancient Egyptians and draw illustrations to go along with their writing.

d. The students watch a movie about King Tut and create free-writing pieces based on what they have seen.

86. Mrs. Canas has had a parent offer to visit her fifth-grade class and provide a sign language seminar. The parent is fluent in American Sign Language and would like to offer her skills to benefit the students. Mrs. Canas thinks the seminar will be very interesting and provide a unique way to hone her students' listening and expressive skills. Which choice identifies another language skill set that would indirectly benefit from this seminar?

a. Students' understanding of how visual messages, including body language, facial expression, and signs inform verbal communication and ideas.

b. Students' fine motor skills and hand-eye coordination.

c. Students' respect for other cultures, specifically the non-hearing community.

d. Students' ability to communicate with other peers and adults in their community.

87. An eighth-grade class will be watching a mystery film in English class over the next two days. Throughout the story, the camera will often focus on objects or clothing that are colored bright red. These objects are always related to clues that lead the character toward solving the mystery. What literary device is the students' teacher planning to introduce in this context?

a. Media deconstruction

b. Color imagery

c. Alliteration

d. Symbolism

88. Middle school students at Ms. Kelso's school are expected to complete a large independent study project to be presented at the end of the second term. The project is the culmination of reading research, writing a paper, and the final element of publishing, or presentation. The students can choose how they present their work and are instructed to use visual aids. Which of the following would be a helpful guideline for Ms. Kelso to offer her students?

a. Whenever possible, use pictures, video, music, charts and graphs to supplement your presentation for the purpose of keeping your audience's interest.
b. Think about any parts of your paper that might be hard to explain. Choose a visual aid to help you show your audience the concept, and then use your words to explain it.
c. Select the most interesting photographs from your research, create color photocopies, and pass them throughout the class during your presentation.
d. Use your main ideas and supporting evidence to create a Power-point slideshow, making note-taking and organization simple and clear.

89. Which of the following visual images would be most appropriate for teaching students about how media images influence their perceptions and attitudes?

a. a photograph found in a journalistic magazine, such as Time
b. an illustration or diagram found in the students' own Social Studies textbook
c. a political cartoon found in the newspaper
d. a non-political cartoon found in another section of the newspaper

Use the following information to answer questions 90 and 91:

A middle school class is working through the process of creating a research project. Since this kind of assignment is completely new, their teacher provides direct instruction and practice assignments to help the students approach the large project.

90. Which of the following approaches would increase a middle-school student's preliminary research skills?

a. Assign and analyze a research paper on a topic of the student's choosing.
b. Require students to submit a separate outline before completing a research paper.
c. Require students to turn in note cards containing relevant information on each source they will use in an upcoming research project.
d. Pre-test on several subjects to determine which area or discipline to explore.

91. What is the first point at which the teacher should meet individually to talk with the student?

a. After the student first chooses a topic
b. After the student turns in research note cards
c. After the student completes the initial outline
d. After the rough draft has been turned in

92. An eighth-grade teacher notices that her students perform very well on scheduled tests in class, but struggle with pop quizzes or other in-class assignments that involve recalling information. In discussing this issue with other teachers on her team, she finds that this is a pattern across all disciplines. What would be the best way to help students retain information on a daily or weekly basis in the absence of the motivation of an upcoming test?

    a. Devote the first few minutes of class on previewing information and tasks and the last few minutes of each class summarizing highlights from class work and homework reading.

    b. Increase the frequency of pop quizzes in hopes that the students will begin to study at home more often.

    c. Give the students a study guide before each quiz so they know what will be tested.

    d. Allow the students to work on the quizzes in groups so that they can help each other with memory and recall.

93. Mr. Katz draws these diagrams on the board at the beginning of English class. Janie and Katherine are the two main characters in the book which his class is currently reading.

Janie's Character Traits		Katherine's Character Traits	
1. Bossy		1. Kind to others	
2.		2.	
3.		3.	

	Same	Different
Janie	1. 2. 3.	1. 2. 3.
Katherine	1. 2. 3.	1. 2. 3.

93. Based on the above diagram, what concept do you think Mr. Katz plans to teach?

    a. Structural Text Analysis

    b. Compare/Contrast

    c. Inferential Comprehension

    d. Use of Graphic/Text Organizers

94. Mrs. Costanza's eighth-grade students bring up some concerns during class time. They complain that their teachers are assigning too much reading for homework and that they are worried that they will never be able to retain the information for tests. Some students say that they don't know how to predict what information is important and what is not. What can Mrs. Costanza do to help them?

    a. Encourage students to allow enough time when studying to effectively memorize all the necessary information in the texts and assigned readings.

    b. Teach the students the SQ3R (Survey, Question, Read, Recite/Write, and Review) method.

    c. Ask other eighth-grade teachers to provide study guides that will outline exactly what will be on each test.

    d. Discuss the importance of taking detailed notes in class and asking relevant questions during class discussions.

95. Ana Velasquez's eighth-grade class at Jones Middle School is beginning a unit in which they will be expected to complete a research project. They will choose from a list of topics and then write a report. Each student is required to have a bibliography that includes at least one entry each from the following sources: the internet, library books, newspaper articles, and magazine articles. Which of the following topics would be the best choice for Ana?

a. Day in the Life of the Velasquez family
b. Hurricane Katrina
c. The History of Jones High School
d. How to get your homework done faster!

Use the following information to answer questions 96 and 97:

A teacher is talking with her students about the best way to retain information learned during a unit or course of study. She wants them to be prepared for high school and college, during which they will rely primarily on their class notes to study for tests and prepare papers. She describes these steps:

1. Read all assigned material before class. Make notes on any new vocabulary, questions or ideas you have as you read.

2. Take notes in class based on discussions and lectures.

3. Before the test, review your notes and assigned readings, spending more time on those segments which you remember the least.

96. In step #2, the teacher shows her students how to divide their note pages in half, using one side of the paper for main ideas or questions, and the other side for details relating to those larger concepts. What is the likely purpose of her demonstration?

a. To help students understand cause and effect relationships, which will assist them in other disciplines such as History and Science.
b. To emphasize the difference between main ideas and details. This emphasis will support an upcoming lesson on constructing a five-paragraph essay with a main idea and supporting evidence.
c. To help students be more orderly and write neatly when it comes to taking notes, which will in turn make studying for tests and papers much easier.
d. To show students how they can begin to organize their information and understanding about a subject as they take notes, constructing meaning from a large amount of information.

97. What step should be included at #3 to supplement her instruction?

a. Meet with a partner for any information you failed to write down during class.
b. Take an audio recorder with you in order to record everything discussed in lectures and class.
c. Review your notes periodically; at least once a week.
d. Read all assigned material at least once more in its entirety.

98. An eighth-grade teacher plans to deliver a test on a book recently read and discussed in class. He plans to include some short answers, multiple choice, fill-in-the-blanks, and 2-3 essay questions. The students are familiar with multiple-choice and fill-ins, but are not accustomed to short answers and essays. He wants to scaffold their attempts to study the large amount of material. What should he do?

    a. Make the test "open-notes."
    b. Provide a copy of the questions ahead of time so that the students can formulate their answers.
    c. Provide several sessions of written practice and instruction with similar short-answer and essay questions, and discuss the students' answers afterward.
    d. Allow the students to re-take the test if they struggle the first time around.

99. Sully is struggling to write his eighth-grade research report. His writing is full of great ideas and generalizations, but few supporting details and little evidence. When his teacher suggests that he needs to provide more supporting information, he looks blankly at her. How can she help him understand this concept and improve his paper?

    a. Tell Sully that his writing topic is too broad, and ask him some guiding questions to narrow it down. These questions could include: "what is most important to you about this subject?" and "what do you most want your readers to learn about?"
    b. As much as it will be frustrating for Sully, explain to him that sometimes it is easiest to start from scratch when a paper does not fit the appropriate format. Instruct him to use his previous paper to make a new outline for a new paper. Help him make the outline in great detail and then encourage him to simply use his previous paper as a source for details when writing the newer version.
    c. Use a graphic organizer that contains two columns: "ideas" and "details/evidence." Guide Sully to pick his top three or four main ideas and fill in the right hand side with appropriate details and information. Encourage him to use this exercise to revise his paper by adding in his evidence and eliminating any information that is not listed on his graphic organizer.
    d. Help him brainstorm a list of facts about his topic from memory and his research. Show Sully how to take his ideas one by one, adding at least two facts or details after each idea. Instruct him to make sure that each idea has supporting evidence and details.

100. Mrs. Bray's students have been performing poorly on in-class quizzes, lately. She gives them notice that there will be quizzes in class, although she does not tell them when they will take place. How can she help improve the students' performance without giving them direct insight about the quiz dates or material?

    a. Provide more opportunities for taking tests and quizzes in order to lower anxiety and increase familiarity with the format.
    b. Talk with the students about how they are preparing for quizzes and suggest alternatives that match the intended outcomes of the quiz.
    c. When covering potential quiz information emphasize and indirectly communicate that students should pay close attention.
    d. Send a note home to parents asking them to study with their children in anticipation of the quizzes.

Answer Key and Explanations

1. C: Oral language skills can be distinguished from specific speech characteristics exhibited by some children. Many students like Rosa, whose first language is not English, will speak with an accent and may be less clear when speaking about a topic that is unfamiliar. In fact, even those who are not English Language Learners may exhibit difficulty speaking on new topics. Greer may avoid oral assignments or speaking in class for a number of reasons, such as self-consciousness. This student could be helped by evaluating oral language skills in a one-on-one environment or by introducing peer scaffolding to help reduce anxiety. Brett's demeanor in group assignments may also be due to social characteristics rather than oral skills; it would be important to evaluate his skills in various contexts. Ashley, however, shows marked problems communicating orally both in class discussion and in prepared assignments. She would benefit from specific instruction related to presenting ideas orally.

2. D: Choice "a" would be appropriate for class work or homework, but is less likely than other choices to provide a deep understanding of the relationships between oral and spoken word. Choice "b" would address multicultural interest, but would not require interpretation since only recitation is assigned. Choice "c" could allow students to learn more about their classmates' backgrounds, but would require more specific parameters to ensure that both the multicultural and oral learning outcomes were achieved. Choice "c" also does not address the assumption that the classmates' family backgrounds are diverse, which may not be the case. Choice "d" requires students to use their research skills to learn more about another culture. By assigning a first-person narrative, Mr. Callas encourages the students to imagine life from the perspective of another person. This assignment also requires the student to make the transition from research to written assignment to spoken word.

3. C: Each answer can be an effective tool in teaching students to build oral language skills. The question makes clear that the objective is to help students evaluate their own oral language skills, which will assist them in both spoken and written assignments. The only answer choice that involves the student himself evaluating his message is answer "c." When the student prepares a review/quiz based upon important information, he or she will be more able to speak specifically to that information. When classmates complete the review, the student can identify any patterns in the questions' answers that give clues as to how well those main ideas were communicated. In this way, the student can evaluate how effective the oral presentation was, without relying on classmates or the teacher.

4. A: Even for the older students who are a bit behind grade level, having a chance to help a younger student can increase their confidence and oral skills. Students are challenged to explain and give feedback to the Kindergarteners and will have to think about how best to explain ideas to another person. By pairing the older students with younger ones, they have a chance to be the "teachers," and must consider their purpose and audience when speaking. Regardless of the older student's reading abilities, he or she can build their confidence and skill in oral language by helping a younger student with basic reading skills.

5. B: The purpose of this exercise is for the older students to build their confidence and oral language skills by helping to teach younger students. By doing this, older students build their skills by thinking critically about how to help a new reader understand basic reading skills. In Choice "a", the English language learner may build reading skills, but will not have a chance to build confidence or oral skills, which are just as important to their language development. In Choice "c", the English language learner may lose confidence in attempting to meet program standards without the necessary language skills. In Choice "d", students practice listening skills, which would only indirectly build oral skills. Choice "b" allows students to learn not only by listening, but by having a chance to explain or assist when he or she has the requisite skills to do so. A skilled student is also there to assist when needed.

6. D: The "Phrase of the Day" appears from the question prompt to be dedicated to certain types of oral language, including analogies and idioms. By asking the students to record interpretations in an informal way (through pictures or the students' own words), he will have insight as to their perceptions about common language. He also directly builds the students' oral language skills by giving them the correct meaning of the phrase with which the students can compare their original answers. In this way, Mr. Campbell assesses and builds skills without the use of a formal test or quiz.

7. B: Oral language skills incorporate speaking, listening, and knowledge of conventional language. In Choice "a", students would be limited to a very specific vocabulary in order to work with the science and math programs, and would not have opportunities to increase their knowledge of language. In Choice "c", students are practicing their listening skills, but are not required to speak or think critically about what they have heard. Choice "d" does involve technology and class discussions; however, the benefit of watching the discussion on tape is relatively unclear. In Choice "b", students not only have a chance to build their speaking and listening skills, but also increase their knowledge of other cultures and ways of speaking.

8. C: In choices "a" and "b," students are primarily using written language in order to present to the class. They are required to use what they have composed as the text for their oral presentations. In Choice "c", students have the chance to learn how to prioritize information they have read and written, and also learn to modify the written word to create an oral presentation based upon specific parameters. This exercise highlights the differences between the written and spoken word. Choice "d" does not necessarily involve all of the students and less directly increases the students' oral skills in a relevant way.

9. D: In this activity, students are practicing a variety of skills related to communication. By analyzing the log sheet, it is apparent that students are expected to work on their conversational skills, including listening and speaking. Choice "a" refers to those points on the log sheet that relate to listening while another person is speaking. Choice "c" also pertains to listening skills, specifically with eye contact and other behaviors that let the student know that his partner was listening and making an effort to understand. Choice "b" refers to the ability to speak clearly (each word can be clearly understood) and effectively (the ideas behind the words make sense to the listener). Choice "d" could potentially come to fruition; however, conflict resolution is not specifically addressed in this activity.

10. C: Oral language skills are almost un-quantifiable because they cover a multitude of competencies. Vocabulary, enunciation, listening, body language, comprehension and many other skills directly affect a student's communicative ability. This particular activity primarily focuses on peer interactions. However, conversing with adults provides opportunities for students to learn new vocabulary and ways of speaking. Choices "a," " b" and "d" are possible outcomes or functions of the teacher's partnering with a new student during each conversation. However, teachers must keep in mind that it is just as important for students to converse with adults in a context that allows them to learn from observation as well as participation.

11. D: In the debate process, it is important for students to take a position and support it with evidence or arguments in order to make their claims effective. Choice "d" requires students to formulate their opinions and supporting arguments, and helps them reduce extraneous information and create "reminders" for their talking points on notecards. Choice "c" requires students to prepare their arguments but encourages reading aloud during the debate rather than actually speaking directly to their opponent or to the crowd. Choice "c" fails to help students distinguish between written language and oral language and their occasionally separate purposes. Choice "b" creates opportunities for informal debate, but does not teach students the parameters for formal debating. Choice "a" is similarly informal and does not familiarize students with the preparation process with respect to formulating arguments, opinions, or preparing to speak in front of a large audience.

12. A: In Choice "a", the teacher guides previewing of information to show students how to put themselves in the right frame of mind to listen carefully for meaning. Students are then able to listen in a guided way based upon the previewing. By varying the type of comprehension assessment, the teacher will get a better understanding of what the students learned. Choice "b" is a good exercise, but does not provide for direct instruction by the teacher or a particularly skilled student. In Choice "c", students are focusing more upon reading comprehension than listening since they must read the story to themselves and then write a report. There is then no way to gauge what they have learned. The final choice would be useful, but does not include teacher-guided previewing, which is very helpful in building comprehension.

13. B: At the start of a new school year, a teacher will likely choose to engage in a series of exercises to help her understand her students' current ability levels. These exercises must provide opportunities for evaluation of the whole class, rather than a select few students. In Choice "a", the teacher is not likely to get a lot of information from each student during class discussion, since not all children may participate. An instruction-level text may also prove too difficult for some students to read without guidance from a fluent reader. Choice "c", while a good exercise for peer-assisted reading, would not provide the teacher chances to evaluate each student's comprehension at once. Choice "d" would be very time-consuming; it would also cause students to influence each other's comprehension (e.g. the students going first may influence the comprehension of those re-telling the story later). Choice "b" allows the teacher to evaluate the students' independent comprehension levels with one assignment.

14. A: Emergent readers are those who are not yet reading fluently (with appropriate speed and accuracy). Choice "b" refers to the practice of reviewing relationships between letters and sounds, which is vital to building reading skills. Choice "c" would help students build vocabulary retention by requiring them to find unfamiliar words in the dictionary. This practice causes the student to analyze and retain spelling of unfamiliar words, as well as reinforces dictionary/reference skills. Choice "d" addresses the fact that many words in the English language are irregularly spelled and cannot be decoded with conventional phonetic instruction. While invented spelling described in Choice "a" may be permitted in emergent readers, this practice is not likely to build specific reading skills.

15. C: Literacy skills encompass a variety of contexts: written, verbal, comprehension, vocabulary, grammar, spelling, etc. Designing class work that touches on these multiple contexts must allow the children to increase not only skills that can be measured on tests or written work. Reading a play gives students a chance to touch on comprehension, vocabulary, and grammar; acting the play out creates the opportunity for increased comprehension and oral interpretation. Each of the alternate answers focuses on one specific aspect of literacy skills, without incorporating multiple contexts.

16. B: Assessment is an ongoing process that involves formal testing and a host of other methods. Students are working at any given time in the school year on a multitude of skills sets, and all of these skills are interrelated and developing simultaneously at different rates. It is impossible to ever provide a "snapshot" of a student's abilities, because each student develops in a unique and complex manner. Choice "a" would only offer insight into a student's reading fluency. Choice "c" would show how a student could perform on standardized tests; however, many factors such as anxiety and test-taking speed affect those scores. Choice "d" relies on the teacher to interpret the student's strengths and weaknesses and would require an almost impossible attention to detail. Choice "b" includes both formal and informal assessments as well as giving insight into writing, vocabulary and other skill sets in a comprehensive portfolio.

17. A: Those who are familiar with the guided oral reading strategy will note that the struggling student must be paired with a fluent and skilled partner. If you are not familiar with this strategy, all of the answer choices could conceivably be a part of the oral reading strategy and appear to be related to one another. However, one choice does not make sense after reading all four options. In answer choices "b" and "d," Valeria's partner is required to read the text aloud and offer correction or feedback when Valeria reads aloud. If Valeria is paired with another struggling student (as suggested in Choice "a", neither "b" nor "d" would prove effective in building her reading fluency.

18. B: Mr. Waleran's purpose is to encourage students to express themselves in written words, interpreting their thoughts into writing. However, there are often children who cannot write well enough to create coherent or legible works. In these cases, it is still possible for students to express themselves in writing. Choice "b" allows Dimitri to express himself by drawing, which will likely make him feel more comfortable with the activity. He will also have the chance to use words he does know and incorporate them into his work. As his skills grow, he can gradually transition into more formal writing. Choices "a" and "c" allow Dimitri to explore his thoughts, but do not build his writing skills. Choice "d" will, in all likelihood, become a chore for Dimitri and reinforce his struggles with reading and writing.

19. D: Part of building literacy skills is showing students how to listen effectively to various types of texts: narrative, poetry, informative, etc. In order to become competent in a variety of literacy skills, students must be able to listen for information and for pleasure/experience. This teacher is not only exposing them to poetry, but creating a forum in which they can actively listen and then discuss what they have experienced or learned. The scenario given in Choice "a" could possibly be true, as could Choice "c". But it is less likely that the teacher would devote an entire month of reading and listening to a specific type of text simply to give her students a break or to make a point about poetry versus prose. Choice "b" assumes that the poetry she reads will rhyme, which is not always the case.

20. B: Mrs. Taylor's project introduces students to an ancient form of expression that was written, but not based upon alphabetic principles, like English. This project is applicable to all levels of readers, as it incorporates various kinds of media to assist comprehension. Students are required to listen and read for information so that they can apply what they have learned to creating their own hieroglyphics. In Choice "b", the answer suggests that what is learned about hieroglyphics will assist students in understanding those with different backgrounds. However, hieroglyphics are not used in any widespread way today, and are much less helpful in building multicultural awareness than perhaps a lesson on modern Egyptian culture or writing.

21. D: Teachers should try to avoid shallow notions of what it means to provide cultural or multi-cultural education; in Choice "a", we cannot presume to understand another person by listening to his favorite music or watching a favorite movie. In Choice "b", there is also the assumption that there is a variety of musical tastes in the class, which may not be the case. In fact, if many students pick the same song, it is possible to use that choice to open up dialogue about what they lyrics mean and why they are so popular with the class. Choice "c" is posed in direct opposition to Choice "d". However, Choice "d" suggests what most teachers know to be true: literacy skills are not just important for schoolwork and class work; students must be able to take meaning from a variety of different sources in order to grow into educated adults. Music is an important medium through which students can express themselves and learn about the world around them through comprehension and listening skills.

22. C: All children learn their letter-sound correspondences at different rates. This particular child may simply be showing his teacher that he has not quite mastered this skill set yet. However, the inconsistence with producing the sounds could possibly be a signal that he needs specialized instruction. It is impossible, however, to know exactly what is going on without providing specialized instruction and giving that instruction time to improve skills. Choice "a" suggests an immediate referral for special-needs testing, which may be unnecessary and too soon in this scenario. Choice "b" states that all children learn differently which is certainly true, but does not provide a plan for helping the child improve. In the final choice, the parents may become needlessly alarmed and spend extra money in a situation where the intervention may not be necessary or even helpful. Choice "c" provides specific instruction in the deficient skill and acknowledges that the child may improve on his own; but if he needs it, extra help can be found.

23. D: Students are expected to be able to express themselves verbally and build upon one another's ideas in class as they complete fourth and fifth grades. However, many students lack the confidence or skills to participate in class discussions or conversations. Rather than leave those students to their own devices, as suggested in choices "a" and "b" a teacher must help instruct the students on how to communicate orally in situations where they can be successful. Choice "c" would require the students to speak out more, but might not alleviate issues with preparedness or confidence as would Choice "d" which allows students to feel more comfortable and get the teacher's guidance.

24. B: This prompt focuses not only on reading fluency skills, but also on the issue of the young reader's confidence. It is very common for students who feel unsuccessful at reading to avoid the skill altogether. The teacher in this question realizes something important: it is vital to build a student's confidence with reading as he or she builds skill. In choice "a" there is a faulty assumption that a student could ever memorize enough words to eliminate the need to decode. While some students with processing disorders or different learning styles do rely more heavily on sight words, this practice should not be solely relied upon. In choice "c" the students will likely feel negatively about being asked to read young children's books; their lack of confidence may be reinforced by this plan. In choice "d" students may also be frustrated by the extra work they are required to do without any evidence of success with this practice. In Choice "b", students can build their fluency skills by creating words with various sounds, which is often easier for students than decoding as they are learning to read. As their knowledge of letter-sound relationships grows, they will become better at decoding words they see on the page. Allowing students to encode will also provide them with more chances to feel successful as they learn.

25. C: Reading fluency is defined as a set of skills including speed, accuracy and inflection when reading words on a page. Reading comprehension generally refers to the ability to understand what is being read. Both sets of skills are important, and reading fluency is vital to comprehension, which is the ultimate goal of the practice of reading. It is possible, even common, to isolate skills for the purpose of skill-building or to compensate for areas in which a student is struggling; however, all skills are inter-related. Children can make progress in some aspects of reading while still working on more difficult areas. Based on these ideas, choices "a" and "d" can be ruled out as possible answers. Comprehension is typically not classified as being part of fluency skills, which eliminates Choice "b". Reading fluency should be considered a vital part of overall reading skills: fluency must be improved so that, ultimately, the student can comprehend what is being read more fully.

26. A: It is important to evaluate specific reading skills, such as phonemic awareness, in a variety of contexts. Reading aloud with Abi allowed his teacher to notice that he consistently misread words beginning with digraphs. Digraphs are sounds in which two distinct letters, when combined, produce a single third sound (e.g. when "s" and "h" produce the "-sh" sound). Blends are words in which two letters produce a third sound which is a combination of both sounds put together (e.g. "b" and "l" combined to make "b"). The only set of words consisting only of digraphs is choice set "a."

27. D: The first three choices are all required standards to be met by eighth-graders. Students at this grade level should, of course, be able to identify grade-level words and understand the phonemes and elements within them. Students at this level should also be familiar with words that cannot necessarily be decoded with typical approaches, but that they will encounter on a regular basis (such as phenomenon or charisma). Eighth-graders should also be able to identify and explain similarities in different kinds of texts, as stated in Choice "b", and differences in points of view, as described in Choice "c". However, an extensive knowledge of cultural literature and its effect on media is required to meet the standard in Choice "d". This type of knowledge base, in addition to advanced deconstruction skills mentioned in Choice "d", is more typical of work done in grades 9-12.

28. A: In the passage, Susannah misspells seven words. Six of these misspelled words, when spelled correctly, have silent letter-sounds (phonemes). If Susannah misspells a particular pattern of words in her writing, she may have difficulty reading the same kinds of words independently. While sight word practice Choice "a" would certainly be helpful, teaching Susannah the concept of a "silent e" would be more effective than instructing her to learn similar words by memorizing them out of context. Choices "c" and "d" are also helpful in building reading skills; however, neither of them targets the specific type of word with which Susannah is struggling.

29. C: In Choice "a", the words prince and princess are capitalized, though they do not have suffixes. In choice "b", the word "multimedia" contains the prefix "multi", but no suffix. Choice "c" contains a word with the root "please," which also has both a prefix and a suffix. The suffix -ing acts as the suffix in displeasing, therefore it is correctly capitalized. Choice "d" correctly has "bookkeeper" capitalized due to the suffix "-er" but neglects to capitalize "examined" even though it also contains a suffix. Choice "c" is the only correct choice available.

30. B: Reading fluency refers to the speed, inflection and accuracy with which students read, either orally or silently. In order to read fluently, students must be able to decode, or break down into segments, words that adhere to the common rules of the English alphabet. For those words that are not easily decoded, students must build their vocabulary of "sight words," which are recognized without the need to decode. In Choice "a", students may or may not be reading fluently or accurately, since the computer program does not monitor how the student reads. In Choice "c", keyboarding practice bears no direct relationship to reading fluency. In Choice "d", again, the computer is simply a source for text, but does not build any specific fluency skill. In Choice "b", students are exposed to sight words and vocabulary in a fun way. Using a computer program allows for an unlimited supply of relevant words and for accurate scoring.

31. C: In Choice "a", parents would take up an inordinate amount of class time discussing literacy, without necessarily building any skills. This choice would also rely on the assumption that parents could speak effectively about this topic. Choice "b" would create inconsistency in grading, since there is interpretation and expertise required even in using a grading rubric. Choice "d" would certainly make the teacher's job easier to manage. However, Choice "c" allows parents with limited training to help students build reading fluency by reading challenging texts and building accuracy and speed. This choice satisfies both of the teacher's needs: taking into account the parents' limited training and helping the students most directly.

32. A: True fluency not only involves reading accurately and with appropriate speed, but using vocal inflection to communicate punctuation and emotion. Many students possess fluency with respect to accuracy or speed, but do not reflect interest or comprehension in their vocal modulation. Choice "b" suggests that volume is most important; however, volume can be considered a part of vocal expression. Choice "c" does not guarantee that the student will read with appropriate inflection or accuracy since interest level does not dictate fluency. At a certain point, students should not continue to increase their reading speed, as reading too quickly negatively affects comprehension. Therefore, Choice "d" is incorrect.

33. B: Much research points to the fact that students can increase their speed, accuracy and inflection when they engage in repeated readings of various texts. By reading assigned pieces more than once, they have a chance to apply feedback which they have received so that they make fewer mistakes and read more quickly. Students will struggle if they are only exposed to phonetic rules, without working on automatic word recognition or practice activities, as is suggested in Choice "a". Applying the same logic to vocabulary, it is necessary to rule out Choice "c". Choice "d" is not a widely accepted method for building reading fluency for student readers in traditional schools.

34. C: Generally speaking, students will read more slowly when introduced to texts and material that is new; speed increases with each subsequent reading. Hence, answer A) describes a normal child's reading pattern. When reading material independently, a student should not find more than approximately 1 in 20 words to be "difficult to read." Therefore, answer "b" is incorrect. Answer "d" refers to a comprehension test, which is not specifically related to the monitoring of fluency skills. This answer can be ruled out based upon its irrelevance. However, a student reading instructional-level material should find no more than 1 in 10 words difficult to read. Therefore, a student finding 1 in 5 questions difficult on an instructional-level test may need extra help or a text more appropriate for his age level.

35. B: Previewing information is a method by which students can work to improve their own unguided reading comprehension. During the previewing process, students consider the topic at hand, what they already know about it, and what they would like to learn or believe they will learn. Previewing helps students to approach reading for the purpose of comprehension ("reading to learn") and retention. In Choice "a", students will already be familiar with the text if they have already seen the movie; therefore, their previewing will be affected by familiarity with the text. The same is true for Choice "c", as the students have already read the novel. In Choice "d", previewing the poetry will indeed increase familiarity with the poems. However, reading poetry is typically not a process that involves "reading to learn." Instead, poetry is more often approached as a pleasure-reading activity or an opportunity for literary analysis. Allowing students to preview science material helps them actively learn to read for information and will aid them in other subjects.

36. B: The object of this unit is to teach students to monitor their own comprehension as they read longer and longer texts. The only choice that involves students analyzing their own understanding is Choice "b". This practice shows students logical points in the text to pause and ask themselves whether or not they understand that which they have read. Summarizing will help them identify main points in the story. Choice "b" is also the only choice that allows the teacher to directly instruct her students on comprehension while reading the book in class.

37. C: Many factors can affect a student's ability to understand what he or she is reading. Building comprehension skills is an ongoing process and can be made difficult if a student lacks the appropriate level of reading fluency. If he or she cannot read accurately or with enough speed, he or she will have much more trouble with comprehension than the average student. It is important to identify any decoding or vocabulary problems that might be affecting comprehension first; if those can be solved, comprehension skills may naturally increase as reading fluency increases.

38. B: The key word in this question is "independently." Students will be required to read a book on their own, synthesize the information they have found, pick out relevant main ideas, and then write about all those things. This multi-step process will require that the students be interested enough in their individual books to complete it, and that the students are actually capable of reading their books. Choice "b" allows students some choice, but ensures that the challenge level is appropriate. In Choice "a", more advanced students may find the process tedious if the books are too easy. Choice "c" suggests that students read books which are challenging, requiring additional comprehension work on top of that which is already assigned. The purpose of the project is to understand and synthesize information; selecting a difficult text may prove too much for some students. It is rarely a good idea to eliminate parameters whatsoever on book choice, because students could choose books which they are incapable of reading, or which would be too easy to challenge them.

39. C: Barron demonstrates the ability to read the words on a page, but struggles with several comprehension skills consistently. There is a pattern to Barron's issues: he has a hard time comprehending anything not stated literally in the text. Karishma may or may not have a hard time forming an opinion; we cannot tell as the prompt only says that she is uncomfortable speaking up in class, which seems to be a confidence problem rather than an academic one. Lynne appears to comprehend different genres of literature, which is a grade-level expectation, and it is common for students to have a bit more trouble with one particular genre. Sebastien is not unusual, as he is capable of intelligent contributions and comprehension, but primarily lacks interest. His is a problem of motivation rather than an academic struggle; he would possibly benefit from a wider text selection or a special project.

40. B: Cloze technique refers to the process of selecting a text to present to a student and deleting various words according to a pattern. Every fifth word has been omitted in this passage. The objective of a cloze-style assessment is to assess and increase reading comprehension. This type of assessment is unique in that there is no "correct" answer—students are only expected to use the context clues to fill in words that make sense in the blanks. If they have been able to create meaningful answers, then the exercise should be deemed a success. Choices "a" and "d" are not generally accepted forms of reading comprehension assessment. Choice "c" is an oft-used form of assessment which utilizes prepared questions and students' responses and should not be confused with the cloze-style technique.

41. A: There are differences in the way reading levels are assigned across research and history. These levels can apply to a variety of assessments, including reading fluency, comprehension, word identification and the like. However, it can be generally agreed upon that there are three broad reading levels: frustration, instructional, and independent. Frustration level indicates that the material is too difficult for the student and may create frustration or disappointment while reading. Frustration level typically refers to various assessment scores of below 40%. Instructional level refers to text that can be used for the improvement of reading skills, wherein a student can get about half of his answers correct, whether identifying words, answering questions, etc. Instructional level ranges from approximately 41% to 60%. Any score above an approximate 60% should be considered independent reading material for the student.

42. D: Teachers know that students are often expected to read works written long ago and whose relevance may not be immediately apparent. It is important that students have the information required to understand how the text was created. In Choice "d", students have the opportunity to learn about the socio-historical context in which the author created the piece. Armed with knowledge about the story's context, students can categorize and comprehend any of its aspects that would ordinarily be unclear. Students can also use this knowledge to find similarities and differences between aspects of their own lives and the context of the characters in the story. In choices "a" and "b," students are given the responsibility of determining what is important or unclear in the story. However, without understanding the work's context, students may not even be aware of the relevant information in the text, or may incorrectly interpret some events in the story. In Choice "c", the sole focus is on vocabulary, which may neglect other important characteristics of the writing.

43. A: In a longer text with chapter titles, these titles can give students an understanding of what the book might be about and allows it to be broken into regular increments. Creating questions that the students can answer during their reading will give them points at which they can stop and think about what they comprehend. In Choice "b", the students would be taught to focus primarily on the ending, which neglects the rest of the aspects of the text. Choices "c" and "d" could inappropriately influence the students' comprehension by causing them to rely on other people's opinions rather than on their own understanding.

44. B: There are many, many factors that affect reading comprehension in various proportions, depending on the student. Generally speaking, students must be able to recognize vocabulary, decode unfamiliar words, and monitor their own understanding in order to comprehend a given text. In Choice "a", all of these factors could affect comprehension; written language development and breakfast, however, are probably less important than the set of factors in Choice "b". In Choice "c", the factors seem to relate primarily to a student's understanding of the words in the text— vocabulary, sight words, and the ability to look up words. However, students must understand more than simply the words on the page; they must understand the relationships between the words and the underlying meaning of the whole text. In Choice "d", classroom participation and performance in other subjects does not necessarily indicate or affect comprehension skills.

45. B: Comprehension is a process of creating meaning from that which a student reads, sees, hears, or experiences. The tools for comprehending are similar across genres. The teacher has specifically chosen a passage and wants the students to compare, not contrast, the pieces. Dickensian writing is not generally considered to be journalistic, as suggested in Choice "a". Choice "c" is correct—you can in fact compare even unlike things. However, Choice "b" provides a richer backdrop for showing students how to link that which they read in school to their own lives and use the same tools to comprehend and take meaning from whatever they read.

46. C: Reading for pleasure is an important part of building students' literacy for life. Often, the more parameters that are established around reading, the less students are apt to read for fun. By removing limitations and requirements on the experience of reading, teachers will increase the likelihood that students can enjoy it. Choice "a" does involve books which the students enjoyed, but would not increase the amount of time spent reading for pleasure, as the books have already been read. Choice "b" simply increases the amount of time spent reading for class, but may or may not be enjoyable for the students. Choice "d" establishes a plan for reading for fun, but does not ensure that the students will adhere to the timeline created. Choice "c" removes the limits on what the students can read and is inclusive of students who may not already like to read by allowing them to choose the type of material. Students also have a chance to discuss the different kinds of elements in texts that they enjoy and share them with the class.

47. A: Choice "b" creates opportunities for students to encounter words they might not read on a daily basis at school or while reading for pleasure. They are likely to employ context clues or dictionaries as a means of understanding the main ideas. Choices "c" and "d" are two different methods to expose students to new and unfamiliar words by hearing them in an instructional context and in conversation with adults. Both choices would create opportunities for indirect vocabulary building as means to understand larger ideas. Choice "a" extends the vocabulary assignment by adding harder words. This strategy would likely increase the number of words a student has learned; however, it would do so by direct instruction (words are directly assigned to be learned by students).

48. C: During the unit on imagery and figurative language, students will learn about how sensory experience can be translated into writing. In order to understand and apply these concepts, students will need an ever-increasing bank of descriptive words which they can identify and define. Choices "a," "b" and "d" would certainly be useful as supplements to this particular unit. However, Choice "c" most accurately addresses the question prompt in that it is an activity that directly increases relevant vocabulary skills. Word games engage students' interest, while building their knowledge of words they will encounter in their studies of imagery and figurative writing.

49. A: The text at hand contains several clues as to the meaning of this word, including the use of the words "peaceful" and "quiet" in the preceding sentence. Students may also recognize that Mom's requests for help with undesirable household chores interrupted Dad's peaceful, quiet 'reverie." Choice "a" is the specific method that would be most appropriate for determining the word's meaning; Choice "b" is a less reliable or systematic way of doing the same thing. Choice "c" would not be helpful in this case since "reverie" is not a word that can be decoded in a traditional manner. Choice "d" would not offer a realistic solution to this question since previewing and reviewing are more helpful in increasing comprehension of informative texts, rather than vocabulary words.

50. B: Inferential comprehension refers to a student's ability to understand ideas not explicitly contained in the text. By reading the paragraph, the student should ideally be able to understand that the girls knew they were getting out of helping with chores, because they grinned at one another conspiratorially and left immediately after gaining permission to do so. Mom also comments that she told everybody at breakfast that they'd need to help her out, which Dad has clearly forgotten. There are enough clues in the paragraph to help the reader understand what is happening without stating it in an obvious way. There are no clues to help the reader answer questions "a" or "c," In question Choice "d", the answer (peace and quiet) is stated explicitly, and would refer to literal comprehension instead of inferential comprehension.

51. D: When students read textual information for another subject, they are expected to pick out important words and concepts and retain them. By outlining the text, the student can keep track of the overall framework of information, as well as word definitions and main ideas. In Choice "a", the primary purpose for reading is likely entertainment. In Choice "b", a more appropriate reading comprehension strategy would not focus on key concepts at the expense of the literary style and tools. In Choice "c", it would be correct to analyze a persuasive essay for main ideas and supportive evidence, rather than an extended free-writing exercise.

52. C: The vocabulary list gives clues as to the type of text the students will be reading. Historical fiction is not likely to contain stories of deities or the supernatural, although the other vocabulary words might match. Poetry is not always considered as narrative text; nor would it necessarily explore culture or dualities (although those are possibilities). Drama, there again, is a possible match for this list, but does not match as well as Choice "c", mythology. Mythology encompasses many stories, typically ancient in origin, that explain and describe aspects of culture. Myths across cultures carry as many similarities as they do differences. Common in mythology are stories of duality, gods and goddesses, heroism, and more.

53. C: The goal of this exercise is to help students learn to interpret data in the form of a chart. This skill is vital to increasing overall comprehension skills and test-taking ability. However, we are not given much information regarding this chart other than types of hobbies and how many students in a particular group reported enjoying them. Therefore, we cannot make a judgment about Choice "a"—we do not know if some students reported enjoying more than one hobby, keeping us from answering that question accurately. Choice "b" offers students a chance to form personal opinions about a given topic, which is not the purpose of this exercise. Choice "d" would be more appropriate for building math skills while incorporating reading skills. Choice "c", however, requires students to analyze the types of hobbies, categorize them into physical exercise or artistic pursuits, and then answer the question.

54. B: Technology should not be relied upon to teach comprehension skills, but can be helpful in providing supplements to classroom instruction. In Choice "a", this particular practice can be very helpful for some students who have trouble recalling what is discussed in class. Choice "c" sets up a reward system to encourage students to finish their work but will not directly increase any specific skill. Choice "d" relies on students to pull comprehension-building information from articles, instead of providing them with direct instruction or explanation. Choice "b" provides interactive tools that will help students organize information that they have read, which is an important comprehension skill.

55. D: The key word in this question is "scaffolding," which refers to a practice of supporting and guiding learners with respect to a particular skill. Talking about reading is an important part of building literacy skills, but is rarely helpful without direct instructions on how to do it respectfully and properly. In Choice "a", students are required to support a particular idea in a relatively high-stress format, in front of other students. Some students may struggle with this exercise while they are learning. Choice "b" removes the teacher or any type of guide from the discussion, which exempts students from direct instruction or scaffolding. Choice "c" may eliminate some students who are not confident speaking in front of large groups, and limits how much students can share at one time. Choice "d" gives students a safe, smaller group within which to discuss reading and also provides teacher moderation and discussion guides.

56. C: In this question, it is best to actually approach the exercise as the student would, reading through the choices and contemplating their relationships. Matching numbers 2 and 4 are easiest to do first because they include girls' names and can be matched with the lettered choices with female pronouns ("she"). Some of the choices could be categorized as facts or opinions, but not so consistently that Choice "a" would make sense. It would be impossible to assert accurately that these choices are main and supporting ideas without more information or sentences to prove this, as suggested in Choice "b". Choice "d" would also require more information to be considered a possible answer to this question. Choice "c" fits best, establishing a valid effect (letters) for each cause (numbers).

57. A: Mr. Garson's assignment is intended to expand his students' understanding of other people's points of view. Creative writing is a constructive process that requires many kinds of thought processes. In Choice "b", Mr. Garson would be undermining Kim's chance to think creatively and would constitute lowering his expectations of her due to the language barrier. In Choice "c", he cannot guarantee that Kim would choose a topic that would encourage her to think creatively about different perspectives. In Choice "d", collaborating with another English-language learner would not likely speed up the process of writing; it also may short-circuit her own creative thinking due to the influence of another person's thoughts. Choice "a" allows Kim to focus on the creative constructive process without the issues associated with writing in a new language. Kim will achieve the intended outcome of the assignment, saving translation and language issues to be dealt with separately with the guidance of a trained teacher.

58. D: The students in this scenario are only given the opportunity to memorize a specific set of words each week. However, they have not been given a chance to stretch their spelling skills through various styles of teaching and assignments. Therefore, their knowledge of spelling conventions and irregular spelling will be limited to their word lists. However, writing requires a more expansive spelling skill set and must be practiced in a variety of styles in order to solidify them. In order to build spelling skills in writing, students must have opportunities to practice their spelling while writing, perhaps by using words in original sentences, learning word groups, reviewing words before and after the weekly tests, etc.

59. B: Because writing is an ongoing developmental process, it is important to monitor students' development in various ways over time. During journal time, students can write freely without concern for being graded on various aspects of their work. This freedom will likely enhance their willingness to explore their ideas. This process allows the teacher to understand which rules of conventional writing have carried over into the students' long-term memories and skill sets. Ideally, students will continually add new writing skills to their free journaling, indicating that their writing instruction is improving their skills without the students needing to consciously apply them. Journaling also allows students to practice that which they have learned without paying undue attention to parameters for grading.

60. A: This letter is difficult to follow because it is not organized according to main ideas and supporting sentences. The letter also displays inconsistent capitalization and punctuation within the body. In Choice "b", the reference to writing style is vague and can be viewed subjectively. Teachers are responsible for teaching writing conventions; however, it is important to teach proper grammar without criticizing the student's specific ideas or style. In choices "c" and "d" references to misuse of active and passive voice are irrelevant to this particular writing passage.

61. C: Organization, punctuation, and capitalization are the primary issues with this piece of writing and the letters written by the class. While there are only a few spelling errors, it is always helpful to review commonly made mistakes, as well as discuss capitalization rules. However, the student in this case does not misuse passive or active verbs. Passive voice refers to the over-use of "to be" verbs and to sentences in which the subject is acted upon, most often including passive participles (i.e., verbs in the –ed form). For instance, a sentence stating that "he robbed a bank" is normally preferable to "the bank was robbed." Therefore, Choice "c" would not be as helpful as the other lesson choices in this case.

62. B: Writing is a complex, subjective process which will never be graded identically amongst teachers. The best teachers, however, know that students write more clearly and more accurately when they know that which is expected of them. In Choice "a", the inclusion of so many details may be confusing and cause the grading process to take too long. Choice "c" is certainly an important action to consider, but will probably not directly affect the students' writing skills. Choice "d" may communicate a certain point, but again, will not necessarily improve the students' skills; it will only affect the grading process. Choice "b" will engage the students actively in the writing process and in the building of skills. They will be able to analyze the rubric and determine how well they understand the assignment and whether or not they may need more practice or help in a particular area.

63. D: Writing is a skill that evolves over time because it is so complex and involves multiple skill sets. Because so many skills are important in writing, it is impossible to apply the same sequence to each new writer. Choice "a" is important for all writers, beginning to advanced, since writing, like reading, is a skill they will use across many contexts. Choice "b" gives students practice with the various aspects of the writing process that often prove difficult for new writers, especially when they are attempting to build content and write accurately at the same time. In Choice "c", students can diminish their fear or lack of motivation for writing because they will be able to explore it in a variety of ways. Choice "d", however, may create the problem of boredom for more advanced students and cause writing progress to be very slow for those still learning.

64. B: In the first sentence, the compound subject of the sentence is "each of the kids." This compound subject with a propositional phrase (of the kids) may trick students into thinking that the subject is plural, making the verb "love." But based on the singular subject, "each," the verb should be "loves." In the second sentence, the subject, "game," should change the verb to "is" instead of the plural "are." In the third sentence, the subject is compound with a prepositional phrase (in our class), but the verb should be singular, "enjoy." The punctuation suggested in Choice "a" and the word choice in Choice "c" is correct in the paragraph. There are no split infinitives.

65. B: Often, it helps writers to show their papers to a trusted friend or family member who is unfamiliar with the piece. A fresh set of eyes can identify errors that the student does not see while revising. Choice "a" creates unnecessary work for the student when only certain corrections need to be made. Choice "c" also requires a lot of work that may turn students off of the process of revision. Choice "d" describes most students' approach to revising their papers. There are, however, many processes at work when creating written pieces and it is very difficult to develop and write your ideas without making mistakes.

66. D: In Choice "a", the teacher is providing remedial instruction or extra help, but is not sharpening the actual skills needed to revise. Many students can perform well on mechanics worksheets and exercises, but have trouble with the process of re-reading and revising. Choice "b" is not correct for the same reason. Choice "c" relies upon the students themselves to identify and correct others' grammar, which may not be consistent or accurate. The final choice helps students practice the re-reading and identification skills needed to revise a piece of writing.

67. A: Curriculum standards are important for determining when specific skills should be introduced and mastered. While most literacy skills evolve simultaneously, there is an applicable sequence that should guide teaching. Choices "b" through "d" are all general expectations for fifth-grade students. All students do not master every skill included in order to matriculate, but effort to expose them to each skill should be made. Choice "a" is a standard that students generally do not master until seventh or eighth grade, unless they are provided with specialized instruction at an earlier time and on a consistent basis.

68. A: In the writing process, the prewriting phase includes actions such as brainstorming, story mapping, and jotting down ideas. Most students need to organize their ideas before beginning to draft, or writing. It often helps students to organize their ideas with the use of drawings or diagrams instead of in a linear fashion. By requiring them to use pencil and paper in this phase of the writing process, teachers create an opportunity for students to use different tools to organize their ideas. Once the writing and publishing phases begin, it is appropriate to allow the use of word processors to that the students' work is legible for revision.

69. C: It is obvious when Mrs. Blaine first comments on Alex's report that he does well with literal comprehension and memory, but has trouble identifying and discussing his opinion about the book. Alex, like many students, is not confident in his ability to clearly state an idea and back it up with supporting evidence or ideas from what he has read. This is the skill she is suggesting he will need to use again and again. Alex has an opinion, that the book was "boring at first," but he "liked the way it ended." He knows how he feels about the book, but does not know how to explain his opinion in writing. Therefore, answer Choice "a" is inaccurate. Choices "b" and "c" are both likely to be necessary for Alex at some point, but are unlikely to be the most important skill Mrs. Blaine mentions.

70. A: Alex is having trouble expressing a logical argument in writing. However, he has an opinion about the book to get him started. By having him write each idea on separate items, Alex can use tangible objects to represent his thoughts. He can then move them around as he thinks through how they are related to one another. In this way, he can start to structure his thoughts with the help of visual aids, rather than attempting to do this abstractly. The remaining three choices might assist Alex with certain assignments, but will not give him concrete tools to help him organize his thoughts and write them in a clear, concise way.

71. A: Mr. Benton wants to use a clear-cut approach to writing, involving students in the process. As a teacher, Mr. Benton should know that there are six commonly agreed-upon writing traits: idea development, organization, voice, word choice, sentence fluency and conventions. These traits encompass the majority of writing skills that students will learn over the course of their studies. In Choice "a", not only does Mr. Benton provide students with this framework for thinking about writing, but helps them prioritize their needs in building their skills. The students can then work from the plan devised from that initial meeting. In choices "b" and "c", students are left primarily to their own devices to build their writing skills. However, if most of the students are struggling with writing (as suggested in the question prompt), it would not be advisable to leave the writing instruction to the students themselves. Choice "d" provides faulty information--there are many types of writing that would not be written in the five-paragraph style or format.

72. B: Part of teaching older students is helping them give voice to what is happening in their lives and connecting that voice to what they are learning in class. In Choice "b", students not only have a voice, but can channel that voice into a particular type of writing. In this case, they will be writing journalistically. They also have a chance to turn their frustration into a positive activity that will give parents the information they would like to know. In Choice "a", the students do not build any particular writing skills, nor does the problem get solved for parents or students. In Choice "c", the students would have a chance to write about their feelings, but this does not eliminate the issue of parents wanting to know what is happening at school. Choice "d" only serves to make more work for the students, without building their writing skills.

73. D: The first two questions suggest that the primary focus of this exercise is word choice and vocabulary. The third question refers to the sound of the words chosen, and could also pertain to Choice "a", sentence fluency. The fourth question would work with choices "a," "c" or "d". But taken together, the questions point strongly to the concept of word choice. Choice "a", sentence fluency, refers to the way the words in sentences work together. Choice "b" refers to the way the students' ideas are developed in the paper. Choice "c" encompasses writing conventions such as punctuation, spacing, and capitalization.

74. B: In persuasive writing, the writer must introduce an opinion or statement about which he or she must provide supporting evidence. The paragraph or paper should start with the main idea and then segue into separate but related supporting details. In this writing sample, the student's ideas are written sequentially, as the student might think about them mentally. Introducing a visual aid to help him separate his primary idea and the ideas that give reasons for it may help him develop the piece into a longer, more logical argument. He already includes personal details and ideas that make the piece interesting to read, contrary to Choice "c". Choice "d" suggests that the student may have many grammatical and conventional corrections to make, which is not correct. While it is always important to encourage, as stated in Choice "a", Choice "b" would be the most direct, concrete way to assist this student in developing his skills.

75. D: When teachers talk to their students about writing, it is important to remember that young writers often leave out important details or information vital to its coherence. Students must learn to communicate clearly through writing and include all pertinent information. The teacher uses the metaphor of the alien from outer space to emphasize this point—an alien would have no prior knowledge that would aid comprehension, therefore the writer must be very thorough. This concept is important in all writing, but would be especially important in explaining to another person how to do something. In Choice "d", a student would choose a favorite activity, sport, or task and explain in a methodical way how to complete or participate in it. Neglecting any piece of information would make the piece irrelevant.

76. B: Many aspects of writing are difficult to teach directly. There are not as many specific exercises that show students how to write in their own voices without being overly colloquial or even incorrect. Students must always be working toward adhering to writing conventions, but also making that which they write personal and interesting. Part of "voice" is personal expression and making writing relevant to the intended audience. Often, the best way to show the students how to do this is to show them that which has already been done well and discuss why the writing is good. The students can use this discussion to improve their own writing through emulation. Choice "a" suggests that personal opinions are always relevant to one's writing, which is not always the case, depending on the type of assignment. In Choice "c", students would be very limited should they only choose subjects with which they are familiar--they would rarely have a chance to grow. The final choice would encourage students to speak in someone else's voice, which would create variety, but would not grow their ability to speak as themselves in any relevant or interesting way.

77. A: Reading this excerpt, it becomes apparent that the student is using a limited writing vocabulary. The words "sweet" or "sweets" are used three times; "like" is used three times as well. The sentences feel very repetitive because many words are used again and again. Working with students to build their vocabulary is one of the most helpful ways to build writing skills. The more words in a student's repertoire, the more interesting and lively his writing will be. Despite the vocabulary deficit, the student's writing conventions and grammar are actually quite good in this excerpt. Choice "d" suggests that the student needs to stretch his writing skill by choosing more challenging topics, but we do not know from this piece whether or not the student is working at an appropriate level of challenge.

78. C: Choice "a" is misleading, as writing a letter is a specific format and kind of exercise; it is not typically considered a catch-all exercise for learning the five-step process or the six traits of writing. While every writing exercise can be a backdrop for these skills, Choice "a" is not the most accurate answer. If you read the question prompt carefully, you see that it is already acknowledged that this opportunity will be a good exercise for showing students how to write a letter well. Therefore, Choice "b" is redundant. Choice "d" is true; students should be careful of their writing conventions so that their writing is easier to read, yet Choice "c" is the skill than can be most directly applied when writing to students of another language and culture; the audience actually encompasses Choice "d", as students would determine in thinking about their French pen pals that they might have a hard time reading English, and that they should be cognizant of that fact.

79. B: By the eighth grade, students should begin to understand the purposes and effectiveness of various media. If the students have been learning about how to deconstruct media messages, they have likely been studying ideas about audience, point of view, and persuasive language. Assigning a project in which the students are guided to think through these concepts will solidify their understanding of how media messages are created. Each of the other answers, "a," "b" and "d" will likely be accomplished through the completion of this project. However, it is not likely that the teacher has designed such a specific kind of assignment in order to increase her students' real-life job skills, as not all of them will go into media-related fields described in Choice "a". Choice "c" assumes that technology will be used in the assignment, although it is possible for students to create the ads and essays without the use of computers or other technology. Choice "d" could be accomplished by any number of assignments and is less likely to be the primary intended outcome.

80. A: Inkblot images are often used to gain insight into an individual's thoughts. The teacher clearly understands that different people will interpret these images in various ways. She asks the students to write their questions down so that they will not be influenced by others' interpretations. While some visual symbols are universal, most images are not inherent as suggested in Choice "b". Choice "c" could possibly be true, but would be irrelevant to a group of sixth graders in most circumstances. Choice "d" supposes that students should confer with one another before forming their own opinions, which should not be a rule of thumb. By allowing students to interpret the messages individually and then share their perceptions, the teacher will demonstrate that the individual's point of view will affect his understanding of visual images.

81. D: Students typically enjoy watching film versions of literature, especially when the text is challenging to read. An important part of media consumption is building skills to deconstruct the embedded ideas and messages. The teacher in this scenario wants the students to think about how the structure and content of the film affects their understanding of a classic story. In choices "a" and "b", students are assigned to state their opinions about certain aspects of the film or play, but are not asked to critically analyze a specific message. Choice "c" simply creates a rather tedious assignment that will yield a rote list of examples. Choice "d" targets the unique setting of the film and encourages students to think about why the film's creators might have chosen to adapt the story in such a way, which is likely to suggest that the content of the story is relevant to people in any era or setting.

82. A: Mr. James is showing students the difference between a main idea (or concept) and its supporting evidence (or details). He has taken an element of a story and provided three details or character traits that provide proof of his claim. The organization of the graph helps students see the relationship between in the ideas, in addition to hearing it. This skill can be directly applied to either constructing meaning from a text or creating a well-planned paragraph. Choice "b" may not always be true, depending on the kind of questions asked. Choice "c" assumes that characters in texts can always be broken down into smaller components. Choice "d" refers to aspects of writing such as punctuation, grammar, spelling, etc.

83. B: Students are expected to have a variety of skills with respect to viewing, representing, and analyzing visual/media images by the time they enter high school. They should be able to

200

understand visual imagery and how it affects or creates meaning. Students must also learn to deconstruct the messages they see and create their own for the purposes of communicating their own ideas. Choice "a" would, perhaps, be the goal of a consumerism or economics class, but is not the best choice for this scenario. This game would create understanding in students about different types of visual images, but they are not likely to be the same images used in their schoolwork at this juncture. Choice "d" is certainly true; the children will likely enjoy the game. However, Choice "b" most closely matches the educational requirements and standards laid out for students of this age.

84. D: Generally speaking, the following story elements take place in sequential order:

Exposition: refers to background information and actions in a story that describe the setting, characters, etc.

Rising action: events in the plot that lead up to the critical event or turning point

Climax: critical event, dramatic scene, or turning point in the story

Falling action: resulting events and actions following the conflict

Resolution: all actions and events are resolved and addressed

Teaching students about the plot elements they can find in most stories will help them develop many skills, including comparisons/contrasts, plot analysis, reading comprehension, etc.

85. B: Ancient Egypt provides a rich backdrop for a myriad of literacy skills. Students can develop their visual literacy skills in a number of ways, even using material and studies that date back thousands of years. In Choice "a", students are creating visual images with costume and dress, but no method for decoding those messages is stated in the answer choice. Drawing illustrations focuses on the same skill: creation of visual images, but no decoding or discussion of those images. In Choice "d", students could build their visual literacy skills if they were to discuss the visual images or representations in the film, but this activity is not included in the answer choice. In the correct answer, B), students are exposed to various representations and exhibits regarding the material in question and then have a chance to discuss and uncover meaning in what they have seen, with the guidance of the teachers.

86. A: If you read the question prompt carefully, you will notice that the question refers specifically to language skills. While Choice "c" is important and would likely result from the exercise, it does not signify a specific language skill. Students' motor skills are not likely to significantly improve over the course of one day, eliminating Choice "b". In Choice "d", the assumption that other individuals in the community would be able to interpret sign language is incorrect. But the seminar would indeed provide an opportunity for students to learn about how visual representations affect meaning. Using sign language allows them to hone listening and expression skills simultaneously, as well as to learn how to decode nonverbal expressions.

87. D: In literature and in media, storytellers often use the color red to symbolize a number of concepts: red can signal importance, danger, love, or simply draw the viewer or reader to the particular object in question. The question prompt tells you directly that the red objects signify that the main character is seeing a clue to solving the mystery. In essence, anything colored red represents, or symbolizes, a clue.

88. B: The primary purpose of visual aids is to extend or enhance meaning. Visuals can sometimes distract from the meaning of the presentation if used too much, as in Choice "a". Choice "c" could also create distractions in that students may be more likely to look at photos directly in front of them than pay attention to the student presenting. The final choice simply encourages students to read the information on screen, and will likely cause the presenting student to read aloud rather than communicate in his own words. Choice "b", however, utilizes the students' thought processes in determining where a visual might help enhance understanding, and requires them to use oral communication as well.

89. C: In teaching about this subject, students must be able to understand the intended meaning of a particular media image. To do this, they have to consider the image-creator's background, point of view, and anything else they might be able to determine from analyzing the image. Students need to be taught tools to dissect the barrage of images that they see on a daily basis. Choice "a" encompasses photos of real-life people and events. While these photos are valuable for many teaching purposes, it cannot be guaranteed that students would be able to apply their tools to current-day media analysis. Choice "b" is the choice least related to media influence in that it refers to a Social Studies text, likely created for didactic purposes. Choice "d" most likely refers to a cartoon found in the Funnies, created to entertain, rather than influence. The political cartoon in Choice "c" is the image most explicitly created to affect and influence public opinion by exaggerating personal traits and personalizing lofty issues.

90. C: Many factors affect the final outcome of a research paper or project, including the selection of sources, interpretation of source information, organization of ideas, and writing skills. The final project described in answer "a" is not always indicative of how efficiently a student has researched a topic because it is the end-result of many language processes at work. The outline mentioned in answer "b" would provide insight about the organization of ideas, but answer "c" would allow the instructor to assess the actual process of gathering and synthesizing sources of information.

91. A: One of the most important aspects of completing a research project is topic selection. A student must choose a topic that is appropriately narrow to avoid being overwhelmed by too much information. If the topic is too broad, the student will not be able to adequately research; if it is too narrow, he or she will get stuck. The student should also think critically about whether or not the topic can be researched. For instance, if a student chooses to study a current event, there may not be enough reliable information published yet to support a real research project. The teacher should play an active role in helping the student select a topic, especially on the student's first try.

92. A: The students tend to do well when they know they will be tested; this probably means that they only sit down to study when they are required to do so, unless they want to risk a poor test score. However, it is important for students to retain information each day and week, rather than cramming and memorizing for a test. By devoting a few minutes each day to preview or prepare students for what they will learn, they will begin to learn how to pay attention to the main ideas and salient details of the readings. By reviewing and summarizing, students can compare what they thought would be important during the preview to what they actually learned. The repetition will help the students retain the information from one day to the next.

93. B: If only the first graph was drawn, it may appear that the students were working simply on character analysis or even inferential comprehension. This first set of boxes creates a framework for analyzing and recording information about two specific characters and their personalities. However, taken with the second chart, it becomes apparent that the purpose of the first chart is to organize information in order to complete the second chart. The second chart requires students to think critically about how the two characters are the same and how they are different. This exercise most closely corresponds with Choice "b", comparing and contrasting, in the context of character traits. Choices "c" and "d" are certainly involved in this process, but are simply tools that are used in order to teach students how to compare and contrast

94. B: The question prompt states that the students' primary problems lie in homework: they are concerned about the volume of reading and ho to know what information is most relevant. Although Choice "d" is important and will help students, it will not improve their ability to deal with independent reading and assignments. Choice "c" will help students score more highly on tests, but will likely not improve their study skills. Choice "a" will simply encourage students to "cram' a lot of information for tests. Choice "b", however, teaching SQ3R, is a method by which students can study, internalize and sort through large amounts of information on an independent basis.

95. B: Writing a research paper is a learned skill that begins with proper topic selection. Students must learn to pick topics with guidance from their teachers that can be researched easily. They must be careful not to pick topics that are too broad or too narrow. In this scenario, students also need to pick a topic that can be found as the subject in a variety of sources, including newspapers, magazines, books, etc. Therefore, the topic should be well-known to most readers. Choice "a" is not likely to be found in these sources unless the Velasquez family is nationally, or at least locally, well-known. Choice "c" is probably not appropriate for the same reason. Choice "d" could be considered for an essay topic or another type of writing assignment, but may not be the best choice with respect to the variety of sources. Choice "b" offers a broad subject about which much will have been written.

96. D: The purpose of this kind of note-taking is, on one level, to help students distinguish between major ideas or concepts and the details that support or relate to them. This kind of note-taking also helps students understand how certain events and ideas influence one another. The most important benefit of this practice is that it helps the note-taker start to build meaning out of the information which they receive in class. Students often complain that they don't know how to pick out what will be on a test, or what is important, as they cannot possibly retain every sentence uttered in class. Students do best when they can pick out main ideas and organize their thinking around these concepts, learning details and supporting ideas as they go.

97. C: As is true with students and adults alike, we remember more information when we review it consistently over time. If a student takes meaningful and accurate notes, reviewing them periodically and consistently will help them retain the information and cut down on time spent studying right before the test. This practice also helps the student identify any ideas or questions that need to be addressed before the test or paper is due. Choices "a" and "b" create the impression that a student will struggle if he does not record (in writing or via tape recorder) every word uttered in class. It is more important for students to learn how to create meaning and understand relationships between all of the facts, figures, and concepts introduced in class. Choice "d" would be very time-consuming and would not guarantee that students are choosing the most important ideas and information for use.

98. C: Allowing the students to practice these types of questions starts to open up their ability to show that which they know. Many students experience stress in the transition to various types of testing that do not provide answer choices in multiple choice form, or lack word banks. Choice "c" shows students how to approach these kinds of questions in a safe, un-graded way, and solidifies their thinking by discussing their attempts afterward. Choice "a" may assist with students' recall of information, but does not provide direct instruction on how to formulate answers. Choice "b" will give students time to approach the questions and revise their answers if necessary. For those students who experience more difficulty, however, it may not be as helpful as Choice "c". Choice "d" might also be helpful for any students who experience test anxiety or are taking a bit longer to understand the process, but will not scaffold their attempts as well as Choice "c".

99. C: In a piece of writing such as Sully's, there are two important things which he needs to do; namely, he must select the most important ideas and focus on those, rather than attempt to include every single idea he may have. Once he has done that, he additionally must include details or evidence to support those ideas. Choice "c" gives him a concrete way to identify the most important ideas and match them with appropriate and relevant evidence. Choices "a" and "b" require him to start over on a project, which is unnecessary. Choice "d" would cause him to create a very lengthy and too-detailed report without much focus.

100. B: Studying can be a mystifying experience for students as they begin to do it more frequently. Often, students do not know how to prepare properly for specific kinds of assignments, and direct instruction is helpful. In Choice "b", Mrs. Bray can identify why the students' preparation is not adequate for the examinations and help them understand alternative methods of preparation. In Choice "a", students may or may not improve their performance while taking more quizzes; in fact, their motivation and confidence may decrease if they continue to receive poor grades. Choice "c" contradicts the question prompt, as Mrs. Bray does not want to give the students too many ideas about what will be covered in the quiz; rather, she wants to improve their study skills. Choice "d" is less accurate and direct as a method for achieving her goals than is Choice "b", because parents do not always have good study skills or knowledge of the classroom.

Thank You

We at Mometrix would like to extend our heartfelt thanks to you, our friend and patron, for allowing us to play a part in your journey. It is a privilege to serve people from all walks of life who are unified in their commitment to building the best future they can for themselves.

The preparation you devote to these important testing milestones may be the most valuable educational opportunity you have for making a real difference in your life. We encourage you to put your heart into it—that feeling of succeeding, overcoming, and yes, conquering will be well worth the hours you've invested.

We want to hear your story, your struggles and your successes, and if you see any opportunities for us to improve our materials so we can help others even more effectively in the future, please share that with us as well. **The team at Mometrix would be absolutely thrilled to hear from you!** So please, send us an email (support@mometrix.com) and let's stay in touch.

> **If you'd like some additional help, check out these other resources we offer for your exam:**
> **http://MometrixFlashcards.com/MTTC**

205

Additional Bonus Material

Due to our efforts to try to keep this book to a manageable length, we've created a link that will give you access to all of your additional bonus material:

mometrix.com/bonus948/mttclanartelem